100 MORNING TREATS

100
MORE
TREA

with Muffins, Rolls, Biscuits, Sweet
and Savory Breakfast Breads, and More

SARAH KIEFFER

NING

TS

CHRONICLE BOOKS
SAN FRANCISCO

Library of Congress Cataloging-in-Publication Data available.

ISBN 978-1-7972-1616-4

Manufactured in China.

FSC
www.fsc.org
MIX
Paper from
responsible sources
FSC™ C169962

Prop and food styling by Sarah Kieffer.

Design by Lizzie Vaughan.

Typesetting by Katy Brown.

Typeset in Intervogue.

10 9 8 7 6 5 4 3 2 1

Chronicle books and gifts are available at special quantity discounts to corporations, professional associations, literacy programs, and other organizations. For details and discount information, please contact our premiums department at corporatesales@chroniclebooks.com or at 1-800-759-0190.

Chronicle Books LLC
680 Second Street
San Francisco, CA 94107
www.chroniclebooks.com

DEDICATION

TO ADAM—

Aimee Nezhukumatathil wrote, "Flour on the floor makes my sandals slip and
I tumble into your arms," and that image sums us up quite nicely. This book, well,
all the books, wouldn't be here without your encouragement and support.
All your dishwashing helped too. Thank you for making me laugh every single day.
Thank you for being my best friend. You're my favorite one.

Contents

1

MUFFINS, SCONES, AND QUICK BREADS

4
LAMINATED PASTRIES

5
THE WEEKEND

Introduction

Throughout college I often worked the morning shift at the Blue Heron Coffeehouse, in Winona, Minnesota. Our front door opened at seven o'clock sharp, so I was scheduled for a disquieting start time, where I began brewing coffee and pulling test shots of espresso as soon as I stumbled through the door. When I moved back to Minneapolis a few years later and began baking full time at Bordertown Coffee, that time moved up even earlier, to five o'clock. All the scones, muffins, and cookies needed to be baked, nestled on trays, and then neatly tucked into the bakery case when our little shop opened for business each morning.

I had never considered myself a morning person before, yet with each new day of rising early, I gradually found myself embracing those morning hours. Yes, when I threw those covers off after hitting the snooze button twice and left my warm bed behind (sometimes in the dead of winter! with wind chills of -20°F!), it was bleak. But after a few splashes of water from the faucet met my sleepy eyes, and as I felt the brisk air hit my face minutes later, I soon grew to love the quiet of the early morning. With most of the city still asleep, those dark hours were mine, and I spent them in solitude, quietly whisking, mixing, and stirring.

Those many mornings alone in the kitchen allowed my mind time to wander on the present and the past. I thought of my grandma Ethel, her towering frame hovering over her speckled countertop, her long fingers confidently rolling out pie dough. Baking scones took me back to the Blue Heron, where pots of soup simmered on the stove top and coworkers hummed along to Joni Mitchell's melancholy falsetto flowing from the cheap stereo speakers. Some days I couldn't shake the news, listening to customers and staff discuss in dismay as individuals, nations, and humanity repeated their mistakes again and again. As I baked each morning, I slowly understood that everything was new, and everything was old, and I was never alone: The ritual of preparing food in the morning connected me with so many people, recipes, and stories across the years. The philosophers were right: We all belong to each other.

Today my alarm now goes off a little later. Ella Fitzgerald and Louis Armstrong greet me each morning with clear voices singing sweetly, and two kittens knead their paws and purr gentle encouragement to prod me out of bed. I am no longer rushing to a coffeehouse but rousing sleepy children and frantically making lunches to go, in desperation not to miss the bus. It's still often chilly at the bus stop here, but a few moments later I'm home, and the house is suddenly quiet. I hold my warm cup of coffee between my hands; often Mary Oliver speaks in the silences between sips: *It is a serious thing / just to be alive / on this fresh morning, / in this broken world.* I am grateful for each of these fresh mornings.

Soon after my cup is empty I make my way to the kitchen counter. I may work from home now, but all the counters I leaned up against

> "I want our summers to always be like this—a kitchen wrecked with love, a table overflowing with baked goods warming the already warm air. After all the pots are stacked, the goodies cooled, and all the counters wiped clean—let us never be rescued from this mess."
>
> —Aimee Nezhukumatathil, "Baked Goods"

throughout the years are still before me. First, I see the yellow laminate counters that my mom always hated but still used to teach me how to roll out cookie dough and stir together boxed cake batter on. The white counters with tiny, colorful speckles at my grandma's house are not as clear, but I remember watching through tears as she shaped bread dough while firmly telling me that I would never find a husband because I couldn't keep my bedroom clean. There was the single foot of counter at the apartment my husband and I made our first home in; I baked so many cakes for so many birthdays in that tiny space, piping borders and flowers with homemade buttercream. Then, of course, all the stainless steel surfaces at the bakeries I worked in, the hours and hours of washing dishes and baking for ten-hour stretches. Last, my own well-worn slab of butcher block that I work at each day, where all my cookbooks, including this one, were created, and where hundred of cookies and cinnamon rolls have been cooled and devoured. Here, at this station, my musings and work from the past intertwine with those of the present, and I imagine a connection to the myriad bakers before me: their delight in creating something beautiful, their laughter in failed attempts, and the pleasure in biting into something delicious that their hands set out to make.

I wrote this book, *100 Morning Treats*, to celebrate the morning hours and to represent the baked goods and pastries I developed while working in coffee shops and in my home. The recipes on the following pages are the result of nearly three decades of baking. My work hasn't always been easy, but there has been so much joy I've discovered along the way. I hope that this book brings you the same joy and fulfillment in your life and in your kitchens in the years to come.

HOW TO USE THIS BOOK

Most of the recipes in this book require basic baking skills, such as creaming butter and adding ingredients to create a batter. A few are a bit more complicated or require more of a time commitment. Be sure to follow the baking tips in the next pages and read through the lists for extra advice.

This book is divided into seven chapters, starting with Muffins, Scones, and Quick Breads, a chapter full of (mostly) quick and delicious breakfast treats. I included simple classics like Blueberry Muffins (page 23, totally revamped from my first book!) and Traditional Scones (page 55), but also some twists on the old standbys, like Lemon Meringue Bread (page 64) and Streusel-Bottom Bread (page 76).

Coffee Cakes and Bundt Cakes are next, and you will want to try Cardamom Bundt Cake with Coffee Glaze (page 104) and the Streusel Coffee Cake (page 83). Creamy Jammy Coffee

Cakes (page 91) are a personal favorite and have become a breakfast staple in my house.

Sweet Yeasted and Fried Treats are tucked cozily in the middle, and you'll find a range of recipes from Buttermilk Cinnamon Rolls (page 117) and Maple Bourbon Caramel Rolls (page 120) to Raspberry Caramel Bubble Bread (page 146) and Everything Breakfast Pretzels (page 151).

Laminated Pastries is a slightly more advanced chapter. I especially love the Sheet Pan Danish (page 194) and Cinnamon Twists (page 197), but you'll also find Kouignettes (page 190) and Rum Raisin Buns (page 188).

Recipes focusing on "The Weekend" follow, and for the first time ever I have included some savory recipes in a cookbook. All the recipes here are perfect for weekend mornings, from the simple Sesame Chocolate Rye Breakfast Cookies (page 254) and Peanut Butter Granola Bark (page 253) to the slightly more elevated Prosciutto Gruyère Croissants (page 227).

The Base Doughs and Breads come next, and they are used repeatedly throughout the book. I am very excited to introduce my Brioche Dough (page 259) and a new, laminated Danish Dough (page 276), as well as Milk Bread Dough (page 262). There are also instructions on how to shape brioche, milk bread, and Danish loaves.

And, as always, I have a chapter of "Extras," recipes to use with other recipes in this book or just by their merry selves: Quick Berry Jam (page 287), Pomegranate Sparkler (page 284), and even an Easy Strawberry Smoothie (page 285).

GENERAL BAKING ADVICE

GETTING TO KNOW A RECIPE It is vital to read the entire recipe through before beginning a baking project. It is essential to know all the ingredients, details, and timing at the start to help ensure the recipe succeeds. Once you feel confident about how a recipe works, you can then think about personalizing it.

MEASURING FLOUR Throughout this book, 1 cup of flour equals 142 g (or 5 oz). This is on the higher end of the scale (1 cup of flour can range anywhere from 4 to 5 oz [113 to 142 g], depending on the baker), but I found that after weighing many cups of flour and averaging the total, mine always ended up around this number.

Because most people scoop flour differently, I highly encourage the use of a digital scale when measuring ingredients to get consistent results, and I have provided weight measurements for that reason.

I recommend the dip-and-sweep method for flour if you are not using a scale: Dip the measuring cup into the bag or container of flour, then pull the cup out with the flour overfilling the cup. Sweep the excess off the top with a knife, so that you have a level cup of flour.

MEASURING SEMISOLIDS Yogurt, sour cream, peanut butter, pumpkin purée, and the like are all examples of semisolids: ingredients that fall somewhere between a liquid and a solid. I always measure these types of ingredients in a liquid measuring cup, which gives a little more volume than a dry measuring cup because the cup is slightly bigger. If you are not using a scale to measure these ingredients, I highly recommend using a liquid measuring cup, so your baked goods will turn out correctly.

PINCH OF SALT This is called for occasionally throughout these pages. It is a little more than ⅛ teaspoon, but less than ¼ teaspoon.

EGG WASH To make an egg wash, use a fork to whisk 1 large egg, a pinch of salt, and 1 tablespoon of water together in a small bowl.

MAKING FREEZE-DRIED BERRY POWDER I often call for freeze-dried berry powder. I find that it really bumps up the flavor of the fresh berries in baked goods and also helps them retain their vibrant color. If a bite of a blueberry muffin lasts three seconds, I find that the fresh blueberries are present for up to two seconds, but the freeze-dried fruit hits in that last third second and really helps the berry flavor linger. In most recipes, though, the powder is optional, and the recipes will still taste good without it. To make berry powder, in a food processor, put an amount of freeze-dried berries equal to the amount of powder called for in the recipe. Pulse until the berries are broken down into a powder. You can sift the powder to get rid of seeds if desired. Store the powder in an airtight container at room temperature. The longer it is stored, the harder it gets, but it will last for 2 weeks.

LINING A PAN WITH A PARCHMENT PAPER SLING A parchment paper sling makes it much easier to get a bread or pastry out of the pan. Cut two pieces of parchment paper the same width as the bottom of your pan, and long enough to come up and over the sides. Spray the pan with cooking spray, and then place the pieces of parchment in the pan, perpendicular to each other so each side has a bit of parchment overhang, making sure to push the sheets into the corners.

TEMPERING CHOCOLATE Tempering chocolate allows it to set properly and gives the chocolate a glossy, smooth finish. Throughout the book I use a "cheater's method" to temper chocolate, which is to melt most of the chocolate called for, and then finely chop the few ounces of chocolate left and stir it into the melted chocolate until they are also melted, so that the finished melted chocolate ends up around 88°F [31°C]. This method isn't foolproof, but it's worked for me 99 percent of the time.

A FEW IMPORTANT NOTES

On Ovens

In his cookbook *A Jewish Baker's Pastry Secrets*, George Greenstein wrote, "Ovens are often like divas or temperamental bakers, and each has its own personality." I couldn't agree more. Ovens are the most important piece of baking equipment and can often be the source of baking issues. Most home ovens have hot spots, and possibly malfunctioning lights, fans, or thermometers—or all of the above. These factors can, of course, cause problems when baking, and it is imperative to really get to know your oven. Take time to know your hot spots, how the temperature fluctuates, and how long your oven takes to preheat. Here are some ways to help your oven out.

BUY AN OVEN THERMOMETER Many ovens are not properly calibrated, and a wrong oven temperature can greatly affect the outcome of your baked goods. If your oven is running too hot, the outsides of your baked goods can bake faster than the insides, resulting in burning and undercooked centers. If it is too cold, your baked goods may not rise properly or brown properly. I have an inexpensive oven thermometer that I keep hanging from the middle rack of my oven, so I can keep an eye on the temperature inside. I also have an instant-read thermometer (the DOT Simple Alarm Thermometer by ThermoWorks), which I use to check my oven temperature once a week.

PREHEAT THE OVEN This ensures that you are placing your pan in the oven at the correct temperature. Most ovens need *at least* 30 minutes to reach the correct temperature.

ROTATE THE PAN HALFWAY THROUGH BAKING Oven walls radiate heat differently, due to how they vary in thickness, as well as other factors. As noted previously, most ovens have hot spots, so shifting the pan can promote even baking. But . . .

DON'T OPEN THE DOOR TOO MANY TIMES Whenever you open the oven door to check on things, hot air spills out, causing the oven temperature to rapidly fall. Most ovens take a while to heat back up, and this can affect baking. Clean your oven window and fix that broken light so you minimize the need to open the oven door.

The Temperature and Humidity of Your Kitchen

Humidity and temperature can greatly impact your baked goods. If your kitchen is too hot or humid, butter can soften and melt faster. If you've let a dough or batter sit out in a hot kitchen, the butter can also separate from the dough, resulting in streaks and uneven baking. Ingredients such as flour, sugar, salt, and baking soda all soak up humidity that is lingering in the air. Over time, they will retain moisture, and this can affect the outcome of the recipe. Storing your ingredients in airtight containers will keep out moisture and help them stay fresh longer.

If your kitchen is too cold, this can cause problems too. Butter will take longer to come to room temperature and to cream with sugar. In all these cases, it important to pay close attention to your environment. Which brings us to . . .

Use Your Senses

I am here to guide you as best I can through each of these recipes, but my oven, equipment, ingredients, weather, and state of mind will be different than yours. External factors can influence baking, but internal factors can too. Feeling depressed or anxious can influence your concentration and, therefore, could possibly alter how you read a recipe. Because I am not there with you to guide you should any of these things occur, you need to rely on your senses. If you open the oven and the cake looks like it is browning too quickly, check to see if it should come out early. If the pumpkin bread is still doughy in the middle even though the baking time has elapsed, keep it in the oven longer. Using your eyes and nose will help you recognize when your baked goods are done. Your palate and hands are also good tools.

INGREDIENTS

The following is a list of ingredients used in this book. Most of these ingredients should be available at your local grocery store, but for the few that are specialty items or hard to find, I have included a resources section at the back of the book (page 298) to help you locate them.

Just like women's pant sizes, many baking ingredients vary from one brand to the next. For example, each brand of flour labeled "all-purpose" on your grocery store shelf contains a different amount of protein, ranging from 9 to 12 percent. Flour protein levels can also vary within a brand from season to season, depending on the harvest. Butter has different levels of water and fat content, depending on the brand. And one brand of granulated sugar may be coarser or finer than the next. These differences can and do affect baking outcomes. In the ingredient categories below, I list the brands I use for many of these staple items to help you achieve similar outcomes.

Dairy and Eggs

BUTTER All the recipes in this book call for unsalted butter. If you are a fan of salted butter and decide to use it instead, you will want to use a little less salt overall in the recipe. European-style butter cannot always be swapped for regular butter; the high fat content can cause extra spreading or other problems. If European-style butter is used, it will be noted in the recipe. For grocery store brands, I prefer Land O'Lakes unsalted butter. I do not suggest substituting oil for butter.

CREAM CHEESE I prefer Philadelphia brand cream cheese in my recipes; it tastes best overall and gives baked goods a "creamier" feel.

CRÈME FRAÎCHE This is a matured cream with a tangy flavor and a smooth texture. It is used occasionally in this book, and there is a recipe for making it at home (page 290) in the "Extras" chapter. I use Vermont Creamery crème fraîche when I'm not making my own.

EGGS All the recipes here call for Grade A large eggs. In its shell, a large egg should weigh 2 oz [57 g]. For egg-rich recipes (such as Pastry Cream, page 288), I like to use local, farm-fresh eggs because they typically have beautiful orange yolks. If the recipe calls for room temperature eggs, you can place the cold eggs in a large bowl, cover them with warm water, and let them sit for 10 minutes. If you need to separate the egg white and yolk, it's generally easier to start with a cold egg because the yolk will be firmer.

HEAVY CREAM Look for a heavy cream that is pasteurized, but not ultra-pasteurized, if possible, especially when making crème fraîche. Heavy cream is also known as double cream.

MILK I tested all the recipes in this book with whole milk unless otherwise noted. In most cases, I don't recommend replacing it with a lower-fat milk, as this may change the outcome of the recipe.

Cooking Oils

CANOLA AND VEGETABLE OIL Canola and vegetable oil are the most common oils you'll find in this book because of their neutral flavor.

OLIVE OIL Use a good-quality extra-virgin olive oil so the flavor shines in the final product.

TOASTED SESAME OIL I love the flavor of toasted sesame oil, and while it is often used in savory cooking, I think pairing it with sugar is delicious. I have a few recipes in the book that include it. I prefer toasted sesame oil over regular sesame oil; I find it has a more intense flavor that works well with sugar and vanilla.

Salt and Spices

FLEUR DE SEL This is a delicate, moist salt that is usually used as a finishing salt. Because the crystals are larger, the salt takes longer to dissolve, and the taste lingers a bit longer.

SPICES Make sure your spices haven't been sitting in your cupboard for years before using them. Although they appear to last forever, they do have a shelf life and can grow stale or rancid over time. Spices retain their freshness for 6 months to 1 year.

TABLE SALT I use table salt rather than kosher salt in all the recipes in this book unless otherwise noted.

Sweeteners

BROWN SUGAR Light brown sugar was used for recipe testing in this book. If dark brown sugar is needed, it will be specified in the recipe.

CONFECTIONERS' SUGAR Confectioners' sugar is also known as powdered sugar and icing sugar.

CORN SYRUP Do not substitute dark corn syrup for light; it has a more robust flavor and is not a good replacement in these recipes.

GRANULATED SUGAR Granulated sugar (also known as white sugar) was used to test all the recipes in this book. Cane sugar can be substituted, but please note that it often has a coarser grain than regular white sugar, which means it won't melt as quickly as more finely ground sugar. If cane sugar is preferred, it can be processed in a food processor until it is finely ground before using.

SANDING SUGAR Sanding sugar is a large-crystal sugar that doesn't dissolve while baking. It is used mainly for decorating.

Flour

ALL-PURPOSE FLOUR Different brands of flours have varying levels of protein, ranging from low to high, which can result in very different outcomes when baking. I've found Gold Medal all-purpose unbleached flour to be the best option for many of the recipes in this book; I use it in all the baked good that don't use yeast. For yeasted doughs that call for all-purpose flour, I like to use King Arthur brand.

ALMOND FLOUR Almond flour is found in most grocery baking aisles or can be ordered online. Look for blanched almond flour, which removes the almond skins before processing.

HAZELNUT FLOUR Hazelnut flour is found in most grocery baking aisles or can be ordered online. To make it, you can pulse skinned hazelnuts in a food processor until finely ground.

Leavenings

BAKING POWDER I use nonaluminum baking powder when I bake, as brands with aluminum can give off the taste of metal. Baking powder can expire. To check if your baking powder is still potent, add a spoonful of it to a cup of hot water. If it bubbles, it is still good to use.

BAKING SODA In order for baking soda to rise, it needs to be paired with an acidic ingredient, such as buttermilk, sour cream, yogurt, vinegar, coffee, molasses, brown sugar, or pumpkin. You can check baking soda for freshness the same way you would check for baking powder.

Nuts

I usually toast nuts as soon as I purchase them and then store them in the freezer, as nuts can turn rancid. To toast nuts: Position an oven rack in the middle of the oven and preheat the oven to 350°F [180°C]. Line a sheet pan with parchment paper and place the nuts in the prepared pan in a single layer. Bake for 5 to 10 minutes, until the nuts darken and are fragrant. Let them cool, and then store them in a plastic freezer bag in the freezer for up to 1 month.

Chocolate

BITTERSWEET AND SEMISWEET CHOCOLATE
When shopping for semisweet and bittersweet bar chocolate to use in baking, look for one that falls between 35 and 60 percent cacao, and don't use anything over 70 percent, as this can alter the taste and texture of the recipe. (*Bittersweet* and *semisweet* can be confusing terms, as both can mean chocolate with a cacao percentage of anywhere from 35 to 99 percent.) Most recipes in this book call for semisweet chocolate.

When melting chocolate, chop the bar into fine pieces. This will help the chocolate melt more quickly and evenly and will give it less opportunity to burn. Make sure that there is no water in your bowl when melting, or on your knife and spatula, as contact with water can cause the chocolate to seize, turning it grainy. Adding 1 or 2 tablespoons of hot water to the seized chocolate and then stirring it can sometimes save it.

To melt chocolate in the microwave: Place the chopped chocolate in a microwave-safe bowl, and microwave the chocolate on medium for 1 minute, then stop and stir the chocolate. Continue to microwave the chocolate in 20-second intervals, stirring after each one, until the chocolate is almost completely smooth. Remove the bowl from the microwave and then stir until completely smooth.

CACAO NIBS Cacao nibs have a complex, bitter flavor and crunchy texture.

CHOCOLATE CHIPS Chocolate chips have less cacao than bar chocolate, which allows them to hold their shape when melted. This does mean, however, that they are not always a good substitute for bar chocolate.

COCOA POWDER There are two kinds of cocoa powder: Dutch-process and natural. Dutch-process cocoa is treated; it is washed with an alkaline solution that neutralizes its acids and gives it a more mellow, nutty flavor and a richer color. Natural cocoa powder is left as is, and is a very acidic, sharp powder. The recipes in this book all call for Dutch-process cocoa powder.

WHITE CHOCOLATE White chocolate is made from cocoa butter. Not all white chocolate is created equal, so use a brand you trust when baking with it; Valrhona is a personal favorite. White chocolate chips do not always melt well. White chocolate also melts more quickly than dark chocolate, so be sure to stir it more frequently than you would dark chocolate, especially when using the microwave.

Vanilla

VANILLA BEANS To use a vanilla bean: With a sharp knife, split the bean lengthwise, and then scrape the seeds out of the bean with the dull side of the knife or a spoon. Use the seeds in the recipe as called for. The leftover pod can be dried and then finely ground in a food processor to make a vanilla bean powder.

VANILLA EXTRACT All the recipes in this book use pure vanilla extract, and I don't recommend substituting artificial vanilla. However, pure vanilla extract is expensive, and if you have a brand of artificial vanilla you enjoy, it will work in these recipes.

CHAPTER 1

Muffins, Scones, and Quick Breads

"I came down as soon as I thought there was a prospect of breakfast."

—Charlotte Brontë, *Jane Eyre*

My blueberry muffin baking experience started with a blue boxed mix, complete with tiny dried blueberries. My mom would often make them to accompany dinner, and we would devour them slathered in too much butter. I started baking them from scratch while working at the Blue Heron Coffeehouse; I always loved that their recipe added nutmeg and I took that little trick with me when I left. This recipe is revamped from my first book, *The Vanilla Bean Baking Book*; I found adding almond flour keeps the crumb tender and light, and bumping up the baking powder helps those muffins dance beautifully over the rim. I did keep nutmeg involved, and incorporated it into a perfectly sugary top.

MAKES
12 MUFFINS

Blueberry Muffins

SUGAR TOPPING

½ cup [100 g] granulated sugar

¾ teaspoon freshly grated nutmeg

MUFFINS

2 cups [284 g] all-purpose flour

½ cup [50 g] almond flour

2 teaspoons baking powder

1 teaspoon salt

1 teaspoon lemon zest

¼ teaspoon baking soda

1 cup [200 g] granulated sugar

¾ cup [180 g] buttermilk, at room temperature

5 tablespoons [70 g] unsalted butter, melted

⅓ cup [75 g] vegetable or canola oil

¼ cup [60 g] sour cream, at room temperature

2 large eggs, at room temperature

1 tablespoon lemon juice

1 teaspoon pure vanilla extract

7½ oz [215 g] fresh or frozen blueberries

1) Position an oven rack in the middle of the oven and preheat the oven to 375°F [190°C]. Grease two standard twelve-cup muffin tins (see Muffin Tins and Greasing the Pans, page 24). 2) FOR THE SUGAR TOPPING In a small bowl, whisk together the granulated sugar and nutmeg. 3) FOR THE MUFFINS In a large bowl, whisk together the all-purpose flour, almond flour, baking powder, salt, lemon zest, and baking soda. Make a well in the center. In a large bowl or liquid measuring cup, whisk together the granulated sugar, buttermilk, melted butter, oil, sour cream, eggs, lemon juice, and vanilla until completely combined.

cont'd

Pour the wet ingredients into the well in the dry ingredients and mix gently until almost combined. Fold in the blueberries until just incorporated, being careful not to overwork the batter. It should not be completely smooth; there should be some visible lumps and bumps. The muffin batter can be stored, covered, in the refrigerator for up to 24 hours before baking. 4) Scoop a scant ⅓ cup of the batter into every other muffin cup (see Muffin Scoops, page 29). The batter should fill the cup and mound slightly (using a scoop helps the tops mound). Sprinkle 1 to 2 teaspoons of the sugar-nutmeg mixture evenly over each muffin. 5) Bake until the muffins are light golden brown and a toothpick inserted into the center of a muffin comes out with a few crumbs, rotating the pan halfway through baking, 17 to 20 minutes. Let the muffins cool in the tin for about 5 minutes, then gently remove them and transfer to a wire rack to cool for a few more minutes before serving. 6) Muffins are best eaten the day they are made, but they can be stored in an airtight container in the refrigerator for up to 2 days.

NOTE If your berries are out of season, adding a little "berry boost" can help ramp up the flavor. Combine 2 tablespoons [8 g] of freeze-dried berry powder (see page 14), 1 tablespoon of granulated sugar, 1 tablespoon of water, a pinch of salt, and the blueberries in a small saucepan. Cook over low heat until the berries are warm and coated in the sugar powder, about 3 minutes. Set aside to cool, then swirl into the recipe where the blueberries are called for.

Greasing the Pans

If you're using muffin liners, you don't have to grease the pan. Otherwise, it is absolutely necessary. Your best bet is to use a pastry brush to "paint" butter into the cavities and then dust them with flour, but pan spray works well too. If the muffins are not in liners, I also like to give the top of the pan a spray, so the muffin tops don't stick as much. I use a floured pan spray in the cavities, and a non-floured pan spray for the top (the flour can burn on the top of the pan). I find this usually ensures an easy release.

Muffin Tins

Standard muffin pans are surprisingly varied. After baking thousands of muffins in dozens of different pans over the last two decades, I can report that nearly every brand of muffin pan is slightly different. Because of this, your muffins may not bake up exactly like mine. When testing recipes for this book, I found that I preferred Nordic Ware Naturals twelve-cup aluminum commercial pans. My round scoop (see Muffin Scoops, page 29) matched the dimensions of the muffin cups perfectly, and I liked the way my muffins baked up. In each recipe, I try to give both the amount of batter for each cup and how full each cup should be. But baking a test muffin in your pan to see how it performs is always a good idea. Muffins also often rise better when every other muffin cavity is filled.

There was a time when I couldn't imagine a muffin that didn't fall into one of four categories: blueberry, lemon poppy seed, chocolate, or cranberry-orange. Those flavor choices held every bake case hostage in my suburbia bubble, and I never questioned my limited options. Then Colleen Wolner happened. She was (and is) co-owner of the Blue Heron Coffeehouse, and the first time I encountered her baking, she had the audacity to put other ingredients in her muffins. Strawberries! Ginger and pear! Chocolate with cardamom! And of course, almonds. There were almonds combined with cherries (a customer favorite) but also almonds and poppy seeds, and I loved those muffins so dearly that they quickly replaced blueberries in my heart. In my version, I swirl in some Almond Cream (page 292) to keep the muffins moist, but your favorite jam would be delicious here too.

Almond Poppy Seed Muffins

MAKES 12
MUFFINS

TOPPING

1 cup [120 g] almonds, toasted and chopped

½ cup [100 g] coarse or fine sugar

MUFFINS

2 cups [284 g] all-purpose flour

½ cup [50 g] almond flour

3 tablespoons poppy seeds

2 teaspoons baking powder

1 teaspoon salt

¼ teaspoon baking soda

1 cup [200 g] granulated sugar

¾ cup [180 g] buttermilk, at room temperature

5 tablespoons [70 g] unsalted butter, melted

⅓ cup [75 g] vegetable or canola oil

¼ cup [60 g] sour cream

2 large eggs, at room temperature

1 teaspoon pure vanilla extract

¾ teaspoon almond extract

½ cup [100 g] Almond Cream (page 292, see Note)

1) Position an oven rack in the middle of the oven and preheat the oven to 375°F [190°C]. Grease a standard twelve-cup muffin tin (see Muffin Tins and Greasing the Pans, page 24). 2) FOR THE TOPPING In a small bowl, combine the toasted almonds and sugar. 3) FOR THE MUFFINS In a large bowl or mixer bowl, whisk together the all-purpose flour, almond flour, poppy seeds, baking powder, salt, and baking soda. Make a well in the center.

cont'd

2

4) In a large bowl or liquid measuring cup, whisk together the granulated sugar, buttermilk, melted butter, oil, sour cream, eggs, vanilla, and almond extract until completely combined. Pour the wet ingredients into the well in the dry ingredients and mix gently until almost combined, being careful not to overwork the batter. It should not be completely smooth; there should be some visible lumps and bumps. Dollop the almond cream over the top of the batter, then use a spatula to swirl it into the batter with two or three turns until just incorporated; there will still be streaks of cream. The muffin batter can be stored, covered, in the refrigerator for up to 24 hours before baking. **5)** Scoop a scant ⅓ cup of the batter into each muffin cup. The batter should fill the cups and mound slightly in each cavity (using a scoop helps the tops mound). Top each muffin with a generous amount of the almond-and-sugar mixture. **6)** Bake until the muffins are light golden brown and a toothpick inserted into the center of a muffin comes out with a few crumbs, rotating the pan halfway through baking, 18 to 23 minutes. Let the muffins cool in the tin for about 5 minutes, then gently remove them and transfer to a wire rack to cool to room temperature. **7)** Muffins are best eaten the day they are made, but they can be stored in an airtight container in the refrigerator for up to 2 days.

NOTE If you do not have almond cream on hand, you can swirl in ⅓ cup [100 g] of lemon curd or your favorite jam.

In between school years during college, I spent my summers working the afternoon/evening shift at the Blue Heron Coffeehouse. This meant several things: I spent my entire shift drinking coffee, I stayed up until dawn arrived because of said coffee, and I spent the mornings sleeping in, only to realize too late that I had minutes to spare before my shift started. I would then frantically ride my bike across campus to relieve the morning barista at three o'clock and make myself an iced latte before business started to pick up. If the fates were kind to me, there would be some kind of berry streusel muffin left in the bake case. My favorite at the time was strawberry; the sweet berries and bitter flavor of the coffee never failed to balance each other out perfectly bite for bite. I still love streusel muffins, but now I enjoy mixing up my berries: blueberry, raspberry, and strawberry are all there.

Mixed Berry Muffins

MAKES
10 MUFFINS

BERRY SWIRL

3 oz [85 g] fresh or frozen raspberries

3 oz [85 g] fresh or frozen blueberries

2 oz [57 g] fresh or frozen strawberries, hulled and chopped into bite-size pieces

2 tablespoons granulated sugar

1 teaspoon lemon juice

MUFFINS

1½ cups [213 g] all-purpose flour

1½ teaspoons baking powder

¼ teaspoon baking soda

½ cup [120 g] buttermilk, at room temperature

2 tablespoons sour cream, at room temperature

1 teaspoon lemon juice

8 tablespoons [1 stick or 113 g] unsalted butter, at room temperature

¾ cup [150 g] granulated sugar

½ teaspoon salt

1 large egg, at room temperature

1 teaspoon pure vanilla extract

1½ cups [210 g] Pecan Streusel (page 291)

1) Position an oven rack in the middle of the oven and preheat the oven to 375°F [190°C]. Line a standard twelve-cup muffin tin with tulip liners or grease the pan (see Muffin Tins and Greasing the Pans, page 24). I prefer tulip liners here, as they keep the streusel in place.

cont'd

3

2) FOR THE SWIRL In a small saucepan, stir together the raspberries, blueberries, strawberries, sugar, and lemon juice. Heat over low heat, stirring and gently mashing the berries, until the sugar has dissolved and the berries are just starting to release their juices but still have some shape, 2 to 4 minutes (this will take longer with frozen berries). Remove from the heat and set aside to cool. 3) FOR THE MUFFINS In a small bowl, whisk together the flour, baking powder, and baking soda. In a large bowl or liquid measuring cup, whisk together the buttermilk, sour cream, and lemon juice. 4) In the bowl of a stand mixer fitted with a paddle, beat the butter on medium speed until creamy, about 1 minute. Add the granulated sugar and salt and beat until light and fluffy, 3 to 5 minutes. Lower the speed to low and add the egg, beating until incorporated and scraping down the sides of the bowl as needed. Beat in the vanilla. Scrape down the sides of the bowl again and, still on low speed, add one-third of the flour mixture, beating until just combined. Beat in the buttermilk mixture and the remaining flour mixture in halves, alternating between the two and ending with the flour mixture, mixing just until combined. 5) Pour the cooled berry mixture into the mixer bowl, and use a spatula to swirl the mixture into the batter with two or three turns until just incorporated; there will still be streaks of fruit. The muffin batter can be stored, covered, in the refrigerator for up to 24 hours before baking. 6) Scoop a scant ⅓ cup of the batter into each tulip liner. Sprinkle the streusel evenly over the tops of the muffins.

7) Bake until the streusel is golden brown and a toothpick inserted into the center of a muffin comes out with a few crumbs, rotating the pan halfway through baking, 25 to 30 minutes. Let the muffins cool in the tin for about 5 minutes, then gently remove them and transfer to a wire rack to cool for a few more minutes before serving. 8) Muffins are best eaten the day they are made, but they can be stored in an airtight container in the refrigerator for up to 2 days.

Muffin Scoops

Every bakery I worked in used a portion scoop to dish the batter into the muffin pans. It ensured both consistency and a well-rounded top, which helped the muffins bake up pretty. I still use one in my home kitchen. I found that the 2 oz scoop from Vollrath works perfectly with my Nordic Ware pans.

Caramel apples always bring to mind crisp autumn afternoons and the sound of crunching leaves underfoot. I didn't grow up with an apple tree in my yard, but at least once every October my mom would pick up a caramel apple kit at the grocery store and we'd dip our Granny Smiths in sticky sweetness. These muffins are a nod to that memory, with rich caramel icing draped over apple muffins.

Caramel Apple Muffins

MAKES
8 MUFFINS

MUFFINS

1½ cups [213 g] all-purpose flour

1½ teaspoons baking powder

½ teaspoon ground cinnamon

¼ teaspoon baking soda

¼ cup [60 g] apple cider, at room temperature

¼ cup [60 g] sour cream, at room temperature

8 tablespoons [1 stick or 113 g] unsalted butter, at room temperature

¾ cup [150 g] granulated sugar

½ teaspoon salt

1 large egg, at room temperature

1 tablespoon applejack brandy (optional)

1 teaspoon pure vanilla extract

1 cup [150 g] grated Gala apples

ICING

3 tablespoons Caramel, homemade (page 289) or store-bought

1 to 3 tablespoons apple cider

1 tablespoon unsalted butter, melted

½ teaspoon pure vanilla extract

Pinch of salt

1 cup [120 g] confectioners' sugar

1 cup [120 g] Candied Pecans (page 291)

1) FOR THE MUFFINS Position an oven rack in the middle of the oven and preheat the oven to 375°F [190°C]. Grease a standard twelve-cup muffin tin (see Muffin Tins and Greasing the Pans, page 24). **2)** In a small bowl, whisk together the flour, baking powder, cinnamon, and baking soda. In a medium bowl or liquid measuring cup, whisk together the apple cider and sour cream. **3)** In the bowl of a stand mixer fitted with a paddle, beat the butter on medium speed until creamy, 1 minute. Add the granulated sugar and salt and beat again on medium speed until light and fluffy, 3 to 5 minutes. Add the egg and beat on low speed until incorporated, scraping down the sides of the bowl as needed. Beat in the brandy, if using, then the vanilla. Scrape down the bowl again and add one-third of the flour mixture.

cont'd

Continue beating on low speed until just combined. Beat in the apple cider mixture and the remaining flour mixture in halves, alternating between the two and ending with the flour mixture, mixing until just combined. Add the grated apple, and then mix until just incorporated into the batter, 30 seconds. 4) Scoop ⅓ cup of the batter into the prepared tin; the batter should fill the cups and slightly mound in each cavity (using a scoop works best here to help the tops mound). Bake until a skewer or toothpick inserted into the center of a muffin comes out with a few crumbs, rotating the pan halfway through baking, 20 to 24 minutes. Let the muffins cool in the tin for about 5 minutes, then gently remove them and transfer to a wire rack to cool for 10 minutes. 5) FOR THE ICING While the muffins are cooling, make the icing. In a medium bowl, combine the caramel, 1 tablespoon of the apple cider, the melted butter, vanilla, and salt. Add the confectioners' sugar and mix until smooth, adding more apple cider, 1 tablespoon at a time, until the desired consistency is reached; the icing should be thick but pourable. Drizzle the icing over the top of each muffin, and sprinkle with the candied pecans. 6) Muffins are best eaten the day they are made, but they can be stored in an airtight container in the refrigerator for 2 days.

Double chocolate muffins probably aren't the most nutritious way to start the day, but adding banana always makes me feel better about indulging in something sweet first thing in the morning. I've made these muffins for years, both in shops and at home, and decided this time around to do some upgrading—a little more banana and a lot more chocolate did the trick.

Double Chocolate Banana Muffins

 MAKES ABOUT
14 MUFFINS

1½ cups [213 g] all-purpose flour

¾ cup [75 g] Dutch-process cocoa powder

2 teaspoons baking powder

¼ teaspoon baking soda

1¼ cups [250 g] granulated sugar

1 cup [227 g] mashed bananas (about 3 bananas)

½ cup [120 g] buttermilk, at room temperature

5 tablespoons [70 g] unsalted butter, melted

3 large eggs, at room temperature

¼ cup [60 g] sour cream, at room temperature

2 teaspoons pure vanilla extract

¾ teaspoon salt

4 oz [113 g] semisweet chocolate, finely chopped

Turbinado sugar, for sprinkling

1) Position an oven rack in the middle of the oven and preheat the oven to 375°F [190°C]. Grease two standard twelve-cup muffin tins (see Muffin Tins and Greasing the Pans, page 24). 2) In a large bowl, whisk together the flour, cocoa powder, baking powder, and baking soda. Make a well in the center.

cont'd

3) In a large bowl or liquid measuring cup, whisk together the granulated sugar, bananas, buttermilk, melted butter, eggs, sour cream, vanilla, and salt until completely combined. Pour the wet ingredients into the well in the dry ingredients and mix gently until almost combined. Fold in the chopped chocolate until just incorporated, being careful not to overwork the batter. It should not be completely smooth; there should be some visible lumps and bumps. 4) Scoop a scant ⅓ cup of the batter into each cup. The batter should fill the cups and mound slightly in each cavity (using a scoop helps the tops mound). Sprinkle the tops of the muffins generously with the turbinado sugar. 5) Bake until a toothpick inserted into the center of a muffin comes out with a few crumbs, rotating the pan halfway through baking, 18 to 23 minutes. Let the muffins cool in the tin for about 5 minutes, then gently remove them and transfer to a wire rack to cool for a few more minutes before serving. 6) Muffins are best eaten the day they are made, but they can be stored in an airtight container in the refrigerator for 2 days.

In Minnesota, rhubarb is the first sign that spring is actually, finally here, and bakers everywhere use it in abundance until berries make their debut later in the year. Rhubarb contains quite a bit of liquid, so I like to cook it down first, which helps ensure the finished muffin is not soggy while also concentrating the flavor.

Rhubarb Cream Cheese Swirl Muffins

MAKES 10
MUFFINS

RHUBARB SWIRL

1½ cups [150 g] chopped rhubarb, in bite-size pieces (see Note)

⅓ cup [65 g] granulated sugar

1 tablespoon water

CREAM CHEESE SWIRL

3 oz [85 g] cream cheese, at room temperature

1 tablespoon granulated sugar

MUFFINS

1½ cups [213 g] all-purpose flour

1½ teaspoons baking powder

¼ teaspoon baking soda

½ cup [120 g] buttermilk, at room temperature

2 tablespoons sour cream, at room temperature

8 tablespoons [1 stick or 113 g] unsalted butter, at room temperature

¾ cup [150 g] granulated sugar

½ teaspoon salt

1 large egg, at room temperature

1 teaspoon pure vanilla extract

1½ cups [210 g] Streusel (page 291)

1) Position an oven rack in the middle of the oven and preheat the oven to 375°F [190°C]. Line two standard twelve-cup muffin tins with tulip liners (see Muffin Tins and Greasing the Pans, page 24). 2) FOR THE RHUBARB SWIRL In a small saucepan, combine the rhubarb, granulated sugar, and water. Heat over low heat, stirring occasionally, until the rhubarb has broken down, 12 to 15 minutes. Remove from the heat and set aside to cool. 3) FOR THE CREAM CHEESE SWIRL In a small bowl, combine the cream cheese and granulated sugar, and stir until smooth.

cont'd

4) FOR THE MUFFINS In a small bowl, whisk together the flour, baking powder, and baking soda. In a medium bowl or liquid measuring cup, whisk together the buttermilk and sour cream. 5) In the bowl of a stand mixer fitted with a paddle, beat the butter on medium speed until creamy, 1 minute. Add the granulated sugar and salt and beat until light and fluffy, 3 to 5 minutes. Lower the speed to low and add the egg, scraping down the sides of the bowl as needed. Beat in the vanilla. Scrape down the sides of the bowl again, and add one-third of the flour mixture. Beat on low speed until just combined. Beat in the buttermilk mixture and the remaining flour mixture in halves, alternating between the two and ending with the flour mixture, mixing until just combined. 6) Pour the rhubarb and cream cheese mixtures into the bowl, and use a spatula to swirl the mixtures into the batter until just incorporated with two or three turns; there will still be streaks of fruit and cream cheese. The muffin batter can be stored, covered, in the refrigerator for up to 24 hours before baking. 7) Scoop a scant ⅓ cup of the batter into each tulip liner. Sprinkle the streusel evenly over the top of each muffin. 8) Bake until the streusel is golden brown and a toothpick inserted into the center of a muffin comes out with a few crumbs, rotating the pan halfway through baking, 25 to 30 minutes. Let the muffins cool in the tin for about 5 minutes, then gently remove them and transfer to a wire rack to cool for a few more minutes before serving. 9) Muffins are best eaten the day they are made, but they can be stored in an airtight container in the refrigerator for up to 2 days.

NOTE If your variety of rhubarb doesn't cook down into a pretty shade of pink (many don't), you can add a thin slice of red beet or a handful of raspberries to the pan with the rhubarb, or add a few drops of pink food coloring to the rhubarb mixture.

Muffin Liners

For many of the recipes in this book I don't use muffin liners, but there are a few exceptions. I like to use tulip liners (which stand taller in the pan) for muffins with streusel, as it helps the streusel stay on the batter, so it won't spill all over the pan and oven floor. If you've never used a liner, you can bake a test muffin and see how it works in your particular pan.

This recipe is based on the Grapefruit Cake Bars from my cookbook *100 Cookies* (which, in turn, is based on a Bundt cake from Yossy Arefi's book *Sweeter Off the Vine*). I love the tart flavor of grapefruit, and Yossy's method of adding the segmented pieces and juice to the batter is genius. "To ease each pale pink segment out of its case so carefully without breaking a single pearly cell" makes for delicious muffins. (Craig Arnold, "Meditation on a Grapefruit")

Grapefruit Glazed Muffins

 MAKES 16 MUFFINS

MUFFINS

1 medium grapefruit

1½ cups [300 g] granulated sugar

3 cups [426 g] all-purpose flour

1 tablespoon baking powder

½ teaspoon baking soda

1 cup [2 sticks or 227 g] unsalted butter, at room temperature

1 teaspoon salt

2 large eggs, at room temperature

1 teaspoon pure vanilla extract

1 cup [240 g] buttermilk, at room temperature

GLAZE

1½ cups [180 g] confectioners' sugar

Pinch of salt

2 to 3 tablespoons grapefruit juice

1 tablespoon grapefruit liqueur (optional)

1) FOR THE MUFFINS Position an oven rack in the middle of the oven and preheat the oven to 375°F [190°C]. Line two standard twelve-cup muffin tins or grease the pan (see Muffin Tins and Greasing the Pans, page 24). Line a sheet pan with parchment paper and set a wire rack on top. **2)** Scrub the grapefruit with warm, soapy water (to remove any excess wax), rinse, then dry the fruit. Put the granulated sugar into a medium bowl and grate the grapefruit zest directly over the sugar, being careful not to include any of the bitter white pith. With your fingers, rub the zest into the sugar until combined and fragrant. **3)** Cut the top and bottom off the grapefruit, then cut away any remaining peel and the white pith from the surface of the fruit. Over a bowl, carefully cut the sections of the grapefruit away from the membrane, letting the fruit and juices fall into the bowl. Remove any seeds that have fallen in, and break up the fruit into small pieces, about ½ in [12 mm] wide.

4) In a medium bowl, whisk together the flour, baking powder, and baking soda. 5) In the bowl of a stand mixer fitted with a paddle, beat the butter on medium speed until creamy, 1 minute. Add the sugar-zest mixture and salt and beat until light and fluffy, 3 to 5 minutes. Lower the speed to low and add the eggs, one at a time, scraping down the sides of the bowl as needed. Beat in the vanilla. Scrape down the bowl again and add one-third of the flour mixture. Beat on low speed until just combined. Beat in the buttermilk and the remaining flour mixture in halves, alternating between the two and ending with the flour mixture, mixing until just combined. Remove the bowl from the mixer and gently fold in the grapefruit segments and their juices. The muffin batter can be stored, covered, in the refrigerator, for up to 24 hours before baking. 6) Scoop a scant ⅓ cup of the batter into the prepared tins; the batter should fill the cups and mound slightly in each cavity (using a scoop helps the tops mound). 7) Bake until a toothpick inserted into the center of a muffin comes out with a few crumbs, rotating the pan halfway through baking, 25 to 30 minutes. Let the muffins cool in the tin for about 5 minutes, then gently remove them and transfer to the rack in the prepared sheet pan and let cool for 15 more minutes. 8) FOR THE GLAZE In a medium bowl, stir together the confectioners' sugar and salt. Whisk in 2 tablespoons of the grapefruit juice and add the liqueur, if using. The glaze should be thick but pourable. If it seems too thick, add a few more drops of grapefruit juice. Pour the glaze over the warm muffins and let set before serving. 9) Muffins are best eaten the day they are made, but they can be stored in an airtight container in the refrigerator for up to 2 days.

Is it cake, or is it a muffin? Today, we will convince ourselves it is a muffin.
Yes, it truly is, even with that generous heap of Brown Butter Cream Cheese Icing.

MAKES 14
MUFFINS

Carrot Cake Muffins

MUFFINS

⅔ cup [150 g] vegetable
or canola oil

¾ cup [150 g] granulated
sugar

¼ cup [50 g] brown
sugar

2 large eggs, at room
temperature

1 tablespoon triple sec
(optional)

1 teaspoon ground
cinnamon

1 teaspoon ground
ginger

¾ teaspoon baking
powder

½ teaspoon baking soda

½ teaspoon salt

Pinch of ground cloves

1½ cups [213 g] all-
purpose flour

2 cups [200 g] finely
grated carrots

**BROWN BUTTER CREAM
CHEESE ICING**

12 tablespoons [1½ sticks
or 170 g] unsalted butter,
at room temperature

¼ teaspoon salt

4 oz [113 g] cream
cheese, at room
temperature

2 cups [240 g]
confectioners' sugar

2 teaspoons pure vanilla
extract

8

1) FOR THE MUFFINS Position an oven rack in the middle of the oven and preheat the oven to 350°F [180°C]. Line two standard twelve-cup muffin tins (see Muffin Tins and Greasing the Pans, page 24); these muffins bake best with liners. **2)** In a large bowl, whisk together the oil, granulated and brown sugars, eggs, triple sec (if using), cinnamon, ginger, baking powder, baking soda, salt, and cloves until completely combined. Add the flour, stirring until just combined, then add the carrots, stirring until incorporated. The muffin batter can be stored, covered, in the refrigerator for up to 24 hours before baking. **3)** Divide the mixture evenly among the fourteen muffin cavities; the batter should come up halfway in each cavity. Bake until a tooth-pick inserted into a muffin comes out clean, rotating the pan halfway through baking, 18 to 22 minutes. Set the pan on a wire rack and let cool for 15 minutes, then remove the muffins and let them finish cooling on the rack before icing.

4) **FOR THE ICING** Brown 8 tablespoons [1 stick or 113 g] of the butter (see page 293). Pour the brown butter into a heatproof, freezer-safe bowl and let cool for 10 minutes. Place the bowl in the freezer until solid, but not frozen, about 30 minutes. Transfer to the bowl of a stand mixer fitted with a paddle. 5) Add the remaining 4 tablespoons [56 g] of butter and the salt to the brown butter and beat on medium speed until smooth, 1 minute. Add the cream cheese and beat again until smooth and creamy. Lower the mixer speed to low and slowly add the confectioners' sugar, beating until well combined and creamy and stopping to scrape down the sides of the bowl as necessary, 4 to 5 minutes. Beat in the vanilla. Using an offset spatula or piping bag, spread or pipe a generous amount of icing over the top of each muffin. 6) Muffins are best eaten the day they are made, but these can be stored in an airtight container in the refrigerator for 3 days.

This recipe is for when I find myself needing a little whole-wheat flour in my life. I use a little all-purpose and almond flour to keep the base light, and mashed bananas and yogurt also contribute to keeping things delicious and moist.

Whole-Wheat Yogurt Muffins

 MAKES 12 MUFFINS

TOPPING

⅓ cup [65 g] granulated sugar

¾ teaspoon ground cinnamon

MUFFINS

1½ cups [213 g] whole-wheat flour

½ cup [71 g] all-purpose flour

½ cup [50 g] almond flour

2 teaspoons baking powder

1 teaspoon salt

¼ teaspoon baking soda

1 cup [200 g] granulated sugar

1 cup [240 g] Greek or full-fat plain yogurt, at room temperature

5 tablespoons [70 g] unsalted butter, melted

⅓ cup [75 g] vegetable or canola oil

2 large eggs, at room temperature

2 tablespoons orange juice

1 teaspoon pure vanilla extract

1 cup [226 g] chopped bananas

½ cup [60 g] pecan halves or your favorite nut, toasted and chopped

½ cup [60 g] raisins, your favorite dried fruit, or mini chocolate chips

1) Position an oven rack in the middle of the oven and preheat the oven to 375°F [190°C]. Grease a standard twelve-cup muffin tin (see Muffin Tins and Greasing the Pans, page 24). **2)** FOR THE TOPPING In a small bowl, whisk together the granulated sugar and cinnamon. **3)** FOR THE MUFFINS In a large bowl, whisk together the whole-wheat flour, all-purpose flour, almond flour, baking powder, salt, and baking soda. Make a well in the center. **4)** In a large bowl or liquid measuring cup, whisk together the granulated sugar, yogurt, melted butter, oil, eggs, orange juice, and vanilla until completely combined. Pour the wet ingredients into the well in the dry ingredients and mix gently until almost combined. Fold in the bananas, pecans, and raisins until just incorporated, being careful not to overwork the batter. It should not be completely smooth; there should be some visible lumps and bumps. The muffin batter can be stored, covered, in the refrigerator for up to 24 hours before baking.

9

Freezing Muffins

To freeze muffins, wrap cooled muffins in plastic wrap and place in an airtight, freezer-safe container or plastic bag. Store in the freezer for up to 2 weeks. The night before serving, put the muffins in the refrigerator to thaw.

5) Scoop a scant ⅓ cup of the batter into each muffin cup. The batter should fill the cups and mound slightly in each cavity (using a scoop helps the tops mound). Sprinkle 1 to 2 teaspoons of the sugar topping evenly over each muffin. **6)** Bake until the muffins are light golden brown and a toothpick inserted into the center of a muffin comes out with a few crumbs, rotating the pan halfway through baking, 18 to 23 minutes. Let the muffins cool in the tin for about 5 minutes, then gently remove them and transfer to a wire rack to cool for a few more minutes before serving. **7)** Muffins are best eaten the day they are made, but they can be stored in an airtight container in the refrigerator for up to 2 days.

10

I can already feel the sideways glance you are giving me for including these muffins in this chapter, but, well, I have two children with birthdays that often fall during a school week. And sprinkled birthday muffins on such a day makes the morning extra special. There isn't as much sugar in the muffin as in a regular cupcake, but the addition of sprinkles and frosting goes a long way.

Happy Birthday Muffins

 MAKES 9
MUFFINS

MUFFINS

1½ cups [213 g] all-purpose flour

1½ teaspoons baking powder

¼ teaspoon baking soda

½ cup [120 g] buttermilk, at room temperature

2 tablespoons sour cream, at room temperature

8 tablespoons [1 stick or 113 g] unsalted butter, at room temperature

¾ cup [150 g] granulated sugar

½ teaspoon salt

1 large egg, at room temperature

1 teaspoon pure vanilla extract

½ cup [75 g] large sprinkles (see Notes)

ICING

8 tablespoons [1 stick or 113 g] unsalted butter, at room temperature

4 oz [113 g] cream cheese, at room temperature

1 tablespoon corn syrup

Pinch of salt

2¼ cups [270 g] confectioners' sugar

2 teaspoons pure vanilla extract

Extra sprinkles, for garnish (optional)

1) FOR THE MUFFINS Position an oven rack in the middle of the oven and preheat the oven to 375°F [190°C]. Grease nine cavities in a large popover tin (see Notes, following, and Muffin Tins and Greasing the Pans, page 24). **2)** In a small bowl, whisk together the flour, baking powder, and baking soda. In a medium bowl or liquid measuring cup, whisk together the buttermilk and sour cream. **3)** In the bowl of a stand mixer fitted with a paddle, beat the butter on medium speed until creamy, 1 minute. Add the granulated sugar and salt and continue beating until light and fluffy, 3 to 5 minutes. Lower the speed to low and add the egg, scraping down the sides of the bowl as needed. Beat in the vanilla.

cont'd

4) Scrape down the sides of the bowl again and add one-third of the flour mixture. Beat on low speed until just combined. Beat in the buttermilk mixture and the remaining flour mixture in halves, alternating between the two and ending with the flour mixture, mixing until just combined. Add the sprinkles and then mix again, just incorporating them into the batter. Remove the bowl from the stand mixer and stir once or twice with a spatula. 5) Divide the batter evenly among the prepared tins; the batter should come up about halfway in each cup. Bake until a toothpick inserted into the center of a muffin comes out with a few crumbs, rotating the pan halfway through baking, 25 to 30 minutes. Let the muffins cool in the tin for about 5 minutes, then gently remove them and transfer to a wire rack to cool completely before icing.

6) FOR THE ICING While the muffins are cooling, make the icing. In a clean bowl of the stand mixer, still fitted with a paddle, beat the butter and cream cheese on medium speed until light yellow and creamy, about 3 minutes. Lower the mixer speed to low and add the corn syrup and salt, beating until combined. Gradually beat in the confectioners' sugar, then increase the speed to medium and beat until smooth and creamy, stopping to scrape down the sides of the bowl as necessary, 2 to 3 minutes. Lower the mixer speed to low and beat in the vanilla. Frost each muffin with a thick layer of icing and top with more sprinkles, if desired. 7) Muffins are best eaten the same day they are made, but they can be stored in an airtight container in the refrigerator for up to 2 days.

NOTES Large sprinkles work best in the batter. They melt slightly and streak beautifully, while smaller sprinkles can melt a lot more and turn the batter a grayish color.

If you do not have popover pans, you can use a regular muffin pan and fill each cup about halfway, as called for in the directions.

Scones come in all shapes, sizes, and flavors, and I make a variety of them in rotation. In this version, the minimal amount of chopped dried apricots and white chocolate scattered throughout the scone base keeps the focus on the creamy flavor of the scone. These can be baked right away, but a rest overnight in the refrigerator allows for early morning baking.

MAKES
8 SCONES

Apricot White Chocolate Overnight Scones

½ cup [120 g] sour cream

1 large egg

3 tablespoons heavy cream, plus more for brushing

½ teaspoon pure vanilla extract

2¼ cups [320 g] all-purpose flour, plus more for dusting

⅓ cup [65 g] granulated sugar, plus more for sprinkling

4 teaspoons baking powder

½ teaspoon salt

10 tablespoons [140 g] cold unsalted butter, cut into ½ in [12 mm] pieces

¼ cup [40 g] dried apricots, chopped into small pieces

3 oz [85 g] white chocolate, finely chopped

1) In a medium bowl or liquid measuring cup, whisk together the sour cream, egg, heavy cream, and vanilla. Refrigerate until ready to use. 2) In a large bowl, whisk together the flour, sugar, baking powder, and salt. 3) Add the butter to the dry ingredients and use a pastry cutter to cut in the butter until the flour-coated pieces are the size of peas. Add the chopped apricots and chocolate and stir to combine. Add the refrigerated wet ingredients and fold with a spatula until just combined. The dough will be shaggy, with some dry bits.

cont'd

4) Transfer the dough to a lightly floured surface and knead eight to ten times: Gently fold the dough over on itself, gather any loose/dry pieces and place them on top, then flatten again. Repeat this process until all the loose pieces are worked into the dough. 5) Shape the dough into a 10 in [25 cm] circle, about 1 in [2.5 cm] thick. Wrap with plastic wrap, then let the dough rest in the refrigerator overnight. 6) When you're ready to bake the scones, position an oven rack in the middle of the oven and preheat the oven to 375°F [190°C]. Line a sheet pan with parchment paper. 7) Move the chilled dough to a gently floured work surface. Use a 2.5 in [6 cm] biscuit cutter to cut out rounds. Place the scones on the prepared sheet pan. The dough can be gently kneaded and patted again to stamp out more scones. Put the scones in the freezer for 30 minutes while the oven preheats (see Notes). 8) Brush the tops of the scones with a little heavy cream, making sure it doesn't drip down the sides. Sprinkle the top of each scone generously with granulated sugar. Place another sheet pan under the scones, so the pans are double-stacked (see Notes). 9) Bake the scones until the tops and bottoms are light golden brown, rotating the stacked pans halfway through baking, 18 to 25 minutes. Transfer the top sheet pan to a wire rack and let the scones cool slightly before serving. 10) Scones are best eaten the same day they are made.

NOTES Double-stacking the sheet pans helps prevent the bottoms of the scones from browning too quickly.

Freezing the scones before baking helps them retain their shape.

VARIATIONS

• **Ginger Chocolate Scones:** *Substitute chopped crystallized ginger for the apricots and mini semisweet chocolate chips for the white chocolate.*

• **Chocolate Orange Scones:** *Substitute chopped candied orange peel for the apricots and mini semisweet chocolate chips for the white chocolate.*

It's impossible for me to choose between banana bread and scones for a favorite morning treat, so here is a way to easily enjoy both. Please don't skip icing the scones! It really makes them shine. If you don't want to use rum, the Maple Icing from the Maple Oatmeal Scones (page 52) makes a good substitute.

Banana Bread Scones

 MAKES 8 SCONES

SCONES

½ cup [113 g] mashed bananas (about 1½ bananas)

⅓ cup [80 g] heavy cream, plus more for brushing

1 large egg

1 teaspoon pure vanilla extract

2¼ cups [320 g] all-purpose flour, plus more for dusting

⅓ cup [65 g] granulated sugar

1 tablespoon baking powder

½ teaspoon salt

12 tablespoons [1½ sticks or 170 g] cold unsalted butter, cut into ½ in [12 mm] pieces

¼ cup [30 g] pecans, toasted and chopped

RUM ICING

1 tablespoon unsalted butter, melted

1 to 2 tablespoons blackstrap rum or other dark rum

Pinch of salt

1 cup [120 g] confectioners' sugar

1) FOR THE SCONES Line a sheet pan with parchment paper. In a medium bowl or liquid measuring cup, whisk together the mashed bananas, heavy cream, egg, and vanilla. Refrigerate until ready to use.
2) In a large bowl, whisk together the flour, granulated sugar, baking powder, and salt.
3) Add the butter to the dry ingredients, and use a pastry cutter to cut in the butter until the flour-coated pieces are the size of peas. Add the chopped pecans and stir to combine. Add the refrigerated wet ingredients and fold with a spatula until just combined. **4)** Transfer the dough to a generously floured surface and knead ten to twelve times, until it comes together, adding a little flour as necessary. Pat the dough into a square and roll it into a 12 in [30.5 cm] square, dusting with flour as necessary. Fold the dough in thirds, like a business letter. Fold the dough in thirds again by folding in the short ends, making a square. Transfer it to the prepared sheet pan and put it in the freezer for 10 minutes.

5) Return the dough to the floured surface, shape it into a 12 in [30.5 cm] square, and fold the dough in thirds again. Turn over the dough, so it's seam-side down, and gently roll out the dough into a 12 by 4 in [30.5 by 10 cm] rectangle. 6) With a sharp knife, cut it crosswise into four equal rectangles, then cut each rectangle diagonally into two triangles. Transfer the triangles to the prepared sheet pan. Freeze the scones for 30 minutes (see Notes, page 48). 7) Position an oven rack in the middle of the oven and preheat the oven to 375°F [190°C]. 8) Brush the tops of the scones with a little heavy cream, making sure it doesn't drip down the sides. Place another sheet pan under the scones, so the pans are double-stacked (see Notes, page 48). Bake the scones, rotating the stacked pans halfway through, until the tops and bottoms are light golden brown, 18 to 25 minutes. Transfer the top sheet pan to a wire rack and let the scones cool slightly. 9) FOR THE ICING While the scones are baking, in a small bowl, whisk together the melted butter, 1 tablespoon of the rum, and the salt. Add the confectioners' sugar and mix together, then whisk until well combined and smooth. Add more rum (or water), 1 tablespoon at a time, if needed, to reach the desired consistency. Use the back of a spoon or an offset spatula to top each scone with the icing. 10) Scones are best eaten the same day they are made.

Maple Oatmeal Scones have been a favorite of mine for decades, and almost all the versions I've made at various bakeries throughout the years were inspired by Ina Garten's version in her *Barefoot Contessa* cookbook. I use a food processor to help break down the oats and make quick work of incorporating the butter into the dough. If you don't have one, see the Note.

Maple Oatmeal Scones

 MAKES
9 SCONES

SCONES

⅓ cup [80 g] buttermilk

⅓ cup [107 g] maple syrup

2 large eggs

1 teaspoon pure vanilla extract

3 cups [426 g] all-purpose flour, plus more for dusting

⅔ cup [70 g] rolled oats, plus more for sprinkling

2 tablespoons granulated sugar

4 teaspoons baking powder

1 teaspoon salt

1 cup [2 sticks or 227 g] cold unsalted butter, cut into ½ in [12 mm] pieces

Heavy cream, for brushing

MAPLE ICING

¼ cup [80 g] maple syrup

1 tablespoon unsalted butter, melted

½ teaspoon pure vanilla extract

Pinch of salt

1 cup [120 g] confectioners' sugar

1) FOR THE SCONES Line a sheet pan with parchment paper. In a medium bowl or liquid measuring cup, whisk together the buttermilk, maple syrup, eggs, and vanilla. Refrigerate until ready to use. **2)** In the bowl of a food processor, combine the flour, oats, granulated sugar, baking powder, and salt and pulse a few times to combine. Add the butter and pulse again until the flour-coated pieces are the size of peas, eight to ten pulses. Transfer the dry ingredients to a large bowl. Add the refrigerated wet ingredients and fold with a spatula until just combined. The dough will be shaggy, with some dry bits. **3)** Transfer the dough to a lightly floured surface and knead four to six times, until it comes together, adding more flour as necessary. Pat the dough gently into a square and roll it into a 12 in [30.5 cm] square, dusting with flour as necessary. Fold the dough in thirds, like a business letter. Fold the dough in thirds again by folding in the short ends of the dough, making

3

a square. Transfer it to the prepared sheet pan and put it in the freezer for 10 minutes. 4) Return the dough to the floured surface, shape it into an 8 in [20 cm] square, about 1 in [2.5 cm] thick. Use a 2.5 in [6 cm] floured biscuit cutter to cut out rounds. Transfer the scones to the prepared sheet pan. The dough can be gently kneaded and patted again to stamp out more scones. Freeze the scones while the oven is preheating (see Notes, page 48). 5) Meanwhile, position an oven rack in the middle of the oven and preheat the oven to 375°F [190°C]. 6) Brush the tops of the scones with a little heavy cream, making sure it doesn't drip down the sides. Place another sheet pan under the scones, so the pans are double-stacked (see Notes, page 48). Bake the scones, rotating the

pans halfway through baking, until the tops and bottoms are light golden brown, 18 to 25 minutes. Transfer the top sheet pan to a wire rack and let the scones cool slightly. 7) FOR THE ICING While the scones are baking, in a small bowl, whisk together the maple syrup, melted butter, vanilla, and salt. Add the confectioners' sugar and mix together, then whisk until well combined and smooth. Use the back of a spoon or an offset spatula to top each scone with the icing and a sprinkling of oats. 8) Scones are best eaten the same day they are made.

NOTE If you don't have a food processor, you can use quick oats to replace the rolled oats. Use a pastry cutter to cut the butter into the dry ingredients.

14

My love affair with scones has mostly been American in nature, what with all the extra butter, heavy cream, and untraditional add-ins, including chocolate. However, several years ago I had an opportunity to try authentic British scones, courtesy of cookbook author Edd Kimber. Edd pointed out that his dough contained whole milk, less butter, and no chocolate (he was very clear about the chocolate). He also kneaded the dough a special way (referred to as chaffing), then let the shaped scones rest at room temperature for an hour before popping them in the oven. I was skeptical after years of freezing my scones before baking, but then I split a warm scone in half and slathered it with clotted cream and jam. It was truly one of the best scones I had ever eaten. I decided to take a stab at making them myself, and after testing scone after scone and calling on the 20 percent of British ancestry that resides in my genes to guide me, here are my British scones made by an American.

MAKES 12
SCONES

Traditional Scones

2 large eggs

¾ cup [180 g] whole milk

½ teaspoon pure vanilla extract

3 cups minus 2 tablespoons [408 g] all-purpose flour, plus more for shaping

4½ teaspoons baking powder

2 tablespoons cornstarch

½ teaspoon salt

6 tablespoons [84 g] unsalted butter, at room temperature

½ cup [100 g] granulated sugar

Egg wash (see page 14)

Butter, for serving

Jam, for serving

Clotted cream, for serving (optional)

1) Line a sheet pan with parchment paper. In a medium-size liquid measuring cup, whisk together the eggs, ¼ cup [60 g] of the milk, and the vanilla. Set aside.

2) Put the flour in the bowl of a stand mixer fitted with a paddle. Add the baking powder, cornstarch, and salt. Add the butter and mix on low speed until the butter is completely worked into the flour and no lumps remain. Remove the bowl from the mixer.

cont'd

3) Add the sugar and use a spatula to stir it into the flour mixture. Add the egg and milk mixture and mix again with the spatula until combined. Add the remaining ½ cup [120 g] of milk, a little at a time, folding the mixture together with the spatula until a sticky dough forms (you may not need all of the milk).

4) Generously dust your work surface with 2 tablespoons of flour and dump the dough on it. Sprinkle the top of the dough with 2 more tablespoons of flour and chaff the dough: Fold the dough in half, give the dough a quarter turn, and fold again. Repeat until the dough is smooth, being careful not to overwork it, about six to eight turns and folds total. The dough will feel almost like a yeasted dough; it will have a slight bounce because of the air worked into it. 5) Very gently pat the dough into a 1 in [2.5 cm] thick circle, 7 to 8 in [17 to 20 cm] wide. Use a floured 2 in [5 cm] biscuit cutter to cut out the scones, and place them on the prepared sheet pan. Gently knead the remaining dough again and cut out more scones. 6) Let the scones rest, uncovered, for at least 1 hour, and up to 2 hours, at room temperature. 7) Position an oven rack in the middle of the oven and preheat the oven to 425°F [220°C]. 8) Use a pastry brush to brush the tops of the scones with the egg wash. Bake for 10 to 12 minutes, until they are risen and the tops and bottoms are light golden brown. 9) Move the pan to a wire rack and let the scones cool until just warm, then split them and serve them with butter, jam, and, if you can find it, clotted cream.

It took me a while to get this recipe just right. I wanted scones with cinnamon and sugar swirled into the batter, but still pretty scones that didn't leak filling or spread too much. There were many failed attempts. Then I discovered Thomas Keller's genius way of incorporating cinnamon butter into his scones. He beats together butter, sugar, cinnamon, and flour, chills the mixture, and distributes it throughout the dough. It worked like a charm, and my scones baked up beautifully, with plenty of cinnamon flavor.

Cinnamon Scones

MAKES
8 SCONES

CINNAMON BUTTER

4 tablespoons [56 g] unsalted butter, at room temperature

1 tablespoon all-purpose flour

1 tablespoon granulated sugar

2 teaspoons ground cinnamon

SCONES

½ cup [120 g] crème fraîche, homemade (page 290) or store-bought, or sour cream

1 large egg

1 large egg yolk

1 teaspoon pure vanilla extract

2¼ cups [320 g] all-purpose flour, plus more for dusting

¼ cup [50 g] granulated sugar

1 tablespoon baking powder

½ teaspoon salt

8 tablespoons [1 stick or 113 g] cold unsalted butter, cut into ½ in [12 mm] pieces

Heavy cream, for brushing

ICING

2 oz [55 g] cream cheese, at room temperature

2 to 4 tablespoons milk

1 tablespoon unsalted butter, melted

½ teaspoon pure vanilla extract

Pinch of salt

1½ cups [180 g] confectioners' sugar

1) FOR THE CINNAMON BUTTER Place the butter, flour, granulated sugar, and cinnamon in a medium bowl and mix with a spatula until completely combined. Pat the butter into a small square, 3 by 3 in [7.5 by 7.5 cm], and wrap with a piece of plastic wrap. Chill the butter in the refrigerator until very firm. **2) FOR THE SCONES** Line a sheet pan with parchment paper. In a medium bowl or liquid measuring cup, whisk together the crème fraîche, egg, egg yolk, and vanilla. Set aside.

cont'd

15

3) In the bowl of a stand mixer fitted with a paddle, combine the flour, granulated sugar, baking powder, and salt. Add the butter and mix on low speed until the flour-coated pieces are the size of peas. 4) Remove the cinnamon butter from the refrigerator and cut into ½ in [12 mm] cubes. Add them to the bowl and mix until the cubes just begin to break down and are about half their original size. 5) Remove the bowl from the mixer and use a spatula to fold the wet ingredients into the dry until just combined. Transfer the dough to a lightly floured surface and knead four to six times, until it comes together, adding more flour as necessary if the dough is sticky. Pat the dough gently into a square and roll it into a 12 in [30.5 cm] square, dusting with flour as necessary. Fold the dough in thirds, like a business letter. Fold the dough in thirds again by folding in the short ends, making a square. Transfer it to the prepared sheet pan and put it in the freezer for 10 minutes. 6) Return the dough to the floured surface, roll it into a 12 in [30.5 cm] square, and fold it in thirds. Turn over the dough so it's seam-side down, and gently roll out the dough into a 12 by 4 in [30.5 by 10 cm] rectangle. With a sharp knife, cut it crosswise into four equal rectangles, then cut each rectangle diagonally into two triangles. Transfer the scones to the prepared sheet pan and freeze the scones while the oven is preheating (see Notes, page 48). 7) Meanwhile, position an oven rack in the middle of the oven and preheat the oven to 375°F [190°C]. 8) Stack the sheet pan with the scones on another sheet pan (see Notes, page 48). Brush the tops of the triangles with a little heavy cream, making sure it doesn't drip down the sides. Bake until the tops and bottoms are light golden brown, rotating the pans halfway through, 18 to 25 minutes. 9) FOR THE ICING While the scones are baking, in a medium bowl, whisk together the cream cheese, 2 tablespoons of the milk, the melted butter, vanilla, and salt until smooth. Add the confectioners' sugar and mix together, then whisk until well combined and smooth. Add more milk, 1 tablespoon at a time, to thin the icing to your preferred consistency; the icing should be thick but pourable. 10) Transfer the top sheet pan to a wire rack and ice the scones immediately, using the back of a spoon or an offset spatula. 11) Scones are best eaten the same day they are made.

The faint flavors of ginger and orange here really make this bread shine, and it stays moist over several days. Since this bread doesn't bake up tall and lofty, I like to bake it in a 12 by 4 in [30.5 by 10 cm] tea loaf pan, but a regular 8 by 4 in [20 by 10 cm] loaf pan will work well too.

Ginger Orange Carrot Bread

MAKES ONE 12 IN [30.5 CM] TEA LOAF
OR ONE REGULAR 8 IN [20 CM] LOAF

⅔ cup [150 g] vegetable or canola oil

¾ cup [150 g] granulated sugar

¼ cup [50 g] brown sugar

2 large eggs, at room temperature

1½ tablespoons ginger paste or grated ginger

1 tablespoon grated orange zest

1 tablespoon triple sec (optional)

¾ teaspoon baking powder

½ teaspoon baking soda

½ teaspoon salt

1½ cups [213 g] all-purpose flour

2 cups [200 g] peeled and finely grated carrots (see Note)

1) Position an oven rack in the middle of the oven and preheat the oven to 350°F [180°C]. Grease a 12 by 4 in [30.5 by 10 cm] tea loaf pan or an 8 by 4 in [20 by 10 cm] loaf pan and line with a parchment sling (see page 14). 2) In a large bowl, whisk together the oil, granulated and brown sugars, eggs, ginger, orange zest, triple sec (if using), baking powder, baking soda, and salt until completely combined. Add the flour, whisking until just combined. Add the carrots, stirring until incorporated. 3) Pour the mixture into the prepared pan and bake until a wooden skewer or toothpick comes out clean, rotating the pan halfway through baking, 45 to 60 minutes. Transfer the pan to a wire rack and let the bread cool for 15 minutes. Use the parchment sling to remove the bread from the pan, peel off the parchment paper, and finish cooling on the wire rack before serving. 4) The bread can be wrapped in plastic wrap and stored at room temperature for up to 2 days, or in the refrigerator for up to 4 days.

NOTE Freshly grated carrots have great flavor, but if you're pressed for time, you can process store-bought shredded carrots in a food processor until they are broken down.

16

17

Colleen had this bread on the menu the last time I went to visit her in Winona, and she kindly sent me home with the recipe. I found myself in the kitchen tinkering with it a bit by adding apple cider–soaked apples and brandy to the batter. I like to leave the peels on the apples, but you can remove them if you like. Please don't skip the streusel!

Apple Brandy Bread

 MAKES ONE 8 IN [20 CM] OR 9 IN [23 CM] LOAF

1½ cups [150 g] chopped Gala apples (1 in [2.5 cm] pieces; about 1 large apple)

½ cup [120 g] apple cider

2 tablespoons applejack or another brandy

1¾ cups [250 g] all-purpose flour

1 tablespoon baking powder

¾ teaspoon salt

¼ teaspoon baking soda

½ cup [120 g] whole milk

6 tablespoons [84 g] unsalted butter, melted

¾ cup [150 g] granulated sugar

2 large eggs, at room temperature

1 teaspoon pure vanilla extract

1 cup [140 g] Pecan Streusel (page 291)

1) Position an oven rack in the middle of the oven and preheat the oven to 350°F [180°C]. Grease an 8 by 4 in [20 by 10 cm] loaf pan or a 9 by 4 by 4 in [23 by 10 by 10 cm] Pullman pan and line with a parchment sling (see page 14). 2) Run your knife through the apple chunks a few times, creating pieces of various sizes, taking care not to leave any full-size pieces. 3) In a small saucepan, bring the apple cider to a boil over medium heat, then simmer until the cider is reduced by half, to about ¼ cup [60 g]. Remove from the heat and add the chopped apples and brandy, stirring to combine. 4) In a large bowl, whisk together the flour, baking powder, salt, and baking soda. In a medium bowl or liquid measuring cup, whisk together the milk, melted butter, granulated sugar, eggs, and vanilla.

5) Pour the liquid ingredients over the dry ingredients and mix together until just combined. Add the reduced cider and apples to the batter and mix again until combined. Pour the batter into the prepared pan and sprinkle evenly with the streusel. 6) Bake the bread until the streusel is golden brown and a wooden skewer or toothpick inserted into the center comes out clean, rotating the pan halfway through baking, 50 to 60 minutes. Transfer the pan to a wire rack and let cool for 20 minutes. Use the parchment sling to lift the loaf out of the pan, and peel off the paper. Let the bread finish cooling on the wire rack before slicing. The bread can be wrapped in plastic wrap and stored at room temperature for up to 2 days, or refrigerated for up to 4 days.

Back in the early days of the Blue Heron Coffeehouse, there was a brief window of time in which Larry made this incredible lemon bread: a moist loaf with a sweet-tart glaze that complemented my iced coffee perfectly. But in the hustle and bustle of running a small business, somehow the recipe was lost in the kitchen and the bread was phased out. Since I was still thinking about this bread twenty years later, I decided it was time to try and recreate it. However, I got sidetracked when I saw a photo for Sweet Potato Tea Cake with Meringue in Elisabeth Prueitt and Chad Robertson's cookbook *Tartine* and immediately decided my bread also needed meringue. This bread gets better the longer it sits; on days two and three it really shines. The meringue is fun to make, but it can be omitted. See the variation for Straight-Up Lemon Bread, which has a simple glaze.

Lemon Meringue Bread

 MAKES ONE 9 IN
[23 CM] LOAF

LEMON BREAD

1½ cups [213 g] all-purpose flour

½ teaspoon salt

¼ teaspoon baking soda

1½ cups [300 g] granulated sugar

1 tablespoon grated lemon zest

3 oz [85 g] cream cheese, at room temperature

½ cup [112 g] vegetable or canola oil

3 large eggs, at room temperature

1 teaspoon pure vanilla extract

¼ cup [60 g] lemon juice

⅓ cup [100 g] lemon curd, homemade (page 288) or store-bought (see Note)

MERINGUE

A few drops of lemon juice

1 cup [200 g] granulated sugar

½ cup [113 g] egg whites (from 3 or 4 large eggs)

⅛ teaspoon cream of tartar

Pinch of salt

1) **FOR THE BREAD** Position an oven rack in the middle of the oven and preheat to 325°F [165°C]. Grease a 9 by 4 by 4 in [23 by 10 by 10 cm] Pullman pan and line with a parchment sling (see page 14).

2) In a small bowl, whisk together the flour, salt, and baking soda. In a medium bowl, combine the sugar and lemon zest and use your fingers to rub the zest into the sugar until evenly distributed and fragrant.

3) Transfer the granulated sugar and zest to the bowl of a stand mixer fitted with a paddle. Add the cream cheese and beat on low speed until combined and fluffy, 2 to 3 minutes. Scrape down the sides of the bowl and, with the mixer still on low, add the oil and beat until completely combined.

cont'd

4) Add the eggs, one at a time, mixing for about 30 seconds on medium speed after each addition and scraping down the bottom and sides of the bowl. Beat in the vanilla. On low speed, add half the flour mixture, followed by the lemon juice, and then the remaining flour mixture, beating after each addition until just combined. Remove the bowl from the mixer and give the batter a few more turns with a spatula to make sure the ingredients have been incorporated. Add the lemon curd and swirl it into the batter with the spatula, using four or five strokes. Pour the batter into the prepared pan and set aside. 5) FOR THE MERINGUE Pour 1 in [2.5 cm] of water into a medium saucepan and bring to a gentle boil. Pour a few drops of lemon juice into the bowl of a stand mixer fitted with a whisk, and use a paper towel to wipe the juice around the inside of the bowl (this helps remove any traces of grease, which can hinder the whites from whipping properly). Add the granulated sugar, egg whites, cream of tartar, and salt to the mixing bowl and stir gently with a rubber spatula until completely combined. 6) Place the bowl over the saucepan, being careful not to let the water touch the bottom of the bowl. Stir with the spatula until the sugar is completely dissolved and the mixture registers 160°F [70°C] on an instant-read thermometer, scraping down the sides of the bowl with the spatula (to ensure no sugar crystals are lurking, which can cook the egg whites), 4 to 5 minutes. 7) Place the bowl in the stand mixer fitted with a whisk and whisk the egg whites on low speed for 1 minute. Slowly increase the speed to medium-high, and beat until stiff, glossy peaks form, 8 to 10 minutes. The bowl should feel cool to the touch at this point.

8) Working quickly, spoon all the meringue over the bread batter, and fold it into the batter gently with a rubber spatula six or seven times, starting at the top and dragging the meringue into the batter almost to the bottom of the pan and back up again. There should still be a visible amount of meringue on the top, which will bake up as a topping. 9) Bake the bread until the top of the meringue is browned and a wooden skewer or toothpick inserted into the center of the loaf comes out clean, 75 to 90 minutes. Let the bread cool in the pan for 15 minutes, then carefully remove it from the pan using the parchment sling, peel off the paper, and transfer to a wire rack. Cool completely before slicing. The bread can be stored in an airtight container at room temperature for up to 4 days, but it is best on the second and third days.

NOTE Not all store-bought lemon curd is created equal! Make sure you use a brand you love here if you're not making it yourself.

VARIATION

• **Straight-Up Lemon Bread:** *Grease and line an 8 by 4 in [20 by 10 cm] loaf pan with a parchment sling and proceed with the recipe, omitting the meringue. Bake the bread until the top is golden and a wooden skewer or toothpick inserted into the center comes out clean, 55 to 65 minutes. While the bread bakes, make a lemon glaze: In a medium bowl, whisk together 2 tablespoons of lemon juice, 1 tablespoon of melted butter, and a pinch of salt. Add ½ cup [113 g] of confectioners' sugar and mix together, then whisk until well combined and smooth. Add more lemon juice, 1 tablespoon at a time, until the glaze is thick but pourable. Pour the glaze over the bread while it is just warm to the touch, then let the bread cool completely before slicing. This bread will not bake up as tall, and is also best on the second and third day.*

I have a banana bread recipe in my first book that I love, but I wanted to come up with a version that didn't require pulling out the stand mixer. Browning a little butter gives this bread a nutty undertone, and the bananas and buttermilk keep things nice and tender. This bread is rich and delicious, always moist, and full of banana flavor.

 MAKES ONE 8 IN [20 CM]
OR 9 IN [23 CM] LOAF

Brown Butter Banana Bread

1½ cups [213 g] all-purpose flour

1 teaspoon baking soda

5 tablespoons [70 g] unsalted butter

1 cup [227 g] mashed very ripe bananas (about 3 bananas)

½ cup [100 g] granulated sugar

½ cup [100 g] brown sugar

⅓ cup [80 g] buttermilk, at room temperature

¼ cup [60 g] vegetable or canola oil

1 tablespoon pure vanilla extract

1 teaspoon salt

2 large eggs, at room temperature

1) Position an oven rack in the middle of the oven and preheat the oven to 350°F [180°C]. Grease an 8 by 4 in [20 by 10 cm] loaf pan or a 9 by 4 by 4 in [23 by 10 by 10 cm] Pullman pan and line with a parchment sling (see page 14). 2) In a small bowl, whisk together the flour and baking soda. 3) Brown the butter (see page 293). Pour the brown butter (and any bits stuck to the bottom of the pan) into a large bowl.

cont'd

4) Add the bananas, granulated and brown sugars, buttermilk, oil, vanilla, and salt, whisk to combine, and let cool to room temperature. Add the eggs and whisk until completely combined. Add the dry ingredients and stir together until combined. 5) Pour the batter into the prepared pan and bake until the top of the bread is dark brown and a wooden skewer or toothpick inserted into the center comes out clean, 50 to 65 minutes. 6) Transfer the pan to a wire rack and let cool for 20 minutes. Using the parchment sling, lift the loaf out of the pan, peel off the paper, and let the bread finish cooling on the wire rack. The bread can be wrapped in plastic wrap and stored at room temperature for up to 2 days, or refrigerated for up to 4 days.

NOTE This bread can be streamlined even more by replacing the brown butter with 4 tablespoons [57 g] melted butter for a more classic banana bread flavor.

VARIATIONS

• **Banana Streusel Bread:** *Sprinkle 2 cups [280 g] of Pecan Streusel (page 291) over the top of the banana bread before baking.*

• **Banana Chocolate Pecan Bread:** *Add 4 oz [113 g] of chopped semisweet or bittersweet chocolate and ½ cup [57 g] toasted, chopped pecan halves to the batter along with the flour.*

This simple quick bread with its subtle maple flavor requires no icing or glaze. However, if you still feel you need some, the Maple Icing on the Maple Oatmeal Scones (page 52) would be delicious here.

Maple Poppy Seed Bread

MAKES ONE 8 IN [20 CM]
OR 9 IN [23 CM] LOAF

1¾ cups [250 g] all-purpose flour

¼ teaspoon baking powder

⅛ teaspoon baking soda

1 cup [2 sticks or 227 g] unsalted butter, at room temperature

1 cup [200 g] granulated sugar

¾ teaspoon salt

⅓ cup [107 g] maple syrup

3 large eggs, at room temperature

1 teaspoon pure vanilla extract

¼ cup [60 g] buttermilk, at room temperature

¼ cup [30 g] poppy seeds

1) Position an oven rack in the middle of the oven and preheat the oven to 350°F [180°C]. Grease an 8 by 4 in [20 by 10 cm] loaf pan or a 9 by 4 by 4 in [23 by 10 by 10 cm] Pullman pan and line with a parchment sling (see page 14).
2) In a medium bowl, whisk together the flour, baking powder, and baking soda. In the bowl of a stand mixer fitted with a paddle, beat the butter on medium speed until creamy, about 1 minute. Add the granulated sugar and salt and beat on medium speed until very light and fluffy, 4 to 6 minutes. Add the maple syrup, beating on low speed until well combined.
3) Scrape down the sides of the bowl and increase the mixer speed to medium. Add the eggs, one at a time, stopping to scrape down the sides of the bowl as needed. Lower the mixer speed to low and beat in the vanilla. Add half the flour mixture and mix until combined. Add

the buttermilk and mix again until combined. Scrape down the sides of the bowl and repeat with the remaining flour mixture. Remove the bowl from the mixer, add the poppy seeds, and use a spatula to mix them into the batter and to make sure all the ingredients are completely incorporated. 4) Pour the batter into the prepared pan and use a spatula to smooth out the top. Bake until a wooden skewer or toothpick inserted near the center comes out clean, 50 to 65 minutes. 5) Transfer the pan to a wire rack and let the bread cool in the pan for 20 minutes. Using the parchment sling, lift the loaf out of the pan, peel off the paper, and let the bread finish cooling on the wire rack. The bread can be wrapped in plastic wrap and stored at room temperature for up to 2 days, or refrigerated for up to 4 days.

Chocolate bread is a favorite, though occasional, indulgence. This bread has a rich chocolate flavor from both the cocoa powder and milk chocolate, and the rye flour adds a little nutty, malty goodness.

Milk Chocolate Rye Bread

MAKES ONE 9 IN [23 CM] LOAF

1½ cups [213 g] all-purpose flour

½ cup [65 g] rye flour

½ cup [50 g] Dutch-process cocoa powder

¾ teaspoon baking soda

¼ teaspoon baking powder

8 tablespoons [1 stick or 113 g] unsalted butter, at room temperature

1½ cups [300 g] brown sugar

½ cup [100 g] granulated sugar

¾ teaspoon salt

1 cup [240 g] buttermilk, at room temperature

2 large eggs, at room temperature

2 large egg yolks, at room temperature

1 teaspoon pure vanilla extract

4 oz [113 g] milk chocolate, melted and cooled

1) Position an oven rack in the middle of the oven and preheat the oven to 350°F [180°C]. Grease a 9 by 4 by 4 in [23 by 10 by 10 cm] Pullman pan and line with a parchment sling (see page 14). 2) In a medium bowl, whisk together the all-purpose flour, rye flour, cocoa powder, baking soda, and baking powder. 3) In a large saucepan, melt the butter over low heat. Add the brown and granulated sugars and the salt, and stir to combine. Off the heat, and whisking to combine between each addition, add the buttermilk, then the eggs, yolks, and vanilla. Add the flour mixture, then add the milk chocolate and whisk gently until combined. 4) Pour the batter into the prepared pan and bake until a wooden skewer inserted into the center comes out with a few crumbs attached, 55 to 70 minutes. Let the bread cool in the pan on a wire rack for 15 minutes. Using the parchment sling, lift the loaf out of the pan, peel off the paper, and return to the wire rack to finish cooling before slicing. The bread can be wrapped in plastic wrap and stored at room temperature for up to 2 days, or refrigerated for up to 4 days.

Pumpkin bread is a necessity during the winter holidays, but I also find myself making it as soon as the first leaves start to fall in September. The pumpkin and spice combination is a comfort, and the smell never fails to bring cheer to a tired teen or husband walking through the door after a long day. If you want to omit the Cream Cheese Icing, this bread is also delicious with a generous sprinkle of sanding sugar.

Pumpkin Bread

 MAKES ONE 9 IN [23 CM] LOAF

PUMPKIN BREAD

1½ cups [213 g] all-purpose flour

1 tablespoon ground cinnamon

1 teaspoon salt

1 teaspoon baking soda

1 teaspoon ground ginger

½ teaspoon baking powder

½ teaspoon freshly grated nutmeg

Pinch of ground cloves

3 large eggs, at room temperature

1½ cups [300 g] granulated sugar

¾ cup [168 g] unsweetened pumpkin purée

¾ cup [168 g] vegetable or canola oil

2 tablespoons maple syrup

1 teaspoon pure vanilla extract

½ teaspoon lemon juice

Sanding sugar, for sprinkling (optional)

CREAM CHEESE ICING

2 tablespoons unsalted butter, at room temperature

2 oz [57 g] cream cheese, at room temperature

Pinch of salt

1½ cups [180 g] confectioners' sugar

1 teaspoon pure vanilla extract

1) FOR THE BREAD Position an oven rack in the middle of the oven and preheat the oven to 350°F [180°C]. Grease a 9 by 5 in [23 by 12 cm] loaf pan or a 9 by 4 by 4 in [23 by 10 by 10 cm] Pullman pan and line with a parchment sling (see page 14).

2) In a medium bowl, whisk together the flour, cinnamon, salt, baking soda, ginger, baking powder, nutmeg, and cloves.

3) In the bowl of a stand mixer fitted with a paddle, beat the eggs on medium speed until combined and slightly frothy, about 1 minute. Add the granulated sugar and beat until pale yellow and doubled in volume, 2 to 3 minutes. Add the pumpkin, oil, maple syrup, vanilla, and lemon juice, mixing on low speed until incorporated. Scrape down the sides of the bowl and add the flour mixture, beating until just combined. Remove the bowl from the mixer and use a whisk to eliminate any remaining lumps in the dough, about 10 seconds.

4) Pour the batter into the prepared pan. Sprinkle the top generously with the sanding sugar only if not making the icing. Bake for 60 to 75 minutes, until a wooden skewer or toothpick inserted into the center comes out clean. If at any point during baking the top of the loaf is browning too quickly, lay a piece of aluminum foil over it. 5) Transfer the pan to a wire rack and let cool for 20 minutes. Using the parchment sling, lift the loaf out of the pan, peel off the paper, and let the bread finish cooling on the wire rack. (The unfrosted bread can be stored in an airtight container at room temperature for up to 3 days.)

6) FOR THE ICING Meanwhile, make the icing, if using: In a clean bowl of the stand mixer fitted with a paddle, beat the butter, cream cheese, and salt on medium speed until smooth and creamy. Add the confectioners' sugar, beating on low speed until combined. Scrape down the sides of the bowl, increase the speed to medium, and beat until the icing is light and fluffy, 3 to 4 minutes. Add the vanilla, mixing on low speed until combined. 7) When the bread has completely cooled, use an offset spatula or knife to spread the icing over the top of the bread. The bread can be stored in an airtight container in the refrigerator for up to 3 days.

There are several vintage coffee cake recipes that place the streusel on the bottom of the baking pan, resulting in a nice and even streusel top when the pan gets flipped. I decided to try this method out with quick bread, and while it looked too wonky after I flipped the bread over, the streusel made a crunchy, surprise layer that I left on the bottom of the loaf.

Streusel-Bottom Bread

MAKES ONE 8 IN [20 CM]
OR 9 IN [23 CM] LOAF

1½ cups [210 g] Streusel (page 291)

1½ cups [213 g] all-purpose flour

½ teaspoon salt

¼ teaspoon baking soda

8 tablespoons [1 stick or 113 g] unsalted butter, at room temperature

3 oz [85 g] cream cheese, at room temperature

1½ cups [300 g] granulated sugar

3 large eggs, at room temperature

1 teaspoon pure vanilla extract

¼ cup [60 g] buttermilk

1) Position an oven rack in the middle of the oven and preheat the oven to 325°F [165°C]. Grease an 8 by 4 in [20 by 10 cm] loaf pan or a 9 by 4 by 4 in [23 by 10 by 10 cm] Pullman pan and line with a parchment sling (see page 14). Pour the streusel into the pan and press down into an even layer.
2) In a small bowl, whisk together the flour, salt, and baking soda.
3) In the bowl of a stand mixer fitted with a paddle, beat the butter and cream cheese on medium-low speed for about 2 minutes. Add the granulated sugar and increase the mixer speed to medium-high. Beat until light and fluffy, periodically scraping down the sides of the bowl with a rubber spatula, 3 to 5 minutes.

4) Add the eggs, one at a time, mixing on medium speed after each addition and scraping the sides of the bowl as needed. Beat in the vanilla. Add half the flour mixture, followed by all the buttermilk, and then the remaining flour mixture, beating on low speed after each addition until just combined. Remove the bowl from the mixer and give the mixture a few turns with a spatula to make sure the ingredients are completely combined. 5) Pour the batter into the prepared pan and tap the pan lightly on the counter to get rid of any air bubbles. Bake the bread until it is golden and a wooden skewer or toothpick inserted into the center comes out clean, 60 to 75 minutes. Move the bread to a

wire rack and let cool in the pan for 15 minutes. Using the parchment sling, lift the loaf out of the pan, peel off the paper, and let the bread finish cooling on the wire rack. The bread can be wrapped in plastic wrap and stored at room temperature for up to 2 days, or refrigerated for up to 4 days.

23

This bread is a treat, a chocolate chip snack cake in quick bread form. The lack of frosting will help convince you that this is, in fact, morning fare. But if you were to slather the top with, say, Cream Cheese Icing (page 74), I wouldn't blame you.

Sour Cream Chocolate Chip Bread

MAKES ONE 8 IN [20 CM]
OR 9 IN [23 CM] LOAF

2 cups [284 g] all-purpose flour, plus 1 tablespoon

2 teaspoons baking powder

¼ teaspoon baking soda

¾ cup [135 g] mini chocolate chips

10 tablespoons [140 g] unsalted butter, at room temperature

1 cup [200 g] granulated sugar, plus more for sprinkling

½ cup [100 g] brown sugar

¾ teaspoon salt

3 large eggs, at room temperature

2 tablespoons vegetable or canola oil

1 tablespoon pure vanilla extract

1 cup [240 g] sour cream, at room temperature

1) Position an oven rack in the middle of the oven and preheat the oven to 375°F [190°C]. Grease an 8 by 4 in [20 by 10 cm] loaf pan or a 9 by 4 by 4 in [23 by 10 by 10 cm] Pullman pan and line with a parchment sling (see page 14). 2) In a medium bowl, whisk together 2 cups [284 g] of the flour, the baking powder, and baking soda. 3) In a small bowl, toss together the chocolate chips and the remaining 1 tablespoon of flour until the chips are well coated. 4) In the bowl of a stand mixer fitted with a paddle, beat the butter on medium speed until creamy, about 1 minute. Add the granulated and brown sugars and the salt and

24

beat until light and fluffy, 2 to 3 minutes. Add the eggs, one at a time, beating on medium speed after each addition and scraping down the sides of the bowl as needed. Beat in the oil and vanilla on low speed, followed by one-third of the flour mixture. Beat in the sour cream and the remaining flour mixture in halves, alternating between the two and ending with the flour mixture, mixing until just combined. Use a spatula to mix in the chocolate chips, and make sure the batter is well blended. 5) Pour the batter into the prepared pan and use an offset spatula to smooth the top. Bake until the bread is golden brown and a wooden skewer or toothpick inserted in the center comes out clean, 55 to 70 minutes. 6) Transfer the pan to a wire rack and let the bread cool for 20 minutes. Using the parchment sling, lift the loaf out of the pan, peel off the paper, and transfer the bread to the wire rack to finish cooling before slicing. The bread can be wrapped in plastic wrap and stored at room temperature for up to 2 days, or refrigerated for up to 4 days.

CHAPTER 2

Coffee Cakes and Bundt Cakes

"The **making** of the cake, the **heating** of the **oven** and the **baking**; nay, you must stay **the cooling too**, or you may chance to **burn your lips**."

—William Shakespeare, *Troilus and Cressida*

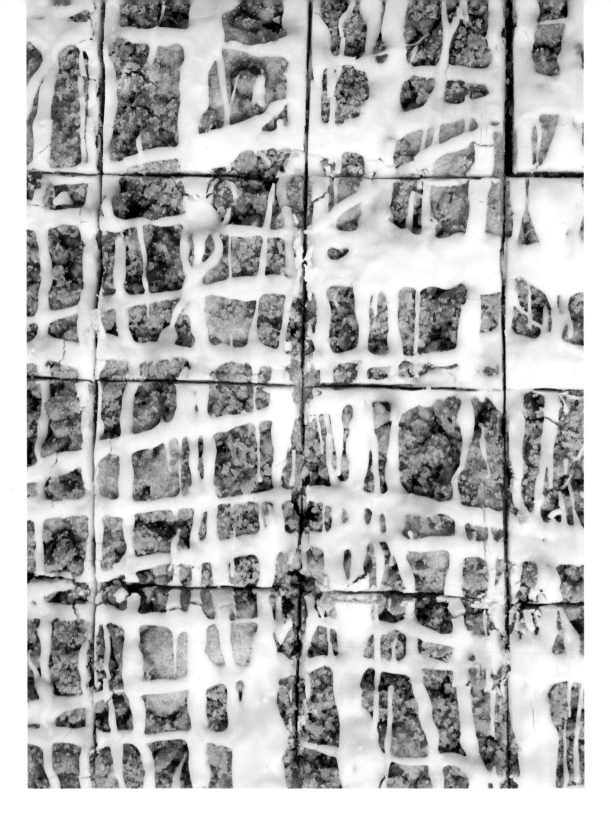

"Mrs Forrester . . . sat in a state, pretending not to know what cakes were sent up, though she knew, and we knew, and she knew that we knew, and we knew that she knew that we knew, she had been busy all morning" goes Elizabeth Gaskell's line in *Cranford*, and while Mrs. Forrester was busy making tea cakes, I always recall this passage when I set out to make this coffee cake. I may be busy for the morning mixing batter and sprinkling streusel, but the time spent is always worth it.

Streusel Coffee Cake

MAKES 12 LARGE OR
16 SMALL SERVINGS

CAKE

1 cup [240 g] whole milk, at room temperature

1 scant cup [210 g] egg whites (from 6 or 7 large eggs), at room temperature (see Notes)

½ cup [120 g] sour cream, at room temperature

1 tablespoon pure vanilla extract

2¾ cups [391 g] all-purpose flour

2 cups [400 g] granulated sugar

4 teaspoons baking powder

1 teaspoon salt

1 cup [2 sticks or 227 g] unsalted butter, cut into 1 in [2.5 cm] pieces, at room temperature

CREAM CHEESE FILLING

4 oz [113 g] cream cheese, at room temperature

2 tablespoons granulated sugar

1½ cups [210 g] Streusel (page 291)

ICING

2 to 4 tablespoons [30 to 60 g] water

1 tablespoon unsalted butter, melted

½ teaspoon pure vanilla extract

1½ cups [180 g] confectioners' sugar

1) FOR THE CAKE Position an oven rack in the middle of the oven and preheat the oven to 350°F [180°C]. Grease a 9 by 13 in [23 by 33 cm] pan and line it with a parchment sling (see page 14). **2)** In a medium bowl or liquid measuring cup, whisk together the milk, egg whites, sour cream, and vanilla. **3)** In the bowl of a stand mixer fitted with a paddle, combine the flour, granulated sugar, baking powder, and salt on low speed. Add the butter, one piece at a time, beating until the mixture resembles coarse sand.

cont'd

25

Gradually beat in a little more than half of the wet ingredients. Increase the speed to medium and beat until the ingredients are combined, about 30 seconds. Lower the speed to low and add the remaining wet ingredients, mixing until just combined. Increase the speed to medium and beat for 20 seconds; the batter may still look a little bumpy. Scrape down the sides and bottom of the bowl and use a spatula to mix the batter a few more times. Set aside 1 tablespoon of the batter for the filling. Pour the rest of the batter into the prepared pan and smooth the top. 4) **FOR THE FILLING AND STREUSEL** In a small bowl, whisk together the cream cheese, granulated sugar, and reserved 1 tablespoon of cake batter. Dollop the cream cheese filling over the cake and use a knife or an offset spatula to swirl it into the batter. Sprinkle the streusel evenly over the top. Tap the pan gently on the counter twice to help get rid of any air bubbles. 5) Bake until the cake is golden brown and a wooden skewer or toothpick inserted into the center comes out with a few crumbs, rotating the pan halfway through baking, 35 to 50 minutes (see Notes). Transfer the cake, in the pan, to a wire rack and let cool for 5 minutes. 6) **FOR THE ICING** While the cake is baking, in a medium bowl, whisk 2 tablespoons of the water, the melted butter, and vanilla until smooth. Add the confectioners' sugar and mix together, then whisk until well combined and smooth. Add more water, 1 tablespoon at a time, to thin the icing as needed; it should be thick but pourable.

7) Pour half of the icing over the warm cake and let sit for 20 minutes until set. Pour the remaining icing over the cake and let sit until the cake finishes cooling. Remove the cake from the pan using the parchment sling and peel off the paper. Cut into pieces and serve. Alternatively, the cake can be left in the pan, covered in plastic wrap, and stored in the refrigerator for up to 2 days.

NOTES Because the egg whites aren't being whipped for volume, store-bought egg whites will work here; just make sure they are 100 percent liquid egg whites.

If, while baking, the streusel sinks toward the middle of the cake, you can sprinkle more on the edges halfway through baking, when you rotate the cake.

When I sent this recipe out to testers, I got back a wide variety of baking times, due to different ovens and different baking pan brands and colors. If at 45 minutes your cake is still very liquidy, please do not panic! Just keep baking the cake, checking frequently to see if it's done. This cake can take up to 1 hour to bake.

Something cold and sweet, bursting with bright flavor, will wake up any sleepyhead, and these breakfast bars hit all those notes just right. They are thin but full of flavor, and the glaze soaks in to make moist bars that last for several days.

Passion Fruit Crème Fraîche Breakfast Squares

MAKES 12 LARGE OR
24 SMALL SQUARES

CAKE

1½ cups [213 g] all-purpose flour

½ teaspoon salt

¼ teaspoon baking soda

12 tablespoons [1½ sticks or 170 g] unsalted butter, at room temperature

1½ cups [300 g] granulated sugar

3 large eggs, at room temperature

1 teaspoon pure vanilla extract

½ cup [120 g] crème fraîche, homemade (page 290) or store-bought

2 tablespoons passion fruit purée

GLAZE

2 to 4 tablespoons passion fruit purée

1 tablespoon unsalted butter, melted

Pinch of salt

1½ cups [180 g] confectioners' sugar

1) **FOR THE CAKE** Position an oven rack in the middle of the oven and preheat the oven to 350°F [180°C]. Grease a 9 by 13 in [23 by 33 cm] pan and line it with a parchment sling (see page 14). **2)** In a medium bowl, whisk together the flour, salt, and baking soda. **3)** In the bowl of a stand mixer fitted with a paddle, beat the butter on medium speed until creamy, about 1 minute. Add the granulated sugar and mix until very light and fluffy, 3 to 5 minutes, scraping down the bottom and sides of the bowl as needed. Add the eggs, one at a time, mixing for about 30 seconds after each addition. Beat in the vanilla. With the mixer still on low speed, add the crème fraîche and passion fruit purée, followed by the flour mixture, beating until just combined.

cont'd

4) Pour the batter into the prepared pan and use an offset spatula to smooth the top. Tap the pan lightly on the counter to remove any large air bubbles. Bake until a wooden skewer or toothpick inserted into the center comes out clean, 18 to 22 minutes. 5) FOR THE GLAZE While the cake is baking, in a medium bowl, whisk together 2 tablespoons of the passion fruit purée, the butter, and the salt. Add the confectioners' sugar and mix together, then whisk until well combined and smooth. Add more passion fruit purée, 1 tablespoon at a time, as needed, until the icing is thick but pourable. 6) Transfer the pan to a wire rack and let the cake cool for 20 minutes. Pour over the glaze and use an offset spatula to spread it evenly. Let the glaze soak into the cake, and cool completely. Carefully cover with plastic wrap and refrigerate for at least 2 hours or overnight. Use the parchment sling to remove the cake from the pan, peel off the parchment paper, and cut into squares. The squares can be served cold or at room temperature, and can be topped with fresh passion fruit if desired. Store leftover squares in an airtight container in the refrigerator for up to 3 days.

Creaming Butter and Sugar

Cream your butter and sugar until light and fluffy. When you cream the butter and sugar together, you are incorporating air into the butter, which in turn helps the cake rise and gives it a good texture. Take your time, and make sure your butter and sugar are very light and fluffy. In the winter months, this can take longer, especially if your kitchen and stand mixer bowl are cold.

Another way to start the day out with chocolate: Swirl some Nutella into your coffee cake and eat it while it's just the slightest bit warm. A perfect morning in our house.

Chocolate Hazelnut Crumb Cake

MAKES 12 LARGE OR
16 SMALL SERVINGS

6 oz [170 g] chocolate hazelnut spread, such as Nutella

¼ cup [60 g] heavy cream

¾ cup [180 g] sour cream, at room temperature

¼ cup [60 g] buttermilk, at room temperature

1 large egg, at room temperature

1 teaspoon pure vanilla extract

2¼ cups [320 g] all-purpose flour

1 cup [200 g] granulated sugar

12 tablespoons [1½ sticks or 170 g] unsalted butter, cut into 1 in [2.5 cm] pieces, at room temperature

½ teaspoon baking powder

½ teaspoon baking soda

½ teaspoon salt

1) Position an oven rack in the middle of the oven and preheat the oven to 350°F [180°C]. Grease a 9 by 13 in [23 by 33 cm] pan and line it with a parchment sling (see page 14). 2) Place the chocolate hazelnut spread in a small heatproof bowl. Heat the heavy cream in a small saucepan until it is just about to boil. Pour the cream over the spread, cover the bowl with plastic wrap, and let it sit for 5 minutes. Remove the plastic and whisk until completely smooth. 3) In a medium bowl or liquid measuring cup, whisk together the sour cream, butter-milk, egg, and vanilla. 4) In the bowl of a stand mixer fitted with a paddle, combine the flour and granulated sugar on low speed. Add the butter one piece at a time, beating until the mixture resembles coarse sand. Remove 1 cup [130 g] of the mixture and set it aside in a small bowl.

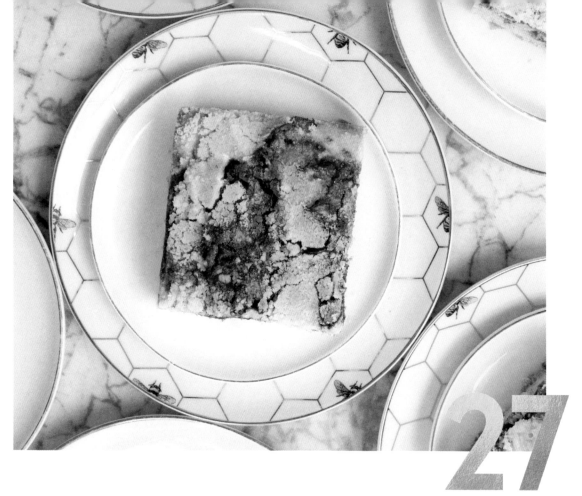

27

5) Add the baking powder, baking soda, and salt to the dry ingredients in the stand mixer bowl and mix on low speed to combine. Beat in the sour cream mixture, mixing until incorporated, about 30 seconds. Remove the bowl from the mixer, scrape down the sides of the bowl, and use a spatula to mix the batter a few more times. Pour the batter into the prepared pan and use an offset spatula to smooth the top. 6) Dollop the Nutella mixture over the cake batter and use a knife or an offset spatula to swirl it into the batter. Sprinkle the reserved flour-sugar-butter mixture evenly over the top.

Tap the pan gently on the counter twice to help get rid of any air bubbles. 7) Bake the cake until golden brown and a wooden skewer or toothpick inserted into the center comes out with a few crumbs, rotating the pan halfway through baking, 26 to 32 minutes. 8) Transfer the pan to a wire rack and let the cake cool to room temperature. Using the parchment sling, lift the cake out of the pan and peel off the paper. Cut into pieces and serve. Alternatively, the cake can be left in the pan, covered in plastic wrap, and stored in the refrigerator overnight.

28

I'm not going to lie; cream cheese swirl is what I'll pick in a bakery case lineup any day. This is one of my favorite recipes in the book: a layer of cake, then cream cheese, tart jam, and streusel topping in every perfect bite. I like to eat them just barely warm, but they are great the next day too.

Creamy Jammy Coffee Cakes

 MAKES EIGHT 4 IN [10 CM] CAKES

CAKE

¾ cup [180 g] sour cream, at room temperature

¼ cup [60 g] buttermilk, at room temperature

1 large egg, at room temperature

1 teaspoon pure vanilla extract

2¼ cups [320 g] all-purpose flour

1 cup [200 g] granulated sugar

12 tablespoons [1½ sticks or 170 g] unsalted butter, cut into 1 in [2.5 cm] pieces, at room temperature

½ teaspoon baking powder

½ teaspoon baking soda

½ teaspoon salt

1 cup [225 g] jam or Lemon Curd (page 288)

CREAM CHEESE FILLING

8 oz [227 g] cream cheese, at room temperature

¼ cup [50 g] granulated sugar

1 large egg, at room temperature

1) FOR THE CAKE Position an oven rack in the middle of the oven and preheat the oven to 350°F [180°C]. Grease eight 4 in [10 cm] cake pans or springform pans, and line the bottoms with parchment. Or prepare a jumbo muffin pan or ramekins (see Note). 2) In a medium bowl or liquid measuring cup, whisk together the sour cream, buttermilk, egg, and vanilla. 3) In the bowl of a stand mixer fitted with a paddle, combine the flour and granulated sugar on low speed. Add the butter, one piece at a time, beating until the mixture resembles coarse sand. Remove 1 cup [130 g] of the mixture and set it aside in a small bowl.

cont'd

4) With the mixer on low speed, beat in the baking powder, baking soda, and salt. Add the wet ingredients and mix until incorporated, about 30 seconds. Remove the bowl from the mixer. Scrape down the sides of the bowl and use a spatula to mix the batter a few more times. Divide the batter evenly among the prepared pans and smooth the tops with an offset spatula or the back of a spoon. Spread 2 tablespoons of jam evenly over the cake batter in each pan. 5) FOR THE FILLING In the stand mixer bowl in which you mixed the cake batter, beat together the cream cheese and granulated sugar on low speed until smooth and creamy. Add the egg and mix until incorporated, scraping down the sides as needed. Divide the cream cheese mixture among the pans and smooth the tops with an offset spatula or the back of a spoon. Divide the reserved flour-butter mixture among the pans, sprinkling it evenly over the tops. Tap the pans gently on the counter twice to help get rid of any air bubbles.

6) Place the cake pans on a large sheet pan and bake until golden brown and a wooden skewer or toothpick inserted into the center comes out with a few crumbs, rotating the pan halfway through baking, 26 to 32 minutes. Transfer the pans to a wire rack and let the cakes cool until barely warm or at room temperature. 7) Remove the cakes from their pans and serve. Alternatively, the cakes can be covered in plastic wrap after cooling and stored in the refrigerator overnight.

NOTE If you don't have 4 in [10 cm] cake pans, you can bake the cakes in jumbo muffin tins or ramekins. Fill the cavities a quarter of the way with batter, and spread only 1 tablespoon of jam on each one. Top with the cream cheese mixture and then the flour-butter mixture. Smaller cakes will bake faster, so start checking them a few minutes earlier.

In my *100 Cookies* book I have a recipe for citrus bars that can be made with any citrus flavor of your choosing. I wanted to do the same thing here with cake, and used the base of my yellow cake recipe to come up with something versatile and simple. This cake is full of sweet-tart flavor, and the almond flour and poured glaze help keep it moist over several days.

Simple Citrus Breakfast Cake

MAKES ONE 8 OR 9 IN [20 OR 23 CM] CAKE

CAKE

⅓ cup [80 g] buttermilk, at room temperature (see Notes)

⅓ cup [80 g] sour cream, at room temperature

2 large eggs, at room temperature

1 large egg yolk, at room temperature

2 tablespoons lemon, lime, orange, or grapefruit juice

2 tablespoons vegetable or canola oil

1 tablespoon pure vanilla extract

1 cup plus 3 tablespoons [166 g] all-purpose flour

1 cup [200 g] granulated sugar

¼ cup [25 g] almond flour

1 tablespoon grated lemon, lime, orange, or grapefruit zest

1 teaspoon baking powder

½ teaspoon plus ⅛ teaspoon salt

¼ teaspoon baking soda

6 tablespoons [84 g] unsalted butter, at room temperature

GLAZE

2 to 4 tablespoons lemon, lime, orange, or grapefruit juice

1 tablespoon unsalted butter, melted

Pinch of salt

1 cup [120 g] confectioners' sugar

1) FOR THE CAKE Position an oven rack in the middle of the oven and preheat the oven to 350°F [180°C]. Grease and flour an 8 or 9 in [20 or 23 cm] springform pan or an 8 or 9 in [20 or 23 cm] cake pan and line the bottom with parchment paper. **2)** In a medium bowl or liquid measuring cup, whisk together the buttermilk, sour cream, eggs, egg yolk, citrus juice, oil, and vanilla.

cont'd

3) In the bowl of a stand mixer fitted with a paddle, mix the flour, granulated sugar, almond flour, citrus zest, baking powder, salt, and baking soda on low speed until combined. Add the butter, one piece at a time, beating until the mixture resembles coarse sand. Slowly add half of the wet ingredients. Increase the speed to medium and beat until incorporated, about 30 seconds. Add the rest of the wet ingredients, beating on low speed until just combined. Increase the speed to medium and beat for 20 seconds; the batter may still look a little bumpy. Scrape down the sides of the bowl and use a spatula to mix the batter a few more times, making sure the batter is well combined. 4) Pour the batter into the prepared pan and use an offset spatula to smooth the top. Tap the pan gently on the counter several times to help get rid of any bubbles. Bake until the cake is golden brown and a wooden skewer or toothpick inserted into the center comes out clean, rotating the pan halfway through baking, 35 to 45 minutes. Transfer the pan to a wire rack and let the cake cool in the pan for 20 minutes, or until just warm to the touch. 5) FOR THE GLAZE While the cake is cooling, in a medium bowl, whisk together 2 tablespoons of the citrus juice, the butter, and salt. Add the confectioners' sugar and mix together, then whisk until well combined and smooth. Add more citrus juice, 1 tablespoon at a time, as needed, until the icing is thick but pourable. If using a springform pan, pour the glaze over the barely warm cake in the pan and let finish cooling to room temperature. Run a knife gently around the cake to help separate it from the pan and then remove the sides of the pan. If using a regular cake pan, turn the barely warm cake out onto a wire rack and remove the parchment paper. Pour the glaze over the top and let sit until the glaze has set. Serve the cake or store in an airtight container at room temperature for up to 2 days.

NOTES The buttermilk and sour cream can be replaced with an equal amount of yogurt or skyr.

If using a springform pan, get it in the oven right after filling, as this batter can leak a little bit if left to sit out.

Room Temperature
Make sure ingredients are at room temperature. If ingredients are added cold, they won't emulsify properly; butter can seize up when hit with cold eggs. In addition, if the eggs are cold, your cake may not rise as well.

This cake came about after many decades of making Bundt cakes; it's evolved slowly over the years, and I've stayed here with this version for quite some time. This recipe is also included in *Baking for the Holidays*, and I make it so often I decided to also include it in this collection. I prefer this cake on the second and third days; the flavor develops and the crumb is tender and perfectly buttery.

Everything Bundt Cake

 MAKES 8 TO
12 SERVINGS

3 cups [426 g] all-purpose flour

½ teaspoon baking soda

½ cup [120 g] sour cream, at room temperature

½ cup [120 g] whole milk, at room temperature

1¼ cups [2½ sticks or 283 g] unsalted butter, at room temperature

3 cups [600 g] granulated sugar

1¼ teaspoons salt

6 large eggs, at room temperature

1 tablespoon pure vanilla extract

2 tablespoons vegetable or canola oil

1) Position an oven rack in the middle of the oven and preheat the oven to 350°F [180°C]. Grease and flour a 10 in [25 cm] one-piece tube pan or 12 cup [2.8 L] Bundt pan. 2) In a medium bowl, whisk together the flour and baking soda. 3) In a medium bowl or liquid measuring cup, whisk together the sour cream and milk until combined. 4) In the bowl of a stand mixer fitted with a paddle, beat the butter on medium speed until creamy, about 1 minute. Beat in the granulated sugar and salt, and continue beating until very light and fluffy, 4 to 6 minutes. Scrape down the sides of the bowl. Add the eggs, one at a time, beating on medium speed until incorporated, stopping to scrape down the sides of the bowl after each addition. Add the vanilla and oil and beat on low speed until combined. Add half the flour mixture until combined. Add the sour cream mixture and mix again. Scrape down the sides of the bowl, add the remaining flour mixture, and mix until incorporated. Increase the speed to medium and beat for 15 to 20 seconds. 5) Pour the batter into the prepared pan and use a spatula to smooth out the top. Bake until a wooden skewer or toothpick inserted near the center comes out clean, 50 to 65 minutes. 6) Transfer the pan to a wire rack and let cool for 10 minutes. Invert the cake onto the rack to finish cooling. The cake can be wrapped in plastic wrap and stored at room temperature for up to 2 days, or in the refrigerator for up to 4 days.

30

VARIATIONS

• **Confetti:** *Add ¾ cup [115 g] sprinkles to the batter after adding the flour mixture and mix gently until combined.*

• **Cream Cheese:** *Use only 1 cup [2 sticks or 227 g] of unsalted butter and add 6 oz [170 g] of cream cheese, at room temperature. Beat the cream cheese with the butter until smooth and creamy, then add the granulated sugar and salt and continue with the recipe.*

• **Lime, Poppyseed, and Chocolate:** *Add 1 tablespoon of grated lime zest along with the granulated sugar. After adding all of the flour mixture, add 2 tablespoons of poppyseeds and 2 oz [57 g] of mini chocolate chips to the batter and mix gently until combined.*

Preparing Pans

Grease and flour your Bundt pan well. After decades of making Bundt cakes, I have found that butter and flour work best for a good release. Using a pastry brush to "paint" on soft butter (making sure to get every ridge and crease!) and then dusting with flour is the best method, but I will admit that I occasionally use a baking spray with oil and flour in it, and that works great too. If I am using a tube pan, I take the extra step of lining the bottom with a circle of parchment paper.

The first time I ever made a Bundt cake I was working the Saturday evening shift at the Blue Heron and the coffeehouse was unusually quiet. Knowing Sunday mornings were quite busy, I decided to open up the kitchen I had just finished cleaning and do some baking. Two hours later and my beautiful Bundt cake was out of the oven, but one sad flip later I had only half a perfect Bundt cake, with one side still stuck. The warm crumbles on the counter proved to be delicious, so I wrapped up the servable portion for the next day and added Bundt cakes to my permanent Saturday evening to-do list, remembering to generously butter and flour the pan.

Tiramisu Bundt Cake

 MAKES 8 TO
12 SERVINGS

MASCARPONE FILLING

4 oz [115 g] mascarpone, at room temperature

2 oz [55 g] cream cheese, at room temperature

CAKE

3½ cups [497 g] all-purpose flour

½ teaspoon baking powder

¼ teaspoon baking soda

2 cups [4 sticks or 454 g] unsalted butter, at room temperature

3 cups [600 g] granulated sugar

1¼ teaspoons salt

6 eggs, at room temperature

1 teaspoon pure vanilla extract

½ cup [120 g] buttermilk

½ cup [85 g] mini chocolate chips

COFFEE SOAK

⅓ cup [80 g] espresso or strong brewed coffee

⅓ cup [65 g] granulated sugar

Pinch of salt

Cocoa powder, for dusting

1) FOR THE MASCARPONE FILLING In a small bowl, mix together the mascarpone and cream cheese until smooth. **2)** FOR THE CAKE Position an oven rack in the middle of the oven and preheat the oven to 350°F [180°C]. Grease and flour a 12 cup [2.8 L] Bundt pan. **3)** In a medium bowl, mix together the flour, baking powder, and baking soda. **4)** In the bowl of a stand mixer fitted with a paddle, beat the butter on medium speed until creamy. Add the granulated sugar and salt, and beat until light and fluffy, 4 to 6 minutes. Add the eggs one at a time, beating well after each addition, stopping to scrape down the sides of the bowl as needed. Add the vanilla and mix on low speed to combine. Add one-third of the flour mixture and mix on low speed to combine. Add half of the buttermilk and mix on low speed to combine. Add half the remaining flour and then the remaining buttermilk, beating on low speed after each addition to incorporate. Add the remaining flour and mix on low speed until just combined. Use a spatula to give the batter a couple of turns to make sure it is fully mixed. Remove ½ cup [110 g] of the batter and mix it with the mascarpone mixture. 5) Pour one-third of the batter into the prepared pan. Dollop half of the mascarpone mixture over the top of the batter and sprinkle with half of the mini chocolate chips. Pour half of the remaining batter over the top, repeat with the remaining mascarpone and mini chocolate chips, and cover with the remaining batter. Drag a knife through the batter, making a figure-eight motion, around the whole Bundt one time. Tap the pan twice on the counter to release any air bubbles. Bake the cake until a wooden skewer or toothpick inserted into the center comes out with the slightest bit of crumb, 65 to 80 minutes. 6) FOR THE COFFEE SOAK While the cake is baking, in a small saucepan, combine the espresso, granulated sugar, and salt. Heat over medium heat until the sugar is dissolved, 3 to 4 minutes. 7) Transfer the cake pan to a wire rack and let cool for 10 minutes. Invert the cake onto the rack and let cool for 15 minutes. 8) Using a pastry brush, brush the coffee soak over the entirety of the cake, using all of the mixture (this will take a few minutes). Let the cake cool completely. Wrap the cake in plastic wrap and chill in the refrigerator overnight. 9) When ready to serve, dust the top of the cake with cocoa powder. The cake can be wrapped in plastic wrap and refrigerated for up to 3 days.

32

Chocolate and vanilla is a classic combination in ice cream, cookies, and even Bundt cakes. This cake is very delicious, and perfect for when you can't decide between these beloved flavors.

Marble Bundt Cake

 MAKES 8 TO 12 SERVINGS

3¼ cups [462 g] all-purpose flour

½ teaspoon baking powder

¼ teaspoon baking soda

2 cups [4 sticks or 454 g] unsalted butter, at room temperature

3 cups [600 g] granulated sugar

1¼ teaspoons salt

1 tablespoon pure vanilla extract

6 large eggs, at room temperature

½ cup [120 g] buttermilk, at room temperature

⅓ cup [33 g] Dutch-process cocoa powder

1) Position an oven rack in the middle of the oven and preheat the oven to 325°F [165°C]. Grease and flour a 12 cup [2.8 L] Bundt pan. 2) In a medium bowl, whisk together the flour, baking powder, and baking soda. 3) In the bowl of a stand mixer fitted with a paddle, beat the butter on medium speed until creamy, about 1 minute. Add the granulated sugar and salt and beat until light and fluffy, 4 to 6 minutes. Scrape down the sides of the bowl and beat in the vanilla. Add the eggs, one at a time, beating until incorporated and stopping to scrape down the sides of the bowl as needed. Add half of the flour mixture, mixing until incorporated. Add the buttermilk, mixing until incorporated. Scrape down the sides of the bowl, add the remaining flour mixture, and mix on low speed until combined. Increase the speed to medium and beat for 15 to 20 seconds.

Use a spatula to give the batter a few final turns, making sure all the ingredients are completely incorporated. 4) Pour half of the batter into a clean bowl and stir in the cocoa powder. 5) Using a spoon or scoop, place equal amounts of the vanilla and chocolate batters into the prepared pan, alternating between the two. Carefully drag a knife through the batters, creating a marbled pattern. Smooth the top of the batter, and then tap the pan on your counter a few times. 6) Bake the cake until a wooden skewer or toothpick inserted into the center comes out clean, 60 to 70 minutes. Transfer the pan to a wire rack and let cool for 10 minutes. Invert the cake onto the rack to finish cooling before serving. The cake can be wrapped in plastic wrap and stored at room temperature for up to 2 days or refrigerated for up to 4 days.

This cake is a dream—an adult version of chocolate pudding cake. The cake itself is moist and rich, with pockets of pudding (secretly a bittersweet chocolate ganache) sinking slightly into the batter. This cake is delicious enough to pass as a birthday cake; my husband prefers it now over regular chocolate cake, but its Bundt cake shape makes it acceptable for breakfast.

Chocolate Pudding Bundt Cake

MAKES 8 TO
12 SERVINGS

GANACHE

6 oz [170 g] bittersweet or semisweet chocolate, finely chopped

½ cup [120 g] heavy cream

CAKE

5 large eggs, at room temperature

1 cup [240 g] crème fraîche, homemade (page 290) or store-bought, or sour cream, at room temperature

½ cup [112 g] vegetable or canola oil

1 teaspoon pure vanilla extract

2 cups [284 g] all-purpose flour

1 cup [200 g] granulated sugar

1 cup [200 g] brown sugar

¾ cup [75 g] Dutch-process cocoa powder, plus more for dusting

1 teaspoon salt

1 teaspoon baking soda

½ teaspoon baking powder

¾ cup [180 g] strong, hot freshly brewed coffee or boiling water

1) FOR THE GANACHE Place the chocolate in a small heatproof bowl. Heat the heavy cream in a small saucepan until it is simmering and just about to boil. Pour the cream over the chocolate, cover the bowl with plastic wrap, and let it sit for 5 minutes. **2)** Remove the plastic and whisk until completely smooth. Refrigerate the ganache until just firm, about 20 minutes. **3) FOR THE CAKE** Position an oven rack in the middle of the oven and preheat the oven to 350°F [180°C]. Grease and flour a 10 in [25 cm] one-piece tube pan. For extra insurance, you can line the bottom of the tube pan with parchment paper. Line a sheet pan with parchment paper and put a wire rack on top. **4)** In a medium bowl or liquid measuring cup, whisk together the eggs, crème fraîche, oil, and vanilla.

5) In the bowl of a stand mixer fitted with a paddle, mix the flour, the granulated and brown sugars, cocoa powder, salt, baking soda, and baking powder on low speed, then slowly add the egg mixture. Increase the speed to medium and beat until combined, 20 to 30 seconds. Add the hot coffee, mixing on low speed until just combined. Using a spatula, give the batter a couple of turns to make sure it is fully mixed.

6) Pour the batter into the prepared pan, tapping the pan on the counter twice to remove any air bubbles. Dollop the chilled ganache over the top of the batter in about 3 tablespoon-size drops. The ganache will sink slightly into the batter. Bake until a wooden skewer or toothpick inserted into the cake comes out clean (find a spot without ganache, which will leave streaks on the skewer regardless, even if the cake is done), 35 to 45 minutes. 7) Transfer the pan to a wire rack and let the cake cool in the pan for 15 to 20 minutes (this cake is a little more tender than a regular Bundt, so it needs a little more time to cool before flipping out of the pan). Invert the cake onto the wire rack on the prepared sheet pan to finish cooling. Serve at room temperature, or wrap the cake in plastic wrap and refrigerate for up to 3 days. Let it come to room temperature and dust with cocoa if you like before serving.

33

This is another cake that had its beginnings at the Blue Heron Coffeehouse. I've been making it for decades, tweaking and fiddling with it in my home kitchen. At the Blue Heron, we always made it with an orange glaze, but I love cardamom and coffee together, so I top it with a light coffee glaze instead.

Cardamom Bundt Cake
with Coffee Glaze

 MAKES 8 TO
12 SERVINGS

CAKE

3 cups [426 g] all-purpose flour

1 tablespoon ground cardamom

¾ teaspoon salt

½ teaspoon baking soda

1 cup [2 sticks or 227 g] unsalted butter, at room temperature

3 cups [600 g] granulated sugar

6 large eggs, at room temperature

1 teaspoon pure vanilla extract

½ cup [120 g] sour cream, at room temperature

½ cup [120 g] heavy cream, at room temperature

GLAZE

2 to 4 tablespoons coffee, at room temperature

1 teaspoon unsalted butter

1 teaspoon pure vanilla extract

Pinch of salt

1½ cups [180 g] confectioners' sugar

1) FOR THE CAKE Position an oven rack in the middle of the oven and preheat the oven to 325°F [165°C]. Grease and flour a 12 cup [2.8 L] Bundt pan. **2)** In a medium bowl, whisk together the flour, cardamom, salt, and baking soda. **3)** In a stand mixer fitted with a paddle, beat the butter on medium speed until creamy, about 1 minute. Add the granulated sugar and beat until light and fluffy, 4 to 6 minutes, scraping down the sides of the bowl as needed. Add the eggs, one at a time, beating after each addition until incorporated and scraping down the sides of the mixing bowl as needed. Add the vanilla and mix on low speed until combined. Add one-third of the flour mixture, mixing until just incorporated. Add the sour cream and mix until just blended into the batter. Add half of the remaining flour, the heavy cream, and then the remaining flour, mixing after each addition until just incorporated into

34

the batter. Use a spatula to scrape down the bowl and make sure the mixture is completely combined. 4) Pour the batter into the prepared pan and use a spatula to even out the top. Bake until a wooden skewer or toothpick inserted into the cake comes out clean, 60 to 75 minutes. 5) Transfer the cake to a wire rack with a piece of parchment underneath and let the cake cool in the pan for 10 minutes. Invert the cake onto the rack and let cool until just warm to the touch, about 20 minutes.

6) FOR THE GLAZE While the cake is cooling, in a small bowl or liquid measuring cup, combine 2 tablespoons of the coffee, the melted butter, vanilla, and salt. Add the confectioners' sugar and mix together, then whisk until well combined and smooth. If needed, add more coffee, 1 tablespoon at time, until the glaze is thick but pourable. 7) Pour the icing over the cake, then let the cake cool completely before serving. The cake can be wrapped in plastic wrap and stored at room temperature for up to 2 days or refrigerated for up to 4 days.

35

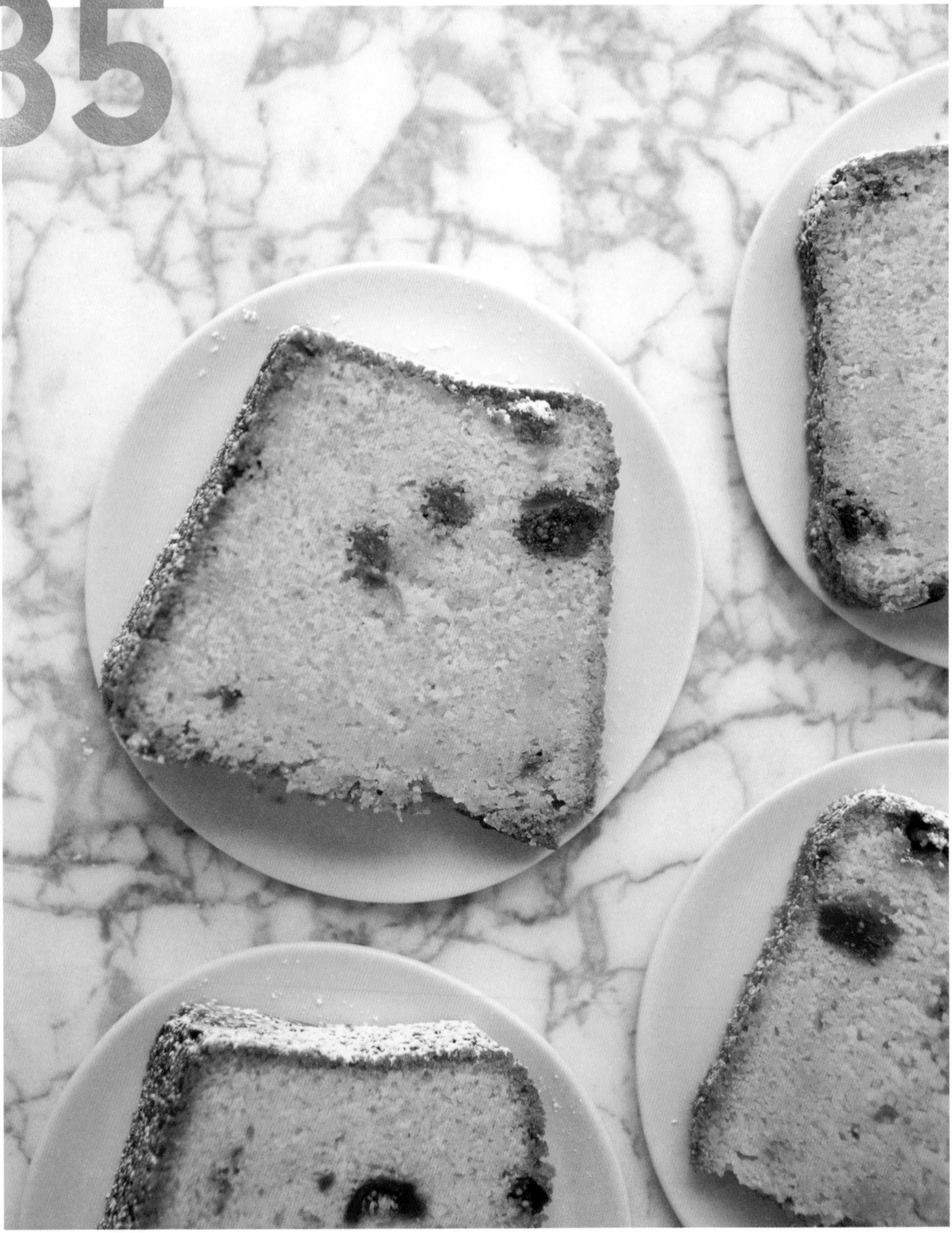

This rich pound cake satisfies both the adult and the child in me. The subtle orange flavor, dried figs, and finely chopped white chocolate are a compatible trio; each bite I take brings me right back to the kitchen cabinet in my childhood home. I am ten years old, I am opening the door, and I know exactly where my dad hid the bag of Fig Newtons. I grab as many as I can hide in my hands and run to my room, eating them quickly before he notices they are gone.

White Chocolate and Fig Pound Cake

MAKES 8 TO 12 SERVINGS

3½ cups [497 g] all-purpose flour

½ teaspoon baking powder

¼ teaspoon baking soda

2 cups [4 sticks or 454 g] unsalted butter, at room temperature

3 cups [600 g] granulated sugar

1 tablespoon grated orange zest

1¼ teaspoons salt

6 large eggs, at room temperature

1 tablespoon pure vanilla extract

½ cup [120 g] buttermilk

5 oz [142 g] dried figs, chopped into bite-size pieces

3 oz [85 g] white chocolate, finely chopped

1) Position an oven rack in the middle of the oven and preheat the oven to 350°F [180°C]. Grease and flour a 12 cup [2.8 L] Bundt pan. 2) In a medium bowl, whisk together the flour, baking powder, and baking soda. 3) In the bowl of a stand mixer fitted with a paddle, beat the butter on medium speed until creamy, about 1 minute. Add the granulated sugar, orange zest, and salt and beat until light and fluffy, 4 to 6 minutes. 4) Scrape down the sides of the bowl and add the eggs, one at a time, beating until incorporated and stopping to scrape down the sides of the bowl as needed. Add the vanilla and mix on low speed until combined. Add half of the flour mixture, and then the buttermilk, mixing after each addition until just incorporated. Scrape down the sides of the bowl and beat in the remaining flour mixture, mixing until just incorporated. Add the figs and white chocolate and use a spatula to mix them into the batter, then give the batter a few extra turns, making sure the ingredients are completely combined. 5) Pour the batter into the prepared pan and use an offset spatula to smooth out the top. Tap the pan twice on the counter to remove any air bubbles. Bake until the top is golden brown and a wooden skewer or tooth-pick inserted near the center comes out clean, 50 to 65 minutes. 6) Transfer the pan to a wire rack and let cool for 10 minutes. Invert the cake onto the rack to finish cooling before serving. The cake can be wrapped in plastic wrap and stored at room temperature for up to 2 days, or refrigerated for up to 4 days.

36

Cakes boasting a doughnut texture and flavor hold different expectations for everyone. This cake will not taste like an old-fashioned doughnut, freshly fried. However, it will faintly remind you of a very good pumpkin doughnut. And, if eaten slightly warm, with plenty of butter, sugar, and cinnamon soaked into the top, it will convince you of the cake itself.

Pumpkin Doughnut Bundt Cake

MAKES 8 TO
12 SERVINGS

CAKE

3 cups [426 g] all-purpose flour

2 teaspoons baking powder

¾ teaspoon freshly grated nutmeg

½ teaspoon ground ginger

¼ teaspoon baking soda

Pinch of ground cloves

1 cup [224 g] unsweetened pumpkin purée

¾ cup [180 g] buttermilk, at room temperature

12 tablespoons [1½ sticks or 170 g] unsalted butter, at room temperature

¾ cup [150 g] brown sugar

½ cup [100 g] granulated sugar

1 teaspoon salt

1 teaspoon pure vanilla extract

3 large eggs, at room temperature

TOPPING

⅔ cup [130 g] granulated sugar

1 tablespoon ground cinnamon

4 tablespoons [57 g] unsalted butter, melted

1) **FOR THE CAKE** Position an oven rack in the middle of the oven and preheat the oven to 350°F [180°C]. Grease and flour a 12 cup [2.8 L] Bundt pan. 2) In a medium bowl, whisk together the flour, baking powder, nutmeg, ginger, baking soda, and cloves. 3) In a liquid measuring cup, mix together the pumpkin purée and buttermilk. 4) In the bowl of a stand mixer fitted with a paddle, beat the butter on medium speed until creamy, 1 minute. Add the brown and granulated sugars and the salt and beat until light and fluffy, 4 to 6 minutes. Beat in the vanilla and then add the eggs, one at a time, mixing after each addition until incorporated and scraping down the bowl as needed.

cont'd

Add one-third of the flour mixture, mixing on low speed until just combined. Beat in the pumpkin-buttermilk mixture and the remaining flour mixture in halves, alternating between the two and ending with the flour mixture. Mix after each addition until just incorporated. Use a rubber spatula to scrape down the bowl and give the batter a few turns, making sure all ingredients are completely combined. 5) Pour the batter into the prepared pan and use an offset spatula to smooth the top. Bake the cake until a wooden skewer or toothpick inserted near the center comes out clean, 45 to 60 minutes. 6) Transfer the pan to a wire rack and let cool for 10 minutes. Invert the cake onto the rack to finish cooling before serving. 7) FOR THE TOPPING In a small bowl, mix together the granulated sugar and cinnamon. Brush the top and sides of the cake with the melted butter, then sprinkle with the cinnamon sugar, using your hands to gently rub it onto the sides. 8) Let cool to room temperature and serve. This cake is best eaten the same day it's made, but it can be stored in an airtight container at room temperature for up to 2 days.

Flipping Your Cake

Knowing when to flip your Bundt cake is the trickiest part of baking one. If the Bundt cake cools too long in the pan, the sugars will begin to set and harden, and this can make removing the cake more difficult. But, of course, if you flip it too soon, the cake will be too warm and crumble into pieces. Ten minutes is a good time frame for resting Bundts, and what I call for (with the exception of the Chocolate Pudding Bundt Cake, page 102). It is also often recommended not to run a knife around the sides of the pan as this can ruin the pan, but if your cake is stuck there might be no other option. I've found a plastic knife can work well and won't leave marks on the pan. If you do use something metal to release it, make sure it is thin, and go slowly and carefully around the edges.

"Ah! The gold and red and the sighing of leaves in the Autumn in Taur-na-neldor!" Tolkien wrote in his poem "Seasons." I sigh too on chilly, rainy autumn days, while layered in sweaters and bundled under blankets. I turn to coffee cake on these blustery days—it works as both breakfast and afternoon snack, and hot coffee or tea complements each bite. This coffee cake incorporates grated pear instead of diced fruit, which gives the cake so much flavor and keeps it moist for days.

Pear Bundt Cake

MAKES 8 TO 12 SERVINGS

CAKE

3 cups [426 g] all-purpose flour

2 teaspoons baking powder

1½ teaspoons ground cinnamon

1 teaspoon salt

½ teaspoon freshly grated nutmeg

¼ teaspoon baking soda

1½ cups [3 sticks or 339 g] unsalted butter, at room temperature

1½ cups [300 g] granulated sugar

1½ cups [300 g] brown sugar

5 large eggs, at room temperature

1 teaspoon pure vanilla extract

1 cup [240 g] sour cream, at room temperature

1 cup [150 g] peeled and grated ripe but still firm Bartlett pears

GLAZE

1 tablespoon unsalted butter, melted

2 to 3 tablespoons apple cider or water

½ teaspoon pure vanilla extract

Pinch of salt

1½ cups [180 g] confectioners' sugar

1) FOR THE CAKE Position an oven rack in the middle of the oven and preheat the oven to 350°F [180°C]. Grease and flour a 12 cup [2.8 L] Bundt pan. Line a sheet pan with parchment paper and put a wire rack on top. 2) In a medium bowl, whisk together the flour, baking powder, cinnamon, salt, nutmeg, and baking soda. 3) In the bowl of a stand mixer fitted with a paddle, beat the butter on medium speed until creamy, about 1 minute. Add the granulated and brown sugars and beat until light and fluffy, 4 to 6 minutes.

cont'd

37

4) Scrape down the sides of the bowl and add the eggs, one at a time, beating until incorporated and stopping to scrape down the sides of the bowl after each addition as needed. Beat in the vanilla. Add one-third of the flour mixture and mix on low speed until combined. Add half the sour cream and mix until incorporated. Scrape down the sides of the bowl, and add half of the remaining flour mixture, then the remaining sour cream, and finally the remaining flour, mixing after each addition to incorporate. Add the pears and use a spatula to mix them into the batter and give a few extra turns to make sure everything is completely combined. 5) Pour the batter into the prepared pan and use an offset spatula to smooth out the top. Bake until the cake is golden and a wooden skewer or toothpick inserted near the center comes out clean, 50 to 65 minutes. 6) Transfer the pan to a wire rack and let cool for 10 minutes. Invert the cake onto the rack to finish cooling before glazing. 7) FOR THE GLAZE While the cake is cooling, in a medium bowl, stir together the melted butter, 2 tablespoons of the apple cider, the vanilla, and salt. Add the confectioners' sugar and mix together, then whisk until well combined and smooth. If needed, add the remaining 1 tablespoon of apple cider until the glaze is thick but pourable. Pour the glaze over the cake while it is still warm, then let the cake cool before serving. The cake can be wrapped in plastic wrap and stored at room temperature for up to 2 days, or refrigerated for up to 4 days.

Scraping Down the Bowl

Even the best stand mixer can leave a little pocket of unmixed ingredients at the bottom. Your ingredients should be completely combined before pouring the batter into a pan, so use a spatula to scrape down the sides and bottom often!

CHAPTER 3

Sweet Yeasted and Fried Treats

"**Why,** sometimes I"ve **believed** as many as **six** **impossible** things before **breakfast.**"

—Lewis Carroll, *Through the Looking Glass*

38

I couldn't leave cinnamon rolls out of a breakfast cookbook; they are my go-to for any type of special occasion that may (or may not) involve breakfast. I have a favorite recipe for cinnamon rolls (made with my Sweet Dough recipe, page 266), which appeared in two of my other books, so I decided to change things up with a buttermilk dough and a slightly different filling. I love both versions equally, but these buns are extra special—they bake up so fluffy and are rich and delicious.

Buttermilk Cinnamon Rolls

MAKES 12
CINNAMON ROLLS

FILLING

6 tablespoons [84 g] unsalted butter, at room temperature

⅔ cup [130 g] brown sugar

4 teaspoons ground cinnamon

Pinch of salt

ASSEMBLY

All-purpose flour, for dusting

1 recipe Buttermilk Dough (page 268)

ICING

8 tablespoons [1 stick or 113 g] unsalted butter, melted

4 oz [113 g] cream cheese, at room temperature

1 teaspoon pure vanilla extract

¼ teaspoon salt

1¼ cups [150 g] confectioners' sugar

1) FOR THE FILLING In a medium bowl, mix together the butter, brown sugar, cinnamon, and salt until completely combined into a thick paste. **2)** TO ASSEMBLE AND BAKE Grease a 9 by 13 in [23 by 33 cm] baking pan; if desired, line it with a parchment sling for easier cleanup (see page 14). **3)** Generously flour your work surface. Roll out the dough into a 12 by 16 in [30.5 by 40.5 cm] rectangle. Use an offset spatula to spread the filling evenly over the surface of the dough. Starting at a long side, roll the dough into a tight cylinder.

cont'd

Pinch the seam gently to seal it and position the dough seam-side down. Use scissors or a sharp knife to cut the dough into twelve equal pieces. *See how-to photos, page 119.* Transfer them to the prepared pan and place them with a spiral side facing up. Cover the pan loosely with plastic wrap and let rise until doubled, 1 to 1½ hours. (The rolls can also do a slow rise in the refrigerator overnight. See "For overnight cinnamon rolls," following.) 4) Position an oven rack in the middle of the oven and preheat the oven to 350°F [180°C]. 5) Remove the plastic and bake the rolls until light golden brown, rotating the pan halfway through baking, 27 to 32 minutes. Transfer the pan of rolls to a wire rack and let cool for 5 minutes. Use the parchment sling to remove the rolls from the pan, peel off the parchment paper, and finish cooling on the wire rack. 6) FOR THE ICING While the rolls are baking, in the bowl of a stand mixer fitted with a paddle, beat the butter and cream cheese on medium speed until smooth and creamy. Add the vanilla and salt and mix on low speed to combine. Add the confectioners' sugar, mixing until incorporated. Scrape down the sides of the bowl, increase the speed to medium, and beat until the icing is light and fluffy, 3 to 4 minutes. 7) With an offset spatula or the back of a spoon, apply a thin layer of the cream cheese icing on the warm rolls, using half of the mixture (see Note). Let the rolls cool for another 15 to 20 minutes. Top with the rest of the icing and serve. 8) Cinnamon rolls are best eaten the same day they are made, but they can be stored in an airtight container in the refrigerator for up to 2 days.

NOTE I like my cinnamon rolls super soft with a gooey center, which is why I put that thin layer of icing over them when they're still very hot. The icing melts into the warm rolls, eliminating any hard corners or edges. If you prefer a little crispy crunch to your cinnamon rolls, you can wait until they have cooled and then top them with all the icing.

FOR OVERNIGHT CINNAMON ROLLS Assemble the rolls and put them in the prepared pan, but do not let them rise at room temperature. Cover them loosely with plastic wrap and place in the refrigerator for 8 hours or up to overnight to do a slow rise. When ready to bake, preheat the oven and let the rolls sit at room temperature (still covered with plastic) for 30 to 45 minutes. Bake as directed, and proceed with the recipe.

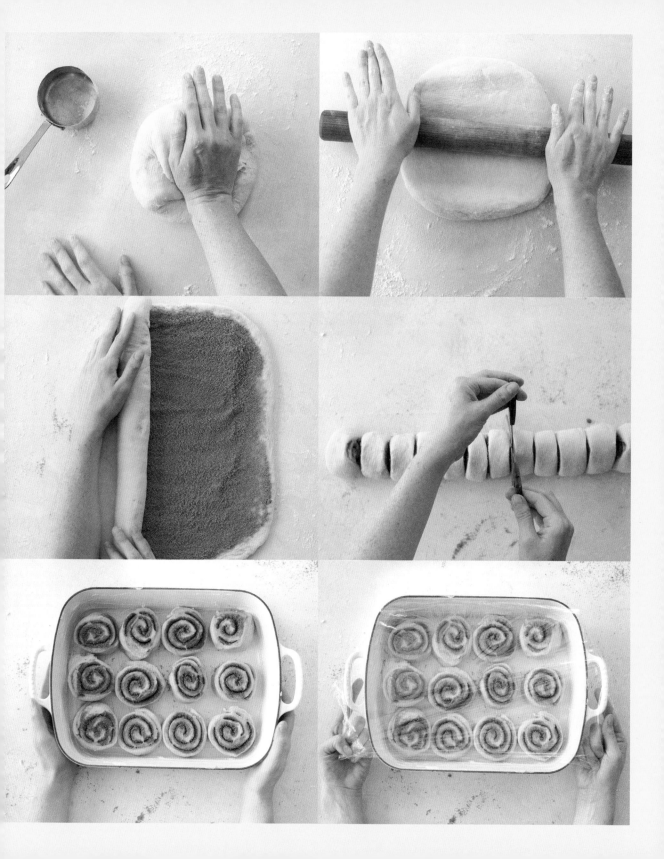

When I was in grade school, I would occasionally need to miss a morning of school for a random appointment. On one of these mornings, instead of taking me back to class, my mom pulled our rusty blue Toyota up to a nearby restaurant and with a wink took me out to breakfast. It was the ultimate treat—skipping school and indulging in a giant sticky bun from the bakery case. I still remember sitting in an oversize brown booth, my legs dangling, and the sunlight streaming in the windows hitting those caramel tops just right, so they gleamed like amber.

Maple Bourbon Caramel Rolls

 **MAKES 12 CARAMEL ROLLS**

MAPLE BOURBON CARAMEL

8 tablespoons [113 g] unsalted butter

1 cup [200 g] brown sugar

1 cup [240 g] heavy cream

⅓ cup [107 g] maple syrup

2 tablespoons corn syrup

½ teaspoon salt

2 tablespoons bourbon

1 teaspoon pure vanilla extract

FILLING

6 tablespoons [84 g] unsalted butter, melted

¾ cup [150 g] brown sugar

1 tablespoon ground cinnamon

¾ teaspoon freshly grated nutmeg

Pinch of ground cloves

Pinch of salt

ASSEMBLY

All-purpose flour, for dusting

1 recipe Buttermilk Dough (page 268)

1 cup [120 g] pecan halves, toasted and chopped

1) FOR THE CARAMEL In a large, heavy-bottom saucepan, combine the butter, brown sugar, heavy cream, maple syrup, corn syrup, and salt. Heat over medium heat until the butter has melted. Increase the heat to medium-high and cook until the mixture has thickened slightly and registers 235°F [113°C] on an instant-read thermometer, 6 to 8 minutes. Remove from the heat and add the bourbon and vanilla, stirring to incorporate. The caramel sauce can be made up to 3 days ahead of time, but bring it to room temperature before using. **2) FOR THE FILLING** In a medium bowl, mix together the butter, brown sugar, cinnamon, nutmeg, cloves, and salt into a thick paste.

3) **TO ASSEMBLE AND BAKE** Grease a 9 by 13 in [23 by 33 cm] baking pan; if desired, line it with a parchment sling (see page 14). 4) Generously flour your work surface. Roll out the dough into a 12 by 16 in [30.5 by 40.5 cm] rectangle. Spread the filling evenly over the surface, pressing it so it adheres. Starting at a long side, roll the dough into a tight cylinder. Pinch the seam gently to seal it and position the dough seam-side down. Use scissors or a sharp knife to cut the dough crosswise into twelve equal pieces. *See how-to photos, page 119.* Transfer them to the prepared pan and place them with a spiral side facing up. Cover the pan loosely with plastic wrap and let the rolls rise until doubled, 1 to 1½ hours. (The rolls can also do a slow rise in the refrigerator overnight; see page 118.) 5) Position an oven rack in the middle of the oven and preheat the oven to 350°F [180°C]. Line a sheet pan with parchment paper. 6) Remove the plastic and bake the rolls until light golden brown, rotating the pan halfway through, 27 to 32 minutes. 7) Invert the pan onto the prepared sheet pan, peel off the parchment, and immediately pour half of the caramel sauce over the rolls, then sprinkle the chopped pecans over the caramel. Let the rolls sit for 10 to 15 minutes. Pour the remaining caramel over the top, covering the rolls evenly. Serve immediately. 8) Caramel rolls are best eaten the same day they are made, but they can be stored in an airtight container in the refrigerator for up to 2 days.

39

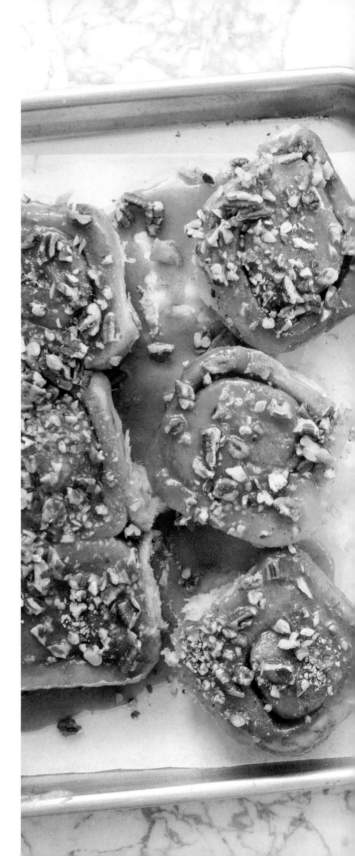

Growing up in the suburban Midwest, I had never encountered toasted sesame oil until I started working at the Blue Heron. Early one morning I opened a bottle to whisk into salad dressing and the nutty smell of the oil washed over me, evoking the same feeling that warm chocolate chip cookies, straight out of the oven, never fails to give me. I paused for a moment to just breathe in the aroma; a new smell is rare the older one gets. I still associate it with something sweet and love to incorporate into my baking whenever I get the chance.

Toasted Sesame Sweet Buns

 MAKES 8
SWEET BUNS

FILLING
⅔ cup [130 g] brown sugar

¼ cup [36 g] sesame seeds, white or black or a combination

1 teaspoon ground cinnamon

1 teaspoon ground ginger

½ teaspoon ground nutmeg

Pinch of ground cloves

Pinch of salt

6 tablespoons [84 g] unsalted butter, at room temperature

ASSEMBLY
All-purpose flour, for dusting

1 recipe Milk Bread Dough (page 262)

ICING
½ teaspoon to 2 tablespoons toasted sesame oil

1 to 2 tablespoons water

1 tablespoon unsalted butter, melted

1 teaspoon pure vanilla extract

1 cup [120 g] confectioners' sugar

White and black sesame seeds, for sprinkling

1) FOR THE FILLING In the bowl of a food processor, pulse the brown sugar, sesame seeds, cinnamon, ginger, nutmeg, cloves, and salt until the sesame seeds are broken down. Add the butter and pulse again until completely combined. **2)** TO ASSEMBLE AND BAKE Grease eight 3 by 2 in [7.5 by 5 cm] 6 oz [180 g] ramekins and line the bottoms with parchment paper (this makes for easier flipping). Place the ramekins on a sheet pan lined with parchment paper. **3)** Generously flour your work surface. Roll out the dough into a 12 by 16 in [30.5 by 40.5 cm] rectangle. Use an offset spatula to spread the filling evenly over the surface. Starting at a long side, roll the dough into a tight cylinder. Pinch the seam gently to seal it and position the dough seam-side down. Use scissors or a sharp knife to cut the dough crosswise into eight equal pieces. *See how-to photos, page 119.* Transfer them to the prepared ramekins, placing them with a spiral side facing up. Cover the ramekins loosely with plastic wrap and let the buns rise until doubled, 1 to 1½ hours. (The buns can also do a slow rise in the refrigerator overnight; see page 118.) 4) Position an oven rack in the middle of the oven and preheat the oven to 350°F [180°C]. Line a sheet pan with parchment paper and set a wire rack on top. 5) Remove the plastic and bake the buns until light golden brown, rotating the sheet pan halfway through baking, 27 to 32 minutes. Transfer the sheet pan to a wire rack and let the buns cool for 3 minutes. Flip each bun out of its ramekin and place on the wire rack.

6) FOR THE ICING While the buns are baking, in a medium bowl, whisk together ½ teaspoon of sesame oil, 1 tablespoon of water, the butter, and vanilla. Add the confectioners' sugar and mix together, then whisk until well combined and smooth. Add the remaining sesame oil to taste, and add water by the tablespoon until the icing is thick but pourable. 7) Pour an equal amount of icing over each hot bun and sprinkle with sesame seeds. Let the buns cool for 20 minutes, and serve while still slightly warm. 8) The buns are best eaten the same day they are made, but they can be stored in an airtight container in the refrigerator for up to 2 days.

What if we took all the things we love best about carrot cake (which for me is the cream cheese frosting), combined that with what we love about cinnamon rolls (more cream cheese frosting, please), and then made it into one gigantic bun? Well, then we'd have this Giant Carrot Cake Cinnamon Roll, a showstopper of a breakfast.

Giant Carrot Cake Cinnamon Roll

MAKES ONE 9 IN
[23 CM] ROLL

FILLING

½ cup [100 g] brown sugar

1 tablespoon ground cinnamon

Pinch of ground cloves

Pinch of salt

ASSEMBLY

All-purpose flour, for sprinkling

1 recipe Pull-Apart Bread Dough, made with the Carrot Sweet Dough variation (page 269)

2 tablespoons unsalted butter, melted

ICING

8 tablespoons [1 stick or 113 g] unsalted butter, at room temperature

4 oz [113 g] cream cheese, at room temperature

¼ teaspoon salt

1 teaspoon pure vanilla extract

1 cup [120 g] confectioners' sugar

1) **FOR THE FILLING** In a medium bowl, mix together the brown sugar, cinnamon, cloves, and salt until well combined. 2) **TO ASSEMBLE** Grease a 9 in [23 cm] springform pan. Generously flour your work surface. Roll out the dough into a 12 by 14 in [30.5 by 35.5 cm] rectangle. Brush the dough with the melted butter and sprinkle the filling evenly over the top, pressing it lightly into the butter so it adheres. Cut the dough crosswise into seven equal strips, each 2 in [5 cm] wide and 12 in [30.5 cm] long. Roll up the first strip into a tight coil. Wrap the next strip around the coil, winding it completely around. Repeat with each remaining strip until you have a giant cinnamon roll. *See how-to photos, page 127.*

cont'd

Place the dough into the prepared pan. Cover loosely with plastic wrap and let rise until doubled in size, about 1 hour. (The roll can also do a slow rise in the refrigerator overnight; see page 118.) 3) Position an oven rack in the middle of the oven and preheat the oven to 350°F [180°C]. 4) Remove the plastic and bake the roll until light golden brown, rotating the pan halfway through, 40 to 55 minutes. If the top of the roll starts to brown too quickly, place a piece of foil over the top. If the center of the roll pops up while baking, use the back of a spoon to gently push it back down into place.

5) FOR THE ICING While the roll is baking, in the bowl of a stand mixer fitted with a paddle, beat the butter, cream cheese, and salt on medium speed until smooth and creamy. Lower the mixer speed to low and beat in the vanilla. Add the confectioners' sugar, mixing until incorporated. Scrape down the sides of the bowl, increase the mixer speed to medium, and mix until the icing is light and fluffy, 3 to 4 minutes. 6) Transfer the pan to a wire rack and run a knife around the edge of the pan to release the sides of the roll. Let the roll cool for 5 minutes. Using an offset spatula or the back of a spoon, apply a thin layer of the icing to the top of the roll, using about half of the mixture. Let the roll cool for another 20 minutes, release the sides of the pan, and then top with the rest of the icing and serve. 7) The roll is best eaten the same day it is made, but it can be stored in an airtight container in the refrigerator for up to 2 days.

I love cherry and rhubarb paired together; the tart flavor of the rhubarb is tamed by the sweet cherries without having to add a lot of extra sugar. These buns are bright and tasty, with a crunchy streusel top. The cherry-rhubarb jam can be made a day ahead of time, if desired.

Cherry Rhubarb Streusel Buns

MAKES
12 BUNS

CHERRY RHUBARB JAM

2 cups [250 g] chopped rhubarb, fresh or frozen, in 1 in [2.5 cm] pieces

6 oz [170 g] fresh or frozen sweet cherries, pitted

½ cup [100 g] granulated sugar

1 to 2 teaspoons lemon juice

Pinch of salt

1 teaspoon pure vanilla extract

ASSEMBLY

All-purpose flour, for sprinkling

1 recipe Sweet Dough (page 266)

2 tablespoons unsalted butter, melted

2 cups [280 g] Streusel (page 291)

ICING

2 oz [57 g] cream cheese, at room temperature

2 to 4 tablespoons lemon juice or water

1 tablespoon unsalted butter, melted

½ teaspoon pure vanilla extract

Pinch of salt

1½ cups [180 g] confectioners' sugar

1) FOR THE JAM In a medium saucepan over medium heat, combine the rhubarb, cherries, granulated sugar, 1 teaspoon of the lemon juice, and the salt and simmer, stirring often, until the cherries have broken down and the jam is thick enough to coat a wooden spoon, 20 to 30 minutes. **2)** Remove the pan from the heat, stir in the vanilla, and allow to cool to room temperature. Taste the jam. If it is a little flat, you can add more lemon juice, ½ teaspoon at a time, to brighten the flavor. **3) TO ASSEMBLE AND BAKE** Grease a 9 by 13 in [23 by 33 cm] baking pan; if desired, line it with a parchment sling (see page 14). Line a sheet pan with parchment paper.

cont'd

4) Generously flour your work surface. Roll out the dough into a 12 by 16 in [30.5 by 40.5 cm] rectangle. Brush the dough with the melted butter and spread ¾ cup [225 g] of the jam evenly over the surface. Starting at a long side, roll the dough into a tight cylinder, then pinch the seam gently to seal it. Place the dough, seam-side down, on the prepared sheet pan and place in the refrigerator to chill for 15 minutes (this makes cutting the buns a little less messy). Place the dough log on a cutting board and use scissors or a sharp knife to cut the dough into twelve equal pieces. *See how-to photos, page 119.* Transfer the pieces to the prepared pan, with a spiral side facing up. Cover the pan loosely with plastic wrap and let the dough rise at room temperature until doubled, 1 to 1½ hours. 5) Position an oven rack in the middle of the oven and preheat the oven to 350°F [180°C]. 6) When the buns are ready, remove the plastic wrap and sprinkle the tops of the buns generously with the streusel, gently pressing it into the buns. Bake the buns until golden brown, rotating the pan halfway through baking, 27 to 32 minutes. Transfer the pan to a wire rack and let the buns cool for 10 to 15 minutes. Use the parchment sling to remove the buns from the pan, peel off the parchment paper, and finish cooling on the wire rack.

7) FOR THE ICING While the buns are baking, in a medium bowl, whisk together the cream cheese, 2 tablespoons of the lemon juice, the melted butter, vanilla, and salt until smooth. Add the confectioners' sugar and mix together, then whisk until well combined and smooth. Add more lemon juice, 1 tablespoon at a time, to thin the icing to your preferred consistency; the icing should be thick but pourable. Drizzle the icing evenly over the warm buns. 8) The buns are best eaten the day they are made, but they can be stored in an airtight container in the refrigerator for up to 2 days.

Working with Cold Dough

Many of the doughs needed for this chapter work best when refrigerated for at least 2 hours, and up to overnight (8 hours). Chilling the dough overnight helps develop flavor, but it also helps with the rolling process. For example, because of the high butter content in brioche dough, it is more apt to stick to your work surface or rolling pin when warm. If that happens, you can put it back in the fridge and let it chill. If your dough is resisting rolling out straight from the fridge, cover it with a tea towel and let it rest for 5 minutes, then try again.

Orange buns: so unassuming at first glance! But don't let them fool you. These buns are light and sweet throughout, with some caramelization on their bottoms from the orange-sugar filling. Then they are topped with an orange-flavored icing that makes for a perfect bite.

Orange Buns

 MAKES
12 BUNS

43

FILLING

6 tablespoons [84 g] unsalted butter, melted

⅔ cup [130 g] brown sugar

1 tablespoon grated orange zest

1 teaspoon ground cinnamon

Pinch of salt

ASSEMBLY

All-purpose flour, for dusting

1 recipe Sweet Dough (page 266)

GLAZE

2 to 4 tablespoons orange juice

1 tablespoon unsalted butter, melted

1 teaspoon pure vanilla extract

Pinch of salt

1½ cups [180 g] confectioners' sugar

1) FOR THE FILLING In a small bowl, mix together the melted butter, brown sugar, orange zest, cinnamon, and salt. **2) TO ASSEMBLE AND BAKE** Grease a 9 by 13 in [23 by 33 cm] baking pan; if desired, line the bottom with a parchment sling (see page 14). **3)** Generously flour your work surface. Roll out the dough into a 12 by 16 in [30.5 by 40.5 cm] rectangle. Using an offset spatula, spread the filling evenly over the dough. Starting at a long side, roll the dough into a tight cylinder.

cont'd

Pinch the seam gently to seal it and position the dough seam-side down. Use scissors or a sharp knife to cut the dough into twelve equal pieces. Transfer the pieces to the prepared pan and place them with a cut side facing up, tucking the loose end underneath the bun. *See how-to photos, page 119.* Cover the pan loosely with plastic wrap and let the dough rise until doubled in size, 1 to 1½ hours. (The buns can also do a slow rise in the refrigerator overnight; see page 118.) 4) Position an oven rack in the middle of the oven and preheat the oven to 350°F [180°C]. 5) When the buns are ready, remove the plastic wrap and bake until light golden brown, rotating the pan halfway through baking, 27 to 32 minutes. Transfer the pan of buns to a wire rack and let cool for 5 minutes. Use the parchment sling to remove the buns from the pan, peel off the parchment paper, and finish cooling on the wire rack. 6) FOR THE ICING While the buns are baking, in a medium bowl, whisk together 2 tablespoons of the orange juice, the butter, vanilla, and salt. Add the confectioners' sugar and mix together, then whisk until well combined and smooth. Add more juice, 1 tablespoon at a time, to thin the glaze to your preferred consistency. Pour the icing over the warm buns, making sure it coats the edges as well as the top. 7) Orange buns are best eaten the same day they are made, but they can be stored in an airtight container in the refrigerator for 2 days.

Kolaches have a cult-like following, and for good reason. Originally brought to Texas by Czech immigrants, they are made with a brioche-like bread dough and are filled with a creamy sweet cheese and the slightest hint of lemon. I spent a lot of time making all kinds of kolache dough variations and came up with a sour cream dough with lots of egg yolks, which has quickly become a family favorite.

Kolaches

MAKES
12 KOLACHES

44

CREAM CHEESE FILLING

12 oz [340 g] cream cheese, at room temperature

3 tablespoons granulated sugar

1 teaspoon lemon juice

POSIPKA (STREUSEL TOPPING)

¼ cup [50 g] granulated sugar

¼ cup [36 g] all-purpose flour

2 tablespoons unsalted butter, at room temperature

ASSEMBLY

All-purpose flour, for dusting

1 recipe Sour Cream Dough (page 270)

Egg wash (see page 14)

¾ cup [168 g] raspberry or apricot jam or Lemon Curd (page 288)

1) FOR THE FILLING In a small bowl, stir the cream cheese to soften, then add the granulated sugar and lemon juice, mixing until smooth. 2) FOR THE POSIPKA In a small bowl, whisk together the granulated sugar and flour. Dollop the butter over the top and use your fingers to work the butter into the dry ingredients until the mixture looks like wet sand. 3) TO ASSEMBLE AND BAKE Line a sheet pan with parchment paper, and generously flour your work surface. 4) Roll out the dough into a 12 in [30.5 cm] square, about ½ in [12 mm] thick. Use a 3 in [7.5 cm] biscuit or cookie cutter to cut out twelve circles.

cont'd

Gather the dough scraps and reroll as needed (see Note). Place the rounds on the prepared pan in four rows, three rounds to a row, spacing the rounds about 1 in [2.5 cm] apart. Cover with plastic wrap and let the dough rise until soft and slightly puffy, 1 to 1½ hours. 5) Position an oven rack in the middle of the oven and preheat the oven to 375°F [190°C]. 6) Grease the bottom of a ⅓ cup dry measuring cup (a drinking glass can also work) and use it to make an indentation in the center of each round. Use your fingers to press the indentation again if it springs back slightly. 7) Brush the dough rounds with the egg wash. Divide the cream cheese filling among the twelve rounds and use the back of a spoon to spread it into the indentations. Dollop 1 tablespoon of jam or lemon curd over the top of the cream cheese filling, then sprinkle the edges with the streusel, trying to avoid the filling. 8) Bake the kolaches until the filling is puffed and the edges are light golden brown, rotating the pan halfway through baking, 20 to 25 minutes. Transfer the pan to a wire rack and let the kolaches cool for 15 minutes. Serve warm. 9) Kolaches are best eaten the same day they are made, but they can be stored in an airtight container in the refrigerator for up to 2 days.

NOTE Extra dough scraps can be rerolled and made into more kolaches, but more filling will be needed if doing so. The dough scraps can also be used to make a small batch of Pumpkin Caramel Monkey Bread (page 162).

In this version of pull-apart bread I roll and cut the dough like a regular cinnamon roll, then flatten each piece to get a cinnamon roll spiral in each slice.

MAKES ONE 9 IN
[23 CM] LOAF

Cinnamon Roll Pull-Apart Bread

FILLING

¾ cup [150 g] brown sugar

1 tablespoon ground cinnamon

Pinch of salt

ASSEMBLY

All-purpose flour, for sprinkling

1 recipe Pull-Apart Bread Dough (page 269)

2 tablespoons unsalted butter, melted and cooled slightly

ICING

2 oz [57 g] cream cheese, at room temperature

2 to 4 tablespoons water

1 tablespoon unsalted butter, melted

½ teaspoon pure vanilla extract

Pinch of salt

1½ cups [180 g] confectioners' sugar

45

1) FOR THE FILLING In a small bowl, mix together the brown sugar, cinnamon, and salt. 2) TO ASSEMBLE AND BAKE Grease a 9 by 4 by 4 in [23 by 10 by 10 cm] Pullman pan and line with a parchment sling (see page 14). 3) Generously flour your work surface. Roll out the dough into a 12 by 20 in [30.5 by 50 cm] rectangle with a short edge facing you. Brush the dough with the melted butter and sprinkle the filling evenly over the surface, pressing it lightly into the butter so it adheres. Starting at a long side, roll the dough into a tight cylinder. Pinch the seam gently to seal it and position the dough seam-side down. Use scissors or a sharp knife to cut the dough into sixteen equal pieces. *See how-to photos, page 119.*

cont'd

With the cut sides facing up, use a rolling pin to roll each piece flat. Fit these flattened pieces into the prepared loaf pan side by side (it will be a tight fit, but it is okay to press them close together). Loosely cover the pan with plastic wrap and let the dough rise in a warm place until almost doubled in size, 45 to 60 minutes. (The bread can also do a slow rise in the refrigerator overnight. See "For overnight pull-apart bread," following.) 4) Position an oven rack in the middle of the oven and preheat the oven to 350°F [180°C]. 5) Bake the bread until the top is golden brown and the bread registers 195°F [92°C] on an instant-read thermometer, 40 to 50 minutes. Check the bread halfway through baking; if the top is browning too quickly, cover loosely with a piece of foil. Transfer the pan to a wire rack set over a piece of parchment paper. 6) FOR THE ICING While the bread is baking, in a medium bowl, whisk together the cream cheese, 1 tablespoon of the water, the melted butter, vanilla, and salt until smooth. Add the confectioners' sugar and mix together, then whisk until well combined and smooth. Add more water, 1 tablespoon at a time, as needed. The icing should be thick but pourable.

7) As soon as the bread is out of the oven, pour half of the icing over it, then let it sit in the pan for 15 minutes. Use the sling to gently remove the loaf from the pan, peel off the paper, then drizzle the remaining icing over the loaf. Let the bread cool slightly before pulling apart and eating. 8) This bread is best eaten the same day it's made, but it can be stored in an airtight container in the refrigerator for up to 2 days.

FOR OVERNIGHT PULL-APART BREAD Assemble the pull-apart bread in the Pullman pan, but do not let it rise at room temperature. Cover the pan loosely with plastic wrap and place in the refrigerator for at least 8 and up to 18 hours. When ready to bake, preheat the oven, and let the bread sit at room temperature (still covered in plastic) for 45 minutes to 1 hour. Bake as directed.

46

This bread is a little more time-consuming to make than the previous cinnamon roll version (page 135), but it's worth the effort—each piece is coated in butter, orange, sugar, and icing. Regular oranges can be substituted for the blood oranges.

Blood Orange Poppy Seed Pull-Apart Bread

MAKES ONE 9 IN
[23 CM] LOAF

FILLING

¾ cup [150 g] granulated sugar

2 tablespoons grated blood orange zest

2 tablespoons poppy seeds

Pinch of salt

ASSEMBLY

All-purpose flour, for dusting

1 recipe Pull-Apart Bread Dough (page 269)

2 tablespoons unsalted butter, melted and cooled slightly

ICING

2 to 4 tablespoons blood orange juice

1 tablespoon unsalted butter, melted

1 tablespoon triple sec (optional)

1 teaspoon pure vanilla extract

Pinch of salt

1½ cups [180 g] confectioners' sugar

1) FOR THE FILLING In a small bowl, mix together the granulated sugar, orange zest, poppy seeds, and salt. 2) TO ASSEMBLE AND BAKE Line a 9 by 4 by 4 in [23 by 10 by 10 cm] Pullman pan with a parchment sling (see page 14). 3) Generously flour your work surface. Roll out the dough into a 12 by 20 in [30.5 by 50 cm] rectangle with a short edge facing you. With a pastry brush, spread the melted butter evenly over the dough. Sprinkle the filling over the dough evenly and press gently into the butter so it adheres. 4) Using a pastry wheel or pizza cutter, cut the dough crosswise into five strips about 4 by 12 in [10 by 30.5 cm] each. Stack the five rectangles on top of each other.

cont'd

5) Slice the stack of rectangles crosswise to create six equal strips, about 4 in [10 cm] long and 2 in [5 cm] wide. Fit these layered strips into the prepared loaf pan side by side, cut edges facing up (it will be a tight fit, but it is okay to press them close together). *See how-to photos, page 140.* Loosely cover the pan with plastic wrap and let the dough rise in a warm place until almost doubled in size, 45 to 60 minutes. (The bread can also do a slow rise in the refrigerator overnight; see page 136.)

6) Position an oven rack in the middle of the oven and preheat the oven to 350°F [180°C].

7) Bake the bread until the top is golden brown and the bread registers 195°F [92°C] on an instant-read thermometer, 40 to 50 minutes. Check the bread halfway through baking; if the top is browning too quickly, cover loosely with a piece of foil. Transfer the pan to a wire rack set over a piece of parchment paper.

8) FOR THE ICING While the bread is baking, in a medium bowl, whisk together 2 tablespoons of the orange juice, the melted butter, triple sec, if using, vanilla, and salt. Add the confectioners' sugar and mix together, then whisk until well combined and smooth. Add more orange juice, 1 tablespoon at a time, to thin the icing, if desired; it should be thick but pourable.

9) Immediately after transfering the pan to the wire rack, set over a piece of parchment paper to catch any drips. Pour half of the icing over the bread, then let it sit in the pan for 15 minutes. Use the sling to gently remove the loaf from the pan, then drizzle the remaining icing over the loaf. Let cool slightly before pulling apart and eating. 10) This bread is best eaten the same day it's made, but it can be stored in an airtight container in the refrigerator for up to 2 days.

VARIATION
• **Lemon Poppy Seed Pull-Apart Bread:** *Replace the orange zest and juice with lemon.*

I've always loved making braided breads; I find so much beauty in the lines of color in the dough, all twisted and wrapped in various shapes and sizes.

Cardamom Pistachio Twist

MAKES ONE 9 IN [23 CM] TWIST

FILLING

½ cup [100 g] brown sugar

¼ cup [30 g] roasted, shelled pistachios, finely chopped (see Note)

2 teaspoons ground cardamon

Pinch of salt

ASSEMBLY

All-purpose flour, for dusting

1 recipe Pull-Apart Bread Dough (page 269)

2 tablespoons unsalted butter, melted

ICING

2 to 4 tablespoons orange juice or water

1 tablespoon unsalted butter, melted

1 teaspoon pure vanilla extract

Pinch of salt

1½ cups [180 g] confectioners' sugar

Roasted, shelled pistachios, finely chopped, for sprinkling

1) FOR THE FILLING In a small bowl, mix together the brown sugar, pistachios, cardamon, and salt. 2) TO ASSEMBLE AND BAKE Grease a 9 in [23 cm] springform pan. Line a sheet pan with parchment paper. 3) Generously flour your work surface. Roll out the dough into a 12 by 20 in [30.5 by 50 cm] rectangle. Brush the dough with the melted butter and sprinkle the filling evenly over the surface, pressing it lightly into the butter so it adheres. Starting at a long side, roll the dough into a tight log. Pinch the seam gently to seal it and position the dough seam-side down. Trim about ¾ in [2 cm] off of each end of the log and discard. Place the log on the prepared sheet pan and transfer it to the refrigerator to chill for 15 minutes (this makes cutting a little less messy). Remove the pan from the refrigerator and place the dough log on your work surface.

cont'd

47

4) With a bench scraper, scissors, or a sharp knife, starting 1 in [2.5 cm] from the end, carefully cut down the center of the log lengthwise, all the way through, so you have two strands of dough attached at the top, with visible layers of dough and filling. With the cut side facing up, gently lift the right strand over the left strand. Repeat, always placing the right strand over the left and keeping the cut sides up (so the filling doesn't fall out), until you have twisted the entire log. Press the ends of the strands together and coil the braid tightly into a spiral, making sure not to leave any gaps. *See how-to photos, page 145.* 5) Transfer the dough to the prepared pan. Loosely cover the pan with plastic wrap and let the dough rise in a warm place until almost doubled in size, 1 to 1½ hours. (The bread can also do a slow rise in the refrigerator overnight; see page 136.)
6) Position an oven rack in the middle of the oven and preheat the oven to 350°F [180°C].
7) Bake until the top is golden brown and set in the center and registers 195°F [92°C] on an instant-read thermometer, 30 to 40 minutes. Check the bread halfway through baking; if the top is browning too quickly, cover loosely with a piece of foil. Transfer the pan to a wire rack and let the bread cool for 10 minutes.

8) FOR THE ICING While the bread is baking, in a medium bowl, whisk together 2 tablespoons of the orange juice, the melted butter, vanilla, and salt until smooth. Add the confectioners' sugar and mix together, then whisk until well combined and smooth. Add more orange juice, 1 tablespoon at a time, to thin the icing, if desired; it should be thick but pourable.
9) Pour the icing over the warm bread in the pan and sprinkle with pistachios. Let sit for 20 minutes. Remove the bread from the springform pan and let cool slightly before slicing and eating. 10) This bread is best eaten the day it's made, but it can be stored in an airtight container in the refrigerator for up to 2 days.

NOTE You can use either salted or unsalted pistachios here; I like the flavor of salted, and it is usually what I have on hand.

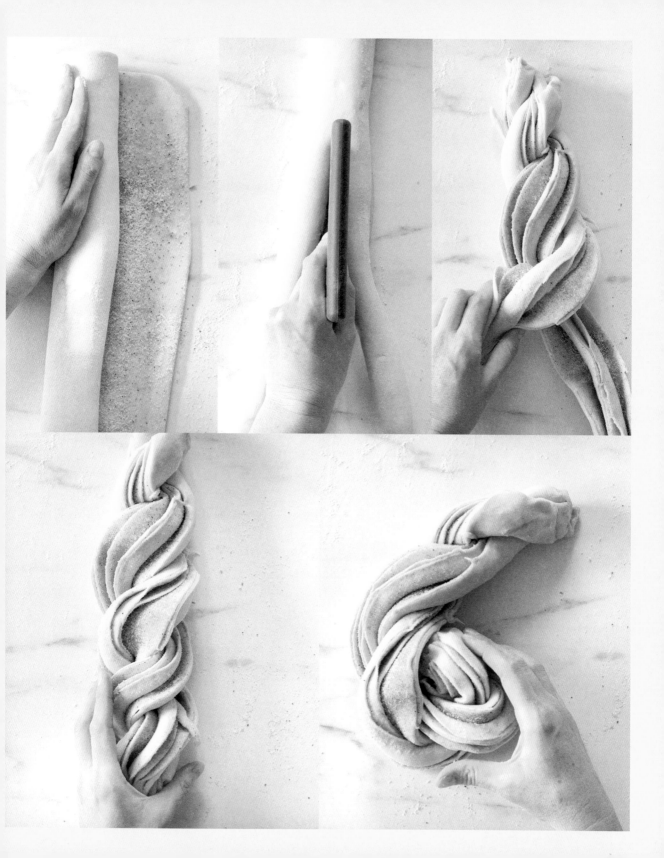

This bread is quite a treat, especially in the summer months, when our raspberry bushes are exploding with fresh berries. Bubble bread is in the same category as monkey bread, with individual pieces tucked in the pan together for a lofty, delicious loaf.

Raspberry Caramel Bubble Bread

MAKES ONE 9 IN
[23 CM] LOAF

RASPBERRY SUGAR

½ cup [100 g] granulated sugar

¼ cup [16 g] freeze-dried raspberry powder (see page 14)

1 tablespoon ground cinnamon

Pinch of salt

ASSEMBLY

All-purpose flour, for dusting

1 recipe Pull-Apart Bread Dough (page 269)

3 tablespoons unsalted butter, melted

4 oz [115 g] fresh raspberries

CARAMEL

¼ cup [50 g] brown sugar

3 tablespoons unsalted butter

Pinch of salt

1 teaspoon pure vanilla extract

ICING

2 tablespoons cream cheese, at room temperature

1 tablespoon unsalted butter, melted

2 to 4 tablespoons water

1 teaspoon pure vanilla extract

1 cup [120 g] confectioners' sugar

1) FOR THE RASPBERRY SUGAR In a small bowl, combine the granulated sugar, freeze-dried raspberry powder, cinnamon, and salt. **2)** TO ASSEMBLE Grease a 9 by 4 by 4 in [23 by 10 by 10 cm] Pullman pan and line with a parchment sling (see page 14). **3)** Generously flour your work surface. Press the dough into a 10 in [25 cm] square and cut into sixteen equal pieces. Shape each piece into a ball. **4)** Put the raspberry sugar in shallow bowl. Brush each ball of dough with some of the melted butter, then roll it in the raspberry sugar. Arrange eight dough balls in the prepared pan and scatter the fresh raspberries over the tops of the dough balls. Cover with the remaining eight dough balls. There will be some space in between the balls, but they will fill in as the dough rises. Sprinkle any leftover raspberry sugar over the top. Cover the pan loosely with plastic wrap and let the dough rise until puffed and almost doubled in size, about 1½ hours.

48

5) Position an oven rack in the middle of the oven and preheat the oven to 350°F [180°C]. Place a sheet pan on a lower rack to catch any drips. 6) TO MAKE THE CARAMEL AND BAKE THE BREAD Right before placing the bread in the oven, in a medium saucepan over medium heat, combine the brown sugar, butter, and salt. Cook until the sugar is completely dissolved. Remove from the heat and add the vanilla. Pour the mixture over the risen bread. 7) Bake until the bread is golden brown and bubbly and registers 190°F [88°C] on an instant-read thermometer, 45 to 60 minutes. Check the bread halfway through baking; if the top is browning too quickly, cover loosely with a piece of foil. 8) FOR THE ICING While the bread is baking, in a small bowl, mix together the cream cheese

and butter until smooth. Add 1 tablespoon of the water and the vanilla and stir to combine. Add the confectioners' sugar and mix together, then whisk until well combined and smooth. Add more water, 1 tablespoon at a time, until the icing is still thick but pourable. 9) Remove the bread from the oven and place on a wire rack set over a piece of parchment paper (to catch any drips). Pour the icing over the top of the hot loaf, so it sinks down into the loaf. Let the bubble bread cool in the pan for 15 minutes, then use the sling to remove it. Let cool on the rack until just warm, and then serve. 10) Bubble bread is best eaten the day it's made, but it can be stored in an airtight container in the refrigerator for up to 2 days.

I never had an authentic New York bagel until I was in my thirties. In fact, bagels were not a regular part of my life until a Bruegger's Bagels opened near my home; my teenage self frequented it often, always ordering a cinnamon bagel, complete with a crunchy, sugared top. This brioche version is far removed from even the chain store bagels I devoured in my youth, and each bite will have you asking questions: *Is it a bagel? Is it brioche?* You may never come to a conclusion. They are delicious plain or sprinkled with everything bagel seasoning, but I've included a version with a cinnamon top too.

MAKES 12 BAGELS

Brioche Bagels

CINNAMON SUGAR TOPPING (OPTIONAL)

½ cup [100 g] granulated sugar

2 teaspoons ground cinnamon

Pinch of salt

2 tablespoons unsalted butter, melted

BAGELS

All-purpose flour, for dusting

1 recipe Brioche Dough (page 259)

5 qt [5.25 kg] water

2 tablespoons nondiastatic malt powder or granulated sugar

1 teaspoon baking soda

Egg wash (see page 14)

Everything bagel seasoning, for sprinkling (optional)

1) FOR THE SUGAR TOPPING If using the sugar topping, put the granulated sugar, cinnamon, and salt in a medium bowl and whisk to combine. Add the melted butter, then use your fingers to mix until it has a sandy texture. 2) FOR THE BAGELS Line a sheet pan with parchment paper and grease the paper lightly with baking spray. 3) Generously flour your work surface. Divide the dough into twelve equal pieces. Shape each one into a ball and let the dough rest, covered, for 10 minutes. 4) Lightly flour your hands, then punch your thumb through the center of each ball of dough to make a hole. Using two fingers, stretch the hole until it is about 2 in [5 cm] wide. Transfer the bagels to the prepared pan and let them rest, covered, for 30 minutes. 5) Position an oven rack in the middle of the oven and preheat to 475°F [245°C]. Line two more sheet pans with parchment paper and dust with flour. 6) In a large stockpot or Dutch oven, bring the water to

49

a boil over high heat. Lower to a simmer, then add the nondiastatic malt powder and baking soda (see Notes). Gently use your fingers to stretch any bagel holes that have closed up during the rise. Drop two of the bagels into the water. They should float. Let them simmer for 1 minute, then flip them over to simmer for another 30 to 45 seconds. They will be very wrinkly. Transfer them to the flour-dusted sheet pan. Repeat with the remaining bagels. When they have all cooled enough to handle, move them to the parchment-lined sheet pan without flour. Grease the bottom of a third sheet pan and place it on top of the bagels (this helps them keep their shape). 7) Bake the bagels for 7 minutes (if using a dark-colored sheet pan on top, check sooner to make sure that the tops aren't browning too quickly), then remove them from the oven and remove the top sheet pan. Brush the bagels with the egg wash and either leave plain, sprinkle with the cinnamon sugar, or top with the bagel seasoning. Return to the oven and bake for another 7 to 10 minutes, until the bagels are golden brown and firm. Place the bagels on a wire rack and let cool to room temperature. 8) Bagels are best eaten straight away, but they can be stored in an airtight container for 2 days; they are also delicious toasted.

NOTES Nondiastic malt powder is used in bagel making to add both sweetness and color. If you can't find it, use granulated sugar.

Boiling the bagels with baking soda gives the crust its shine and helps with caramelization.

50

Homemade soft pretzels are a bit of work, but my children reassure me each time I make them that it is worth my effort. I learned how to shape pretzels while working with cookbook authors Zoë François and Jeff Hertzberg; I was both a baker and a food stylist on several photo shoots for their *In Five Minutes a Day* series on artisan breads, and spent time shaping, boiling, flipping, and then styling these twisted treats. I use Milk Bread Dough here for very soft pretzels.

Everything Breakfast Pretzels

MAKES
6 PRETZELS

All-purpose flour, for dusting

1 recipe Milk Bread Dough (page 262)

5 qt [5.25 kg] water

¼ cup [24 g] baking soda

2 tablespoon granulated sugar

Everything bagel seasoning, for sprinkling

Kosher salt, for sprinkling (see Note)

1) Line a sheet pan with parchment paper and grease the paper lightly with baking spray. 2) Generously flour your work surface. Divide the dough into six equal pieces, weighing about 4 oz [113 g] each. Roll a piece back and forth with your hands to form a long rope about 24 in [60 cm] long, flouring lightly as needed. As you make the rope, leave the center slightly fatter and gradually taper the ends. 3) Twist the rope into a pretzel shape: Bring the ends of the rope away from you and form a *U* or horseshoe shape. Bend the ends to bring them toward the bottom of the *U*, crossing them over each other and then twisting them, if desired. Rest the ends on top of the base of the pretzel or tuck them underneath. *See how-to photos, page 153.* Transfer the shaped pretzels to the prepared sheet pan, leaving about 3 in [7.5 cm] of space in between them, and cover loosely with plastic wrap. Repeat with the remaining pieces of dough, shaping them into pretzels and covering them. Let the pretzels rise for 45 minutes. 4) Position an oven rack in the middle of the oven and preheat the oven to 450°F [230°C]. Line two more sheet pans, one with parchment paper lightly dusted with flour and another with just parchment paper.

cont'd

5) In a large stockpot or Dutch oven, bring the water to a boil over high heat. Lower the heat so the water is simmering, then add the baking soda and granulated sugar to the water. Drop one pretzel into the water; it should float. Simmer for about 1 minute, then flip it over and simmer for another 30 to 45 seconds. Transfer to the flour-dusted sheet pan. When it has cooled for 1 or 2 minutes, transfer to the parchment-lined sheet pan. Repeat with the remaining five pretzels. 6) Put ¼ cup [60 g] of the simmering cooking water in a small heatproof bowl or measuring cup and use a pastry brush to brush the tops of the pretzels lightly with the water. Sprinkle with the bagel seasoning and salt. 7) Bake until the pretzels are golden brown and firm, 12 to 15 minutes. Transfer the sheet pan to a wire rack and let cool until the pretzels are just warm. 8) Pretzels are best eaten when they have firmed up a bit but are still warm to the touch, but they can be stored in an airtight container at room temperature for up to 2 days.

NOTE Everything bagel seasoning differs in the amount of salt it contains from one brand to the next. Salt your pretzel accordingly, but don't skimp! The salt really makes the pretzel.

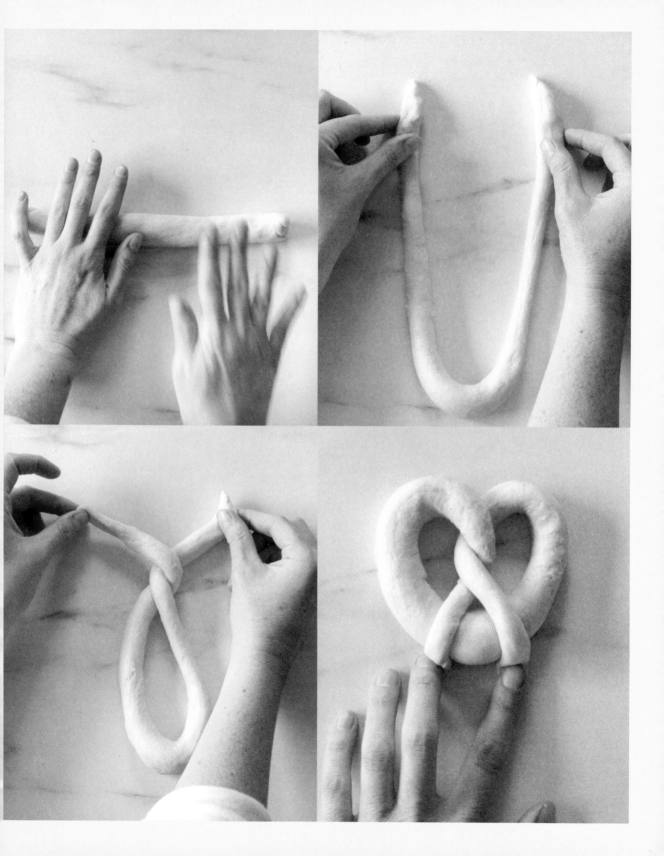

The first time I tried bostok was at Rustica Bakery, in Minneapolis. The bake case was almost empty—my beloved chocolate orange scones were gone, as were the almond croissants. On a whim I ordered the bostok, having no idea what it was. The first bite sold me—the rich brioche soaked in simple syrup, then covered in almond cream and more almonds, was divine, and it instantly became a favorite treat. This recipe works great with leftover brioche, but Milk Bread (page 262) will work well too.

Lemon Curd Bostok

 MAKES
8 BOSTOK

SIMPLE SYRUP

⅓ cup [80 g] water

⅓ cup [65 g] granulated sugar

1 tablespoon triple sec

Pinch of salt

ASSEMBLY

8 slices brioche bread, ½ in [12 mm] thick, from a homemade (page 259) or store-bought loaf

1 cup [300 g] Almond Cream (page 292), at room temperature

1 cup [320 g] Lemon Curd (page 288), at room temperature

1 cup [100 g] sliced almonds

Confectioners' sugar, for dusting

1) FOR THE SYRUP In a small saucepan, combine the water, granulated sugar, triple sec, and salt, and heat over medium heat until the sugar and salt have dissolved. Remove from the heat and let cool to room temperature. 2) TO ASSEMBLE AND BAKE Position an oven rack in the middle of the oven and preheat the oven to 375°F [190°C]. Double stack two sheet pans and line with parchment paper (this helps prevent the bostok from getting too crisp on the bottom). 3) Place the brioche on the prepared pan and brush the top of each slice with the syrup, making sure to cover the entire surface. Spread a layer of almond cream over each slice, then spread a thin layer of lemon curd over the cream. Sprinkle an equal amount of the almonds over each slice. 4) Bake the brioche until the bread is golden and toasted, 18 to 22 minutes. Place the top sheet pan on a wire rack and dust each slice with confectioners' sugar. Let the bostok cool until just warm and serve. 5) Bostock is best eaten the day it's made, but it can be stored in an airtight container at room temperature for up to 2 days.

51

When I was growing up, my mom always had a loaf of cinnamon swirl bread in the cupboard. It became an "everything" bread for our family; we ate it fresh, and then toasted with plenty of butter for both breakfast and after-school snacks. It also made an exceptional French toast on the weekends. The cinnamon swirl in this version is subtle, but perfect, and now my family snacks on it both toasted and not. In a final act of history repeating itself, it also makes a fabulous French toast (see page 216).

Cinnamon Swirl Bread

FILLING

¾ cup [150 g] brown sugar

1 tablespoon ground cinnamon

Pinch of salt

ASSEMBLY

All-purpose flour, for dusting

1 recipe Milk Bread Dough (page 262)

1 egg white, lightly beaten

1 cup [140 g] Pecan Streusel (page 291)

MAKES ONE 9 IN [23 CM] LOAF

1) FOR THE FILLING In a medium bowl, combine the brown sugar, cinnamon, and salt. 2) TO ASSEMBLE AND BAKE Grease a 9 by 4 by 4 in [23 by 10 by 10 cm] Pullman pan or 9 in [23 cm] loaf pan and line with a parchment sling (see page 14). 3) Generously flour your work surface. Roll the dough into a 16 in [40 cm] square. Brush a thin layer of egg white over the dough, then sprinkle the filling over the top, pressing it lightly into the egg white so it adheres. Roll the dough into a tight cylinder. 4) Pinch the seam gently to seal it. Cut the dough into two pieces, each 8 in [20 cm] long. Place one log of dough over the other to make an *X*, then twist the two loaves together two to four times as able. *See how-to photos, page 159.* Place the loaf in the prepared pan, pressing the dough gently into the corners of the pan. Cover with plastic wrap and let rise in

a warm place for 1 to 1½ hours, until doubled in size. 5) Position an oven rack in the middle of the oven and preheat the oven to 350°F [180°C]. 6) Remove the plastic wrap and brush the top of the bread with the remaining egg white. Sprinkle the streusel over the bread. Bake the bread until the top is golden brown and registers 190°F [88°C] on an instant-read thermometer, 35 to 50 minutes. 7) Transfer the pan to a wire rack and let cool for 10 minutes. Carefully remove the bread from the pan using the parchment sling, peel off the paper, and let the bread finish cooling. When the bread has cooled completely, slice and serve. 8) This bread is best eaten the day it's made, but it can be stored in an airtight container for up to 3 days at room temperature. Leftovers are delicious toasted.

52

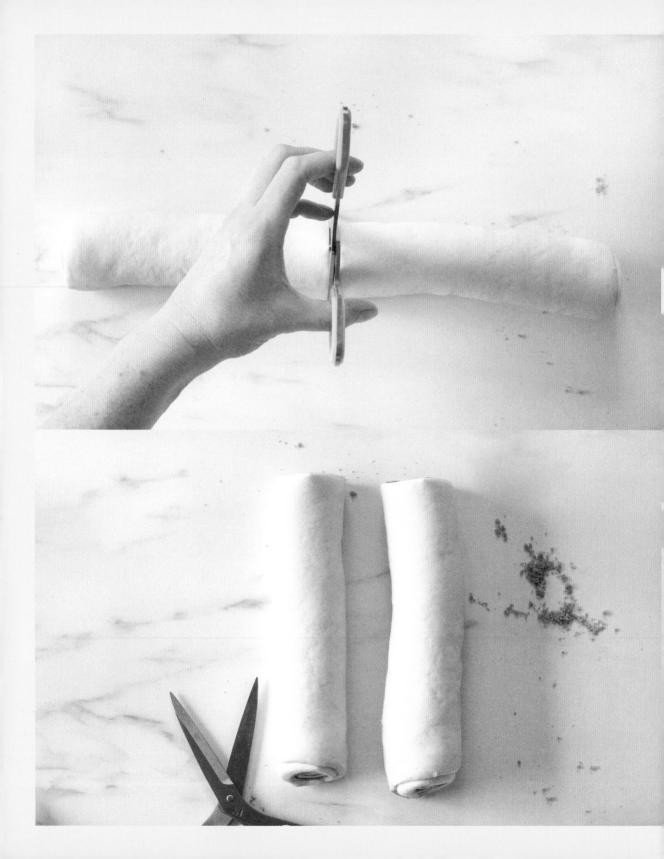

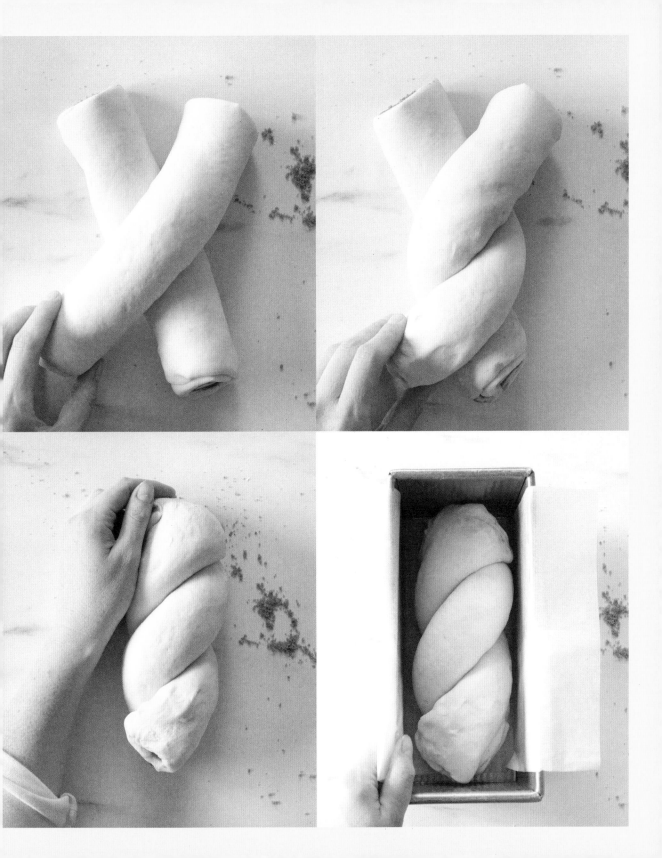

Another twist (pun intended) on braided bread. These little knots are laced with strawberry and sugar, and are as pretty as they are tasty.

Strawberry Knots

FILLING

1 cup [200 g] granulated sugar

¼ cup [16 g] freeze-dried strawberry powder (see page 14)

Pinch of salt

ASSEMBLY

All-purpose flour, for dusting

1 recipe Milk Bread Dough (page 262)

1 egg white, lightly beaten

 MAKES 6 KNOTS

1) FOR THE FILLING In a medium bowl, combine the granulated sugar, freeze-dried strawberry powder, and salt. 2) TO ASSEMBLE Line a sheet pan with parchment paper. 3) Generously flour your work surface. Cut the dough into six equal pieces, then roll each piece into a 14 by 6 in [35.5 by 15 cm] rectangle (the dough will be thin). Brush a thin layer of egg white over the dough, then sprinkle 3 to 4 tablespoons of the filling over the top of each rectangle, pressing it lightly into the egg white so it adheres. Starting at a long side, roll the dough into a tight cylinder. Pinch the seam gently to seal it and position the dough seam-side down. Using a bench scraper or scissors, carefully cut down the center of the log lengthwise, so the layers of dough and filling are visible. With the cut sides facing up, gently lift the right side over the left strand, and continue strand over strand, keeping the cut sides up (so the filling doesn't fall out), until you have twisted the entire

roll. Press the ends together. Twist the dough and form it into a knot, then carefully transfer the dough to the prepared pan. *See how-to photos, page 145.* Repeat with the remaining dough. Cover with plastic wrap and let rise in a warm place for 1 to 1½ hours, until doubled in size. 4) Position an oven rack in the middle of the oven and preheat the oven to 350°F [180°C]. 5) Bake the bread until the top is golden brown and the center is set, 20 to 25 minutes. Transfer the pan to a wire rack and let cool for 10 minutes. Move the knots to the wire rack to finish cooling; wait until the knots have cooled completely before serving. 6) Knots are best eaten the same day they're made, but they can be stored in an airtight container at room temperature for up to 2 days.

VARIATION

• **Cardamom Knots:** *Omit the freeze-dried strawberry powder. Combine 1½ tablespoons of ground cardamom with the granulated sugar, and proceed with the recipe as directed.*

53

Monkey bread baked in a single layer is not only an easy way to prepare it, but each piece has more room to expand in the pan (verses two layers in a Bundt pan) and makes for a better bite of bread, in my opinion. This pumpkin caramel version is delicious, and perfect for holiday baking. If you decide to omit the bourbon, increase the vanilla to 1 tablespoon.

Pumpkin Caramel Monkey Bread

MAKES 40 PIECES OF MONKEY BREAD

COATING

7 tablespoons [98 g] unsalted butter, melted

1¼ cups [250 g] granulated sugar

2 teaspoons ground cinnamon

1 teaspoon ground ginger

½ teaspoon freshly grated nutmeg

Pinch of ground cloves

Pinch of salt

ASSEMBLY

All-purpose flour, for dusting

1 recipe Sour Cream Dough (page 270)

PUMPKIN CARAMEL

½ cup [112 g] unsweetened pumpkin purée

6 tablespoons [84 g] unsalted butter

¾ cup [150 g] brown sugar

¼ cup [50 g] granulated sugar

3 tablespoons corn syrup

¼ teaspoon salt

1 tablespoon bourbon or rum (optional)

1 teaspoon pure vanilla extract

1) FOR THE COATING Pour the melted butter into a pie plate or shallow dish. In another dish, whisk together the granulated sugar, cinnamon, ginger, nutmeg, cloves, and salt. 2) TO ASSEMBLE Grease a 9 by 13 in [23 by 33 cm] pan. Generously flour your work surface. Using a bench scraper or scissors, divide the dough into forty equal pieces and roll each one into a ball. 3) Working with a few at a time, brush the dough balls with the melted butter, then toss them in the sugar mixture to coat. Place the balls in the prepared pan in five rows of eight balls. Cover the pan with plastic wrap and let the dough rise in a warm place until doubled in size, 1 to 1½ hours. (Monkey bread can also do a slow rise in the refrigerator overnight; see page 118.)

4) FOR THE PUMPKIN CARAMEL While the dough is rising, in a medium saucepan over medium heat, combine the pumpkin, butter, brown and granulated sugars, corn syrup, and salt. Bring the mixture to a boil, stirring often until the sugars are dissolved. Turn the heat down and simmer until thickened, 6 to 8 minutes. Remove from the heat and stir in the bourbon, if using, and vanilla and let cool slightly. Pour the caramel over the risen dough. **5)** TO BAKE Position an oven rack in the middle of the oven and preheat the oven to 350°F [180°C]. Place a large sheet pan on a lower rack to catch any caramel that may bubble over. **6)** Bake the monkey bread until it is puffed and golden and registers 190°F [88°C] on an instant-read thermometer, 26 to 32 minutes. **7)** Let the bread cool in the pan on a wire rack for 3 to 4 minutes, then invert it onto a platter or parchment-lined sheet pan. Serve the monkey bread warm. **8)** Monkey bread is best eaten the same day it's made, but it can be stored in an airtight container in the refrigerator for up to 2 days.

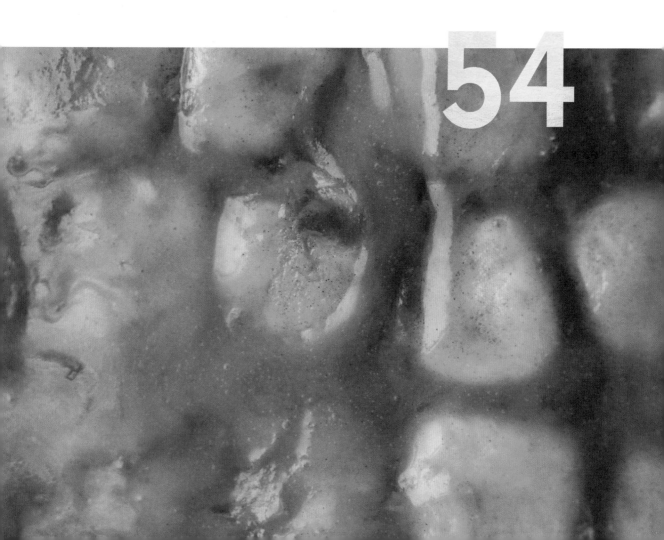

54

55

I have many wonderful memories involving a chocolate glazed doughnut, but my favorite ones are sharing them with my grandma. We often scheduled driving dates around the lakes near her house; she would be waiting anxiously for me to pick her up, clutching her worn-out black purse and talking quietly to herself, her front porch smelling faintly like Pantene hair products and black coffee. Java Jacks was our favorite stop on the route, and I would pick up a giant "Texas" glazed chocolate doughnut and iced mochas to share. We would munch and sip, Louis Prima and Keely Smith swinging for us, and she would tap her hands on her knees, clicking her tongue to the music while admiring the beautiful homes decorating the lakefront.

Chocolate Glazed Doughnuts

 MAKES ABOUT
10 DOUGHNUTS

DOUGHNUTS

½ cup [120 g] whole milk

¼ cup [60 g] sour cream

¼ cup [50 g] granulated sugar

2 tablespoons honey

1½ teaspoon salt

1 tablespoon active dry yeast

1 large egg, at room temperature

2 large egg yolks, at room temperature

1 tablespoon pure vanilla extract

3 cups [426 g] all-purpose flour, plus more for dusting

8 tablespoons [113 g] unsalted butter, cut into 1 in [2.5 cm] pieces, at room temperature

Vegetable oil, for frying (enough to fill a medium to large Dutch oven or stockpot 4 in [10 cm] from the top)

CHOCOLATE GLAZE

5 tablespoons [70 g] unsalted butter

¼ cup [60 g] half-and-half

2 tablespoons corn syrup

Pinch of salt

5 oz [142 g] semisweet chocolate, finely chopped

2 cups [240 g] confectioners' sugar

1 teaspoon pure vanilla extract

cont'd

1) **FOR THE DOUGHNUTS** In a medium saucepan, combine the milk, sour cream, granulated sugar, honey, and salt. Heat until the mixture is just simmering and the sugar and salt have dissolved, stirring constantly, 2 to 3 minutes. Set aside to cool until the milk registers 100 to 110°F [35 to 42°C] on an instant-read thermometer.

2) In the bowl of a stand mixer fitted with a dough hook, combine the warm milk mixture and yeast, and let sit until foamy, 5 minutes. Add the egg, egg yolks, and vanilla and stir to combine. Add the flour and mix on low speed until all the ingredients are incorporated, 2 to 3 minutes. The dough will be shaggy at first, and you may need to scrape down the hook. Knead the dough on medium speed for 6 to 8 minutes, scraping down the sides of the bowl as needed, until the dough is smooth and elastic. The dough will start to pull away from the sides, although it will be sticky. Add the butter one piece at a time, mixing on low speed until completely combined (this will take a few minutes). Increase the speed to medium-low and knead for 2 to 3 minutes more, until all the butter is incorporated and the dough is smooth. If the dough is sticking to the sides of the bowl, add 1 tablespoon more of flour and knead until incorporated. Place the dough inside a large greased bowl. Cover with plastic wrap and let rise in a warm, draft-free area until it has puffed up and is almost double in size, 1½ to 2 hours. Refrigerate for 2 hours and up to overnight.

3) When you're ready to make the doughnuts, move the dough to a lightly floured work surface. Cut twelve 5 in [12 cm] squares of parchment paper, arrange them on two sheet pans, and lightly spray them with baking spray. (The parchment paper will help the doughnuts keep their shape when transferring them to the hot oil.) 4) Roll out the dough into a ¾ in [2 cm] thick rectangle. Using a doughnut cutter or 3 in [7.5 cm] biscuit cutter, cut the dough into rounds, and then use a smaller cutter to cut a hole in the center of each dough round. Transfer the dough to the prepared parchment paper on the sheet pan. Scraps of dough can be rerolled and used one more time, although those doughnuts won't turn out quite as pretty. Scraps can also be used to make doughnut holes. 5) Cover the doughnuts with greased plastic wrap and let rise in a warm, draft-free spot for 1½ hours; the doughnuts should almost double in height. (Doughnuts can also do a slow rise in the refrigerator overnight. See "For overnight doughnuts.") 6) When the doughnuts are ready to fry, heat the oil in a large Dutch oven, wok, or deep fryer to 340°F [170°C] on a candy thermometer (see Note). Set a wire rack over paper towels. Place the doughnuts in a wire basket skimmer one at a time, with their parchment papers, and gently drop them into the hot oil. Use tongs to pluck out the papers. Fry the doughnuts in small batches, being careful not to crowd them, until golden brown on the bottom, about 1 minute. Use the skimmer to flip them over and fry again for about 1 minute, monitoring the oil temperature and adjusting the heat as needed. Use the

skimmer to transfer the doughnuts to the wire rack; let the doughnuts cool before glazing.

7) FOR THE GLAZE While the doughnuts are cooling, combine the butter, half-and-half, corn syrup, and salt in a medium saucepan and heat over medium heat until the butter has melted. Turn down the heat and add the chocolate, whisking until completely melted. Remove from the heat, whisk in the confectioners' sugar and vanilla, and continue whisking until the glaze is smooth. Dip the top of each warm doughnut in the glaze, allowing the excess to drip off back into the saucepan. Place the glazed doughnuts back on the wire rack until the glaze has set. Doughnuts are best eaten the same day they are made.

FOR OVERNIGHT DOUGHNUTS After cutting out the doughnuts and placing them on the parchment squares, cover the pan loosely with plastic wrap and refrigerate for at least 8 hours and up to 18 hours. Before you fry them, let the doughnuts sit at room temperature (still covered in plastic wrap) for 1 to 1½ hours, until doubled in size. Heat the oil and fry and glaze as directed.

NOTE I do have a deep fryer, which I find very helpful for making doughnuts. I don't have to worry about the constantly changing temperature of the oil and can just focus on the doughnuts. However, a large Dutch oven or large stockpot and a candy thermometer will work just fine.

Frying Doughnuts

I've always had a frustrating experience frying yeasted doughnuts; I was taught to fry at 360°F [185°C] for perfect doughnuts, but I found that often at this temperature the outside will be overly golden and the inside undercooked, especially when frying with a candy thermometer vs. a deep fryer. Then I read Vallery Lomas's cookbook *Life Is What You Bake It* and noticed all her beautiful doughnuts, all fried at a much lower temperature. I followed suit and lowered my fry temperature to 340°F [170°C] and was ecstatic with the light golden and perfectly fried doughnuts I was able to create. I've kept the temperature low ever since.

56

Old-fashioned doughnuts fry up differently than a raised doughnut; they are made without yeast and are slightly dense, with lots of cracks and craggy edges. They are also easier to whip up than a yeasted treat, and they melt in your mouth better than any candy can. I've found most old-fashioned doughnut recipes to be very similar in structure. Here I've added a little cornstarch to lighten the flour and use a combination of sour cream and buttermilk for the best flavor.

Old-Fashioned Doughnuts

 MAKES ABOUT 12 DOUGHNUTS

DOUGHNUTS

2¼ cups [320 g] all-purpose flour, plus more for dusting

3 tablespoons cornstarch

1 teaspoon salt

½ teaspoon baking powder

½ teaspoon baking soda

¼ teaspoon freshly grated nutmeg

⅔ cup [160 g] buttermilk, at room temperature

½ cup [100 g] granulated sugar

⅓ cup [80 g] sour cream, at room temperature

4 large egg yolks, at room temperature

3 tablespoons unsalted butter, melted and cooled

1 tablespoon lemon juice

1 teaspoon pure vanilla extract

Vegetable oil, for frying (enough to fill a medium to large Dutch oven or stockpot 4 in [10 cm] from the top)

GLAZE

2 tablespoons unsalted butter, melted

2 to 4 tablespoons water

1 to 2 teaspoons lemon juice

½ teaspoon pure vanilla extract

Pinch of salt

2 cups [240 g] confectioners' sugar

1) **FOR THE DOUGHNUTS** In a large bowl, whisk together the flour, cornstarch, salt, baking powder, baking soda, and nutmeg. In a medium bowl, stir together the buttermilk, granulated sugar, sour cream, egg yolks, melted butter, lemon juice, and vanilla. 2) Add the wet ingredients to the dry, stirring until combined. The finished dough will be thick and rather sticky. Cover the bowl with a greased piece of plastic wrap and refrigerate for at least 2 hours or overnight. 3) Line a sheet pan with parchment paper and grease the paper. Line a second sheet pan with paper towels and place a wire rack on top.

cont'd

4) Heat the oil in a large Dutch oven, wok, or deep fryer to 340°F [170°C] on a candy thermometer. While the oil is heating, lightly flour a work surface and roll out the dough ½ in [12 mm] thick. Use a well-floured doughnut cutter or 3 in [7.5 cm] biscuit cutter to cut the dough into rounds, and then a smaller biscuit cutter to cut out a hole in the center of each dough round. The dough will be sticky, so flour your hands and the work surface as needed. The scraps of dough can be rerolled and cut out for more doughnuts, but they won't turn out quite as pretty. Transfer the cut-out doughnuts to the greased parchment paper and refrigerate until the oil is hot. 5) Place the doughnuts in a wire basket skimmer one at a time, and gently drop them into the hot oil, making sure not to crowd them; the doughnuts will expand as they cook. The doughnuts will sink and then slowly rise to the surface. Fry the doughnuts until they are golden brown, flipping them several times, 2 or 3 minutes total on each side, using tongs or skimmer to flip them (see Note). Transfer to the wire rack and let cool until all the doughnuts are cool enough to touch. While the doughnuts are cooling, make the glaze. 6) FOR THE GLAZE In a medium bowl, mix together the melted butter, 2 tablespoons of the water, 1 teaspoon of the lemon juice, the vanilla, and salt. Add the confectioners' sugar and mix together, then whisk until well combined and smooth. Add more water if needed; the glaze should be thick but pourable. Taste the glaze and add more lemon juice if the flavor needs to be brightened; the glaze shouldn't taste like lemon. 7) Dip the top of each warm doughnut in the glaze, allowing the excess to drip off back into the bowl. Place the glazed doughnuts back on the wire rack until the glaze has set. Serve slightly warm. Old-fashioned doughnuts are best eaten the same day they are made.

NOTE Frying the doughnuts at a lower temperature and flipping them several times helps create the crispy outer texture that old-fashioned doughnuts are known for.

A cruller is an egg-based fried doughnut that is made without any chemical leavenings, such as baking soda or baking powder. The base of a cruller is a French choux pastry, which relies on a high moisture content to create steam, which, in turn, puffs the pastry. These crullers bake up light and crisp and are perfect for a chilly autumn day.

Apple Cider Crullers

MAKES ABOUT
14 CRULLERS

CRULLERS

1 cup [240 g] apple cider

8 tablespoons [1 stick or 113 g] unsalted butter

½ cup [120 g] milk

1 tablespoon granulated sugar

1 teaspoon salt

1 teaspoon pure vanilla extract

1¼ cups [178 g] all-purpose flour

3 large eggs, at room temperature

1 or 2 large egg whites, at room temperature

Vegetable oil, for frying (enough to fill a medium to large Dutch oven or stockpot 4 in [10 cm] from the top)

GLAZE

2 to 4 tablespoons apple cider

1 tablespoon unsalted butter, melted

1 teaspoon pure vanilla extract

¼ teaspoon ground cinnamon (optional)

Pinch of salt

1½ cups [180 g] confectioners' sugar

1) FOR THE CRULLERS Cut fourteen 3 in [7.5 cm] squares of parchment paper and trace a 2 in [5 cm] circle on each one. Put the squares, penciled-side down, on a sheet pan and set aside. Line a sheet pan with paper towels and place a wire rack on top.

2) In a medium saucepan over medium-high heat, boil the apple cider until it is reduced to ½ cup [120 g], 4 to 5 minutes. Turn the heat down to low and add the butter, milk, granulated sugar, salt, and vanilla, stirring until the butter has melted.

cont'd

57

Turn up the heat again to medium-high and bring to a rolling boil. Remove the pan from the heat and add the flour, stirring with a wooden spoon until the dough pulls together into a ball. Return the pan to medium-high heat and cook, stirring, until there is a thin layer of dough coating the bottom of the pan, 2 to 3 minutes. It will register about 175°F [80°C] on an instant-read thermometer. 3) Transfer the dough to the bowl of a stand mixer fitted with a paddle and let cool enough so the eggs don't cook when they are added, about 135°F [57°C]. You can speed up this step by beating the hot dough in the stand mixer until no more steam rises out of the bowl, 2 to 3 minutes. When the dough is cool enough, add the eggs, one at a time, beating on medium-low speed after each addition until the egg is incorporated, and scraping down the sides of the bowl. Add 1 tablespoon of the egg whites and beat until combined. Keep adding egg whites, 1 tablespoon at a time, until the dough is smooth and shiny and is a pipeable consistency; thick, but loose enough to pipe with (you may not use all of the egg whites). Continue beating until the dough is smooth and glossy, about 1 minute. 4) Heat the oil in a large Dutch oven, wok, or deep fryer to 350°F [180°C] on a candy thermometer. While the oil is heating, shape the crullers: Transfer the dough to a large piping bag fitted with a ½ in [12 mm] star piping tip. Pipe circles onto the parchment squares, using the pencil marks for guidance. Place the doughnuts in a wire basket skimmer one at a time, with their parchment papers, and gently drop them into the hot oil, making sure not to crowd them; the doughnuts will expand as they cook. Use tongs to pluck out the papers. Fry the crullers in small batches until they are golden brown, 2 to 3 minutes per side. Transfer the crullers to the prepared wire rack and let cool while you make the glaze. 5) FOR THE GLAZE In a medium bowl, whisk together 2 tablespoons of the apple cider, the butter, vanilla, cinnamon, if using, and salt. Add the confectioners' sugar and mix together, then whisk until well combined and smooth. If needed, add more apple cider, 1 tablespoon at a time, until the glaze is thick but pourable. 6) Dip the top of the crullers into the glaze, one at a time, letting any excess drip back into the bowl. Return to the wire rack and let sit until the glaze sets. Serve slightly warm. Crullers are best eaten the day they are made.

The base of this recipe comes from my mother-in-law. It is a genuine, treasured, handwritten recipe card recipe. When my husband was growing up, his mom made them frequently with apples, and they always dusted them with confectioners' sugar or ate them with a generous glug of maple syrup. But Rum Icing (page 50) is a divine alternative. I think they are even delicious without any sugary topping at all, just perfectly crisp and warm.

Banana Fritters

 MAKES ABOUT
2 DOZEN FRITTERS

Vegetable oil, for frying (enough to fill a medium to large Dutch oven or stockpot 4 in [10 cm] from the top)

1 cup [227 g] mashed bananas, plus 1 cup [227 g] chopped bananas (bite-size pieces, about 6 bananas total)

⅔ cup [160 g] milk, at room temperature

2 large eggs, at room temperature

2 tablespoons granulated sugar

2 teaspoons baking powder

1 teaspoon pure vanilla extract

½ teaspoon baking soda

½ teaspoon salt

1¼ cups [178 g] all-purpose flour

Confectioners' sugar, for dusting

Warm maple syrup, for serving

58

1) Heat the oil in a large Dutch oven, wok, or deep fryer to 360°F [180°C] on a candy thermometer. Line a sheet pan with paper towels and place a wire rack on top. **2)** In a large bowl, whisk together the mashed bananas, milk, eggs, granulated sugar, baking powder, vanilla, baking soda, and salt. Add the flour and stir until just incorporated. Add the chopped bananas and stir just enough to distribute them evenly in the batter. **3)** Fry the fritters in batches. Using a small cookie scoop or a spoon, drop mounds of batter about 1½ in [4 cm] in diameter into the hot oil, making sure not to crowd the pan. Fry the fritters on both sides until deep golden brown, about 2 minutes per side. Use a slotted spoon or wire basket to remove them from the oil, then place them on the wire rack to cool for 10 minutes. **4)** Dust the fritters with confectioners' sugar and serve with warm maple syrup while still warm. Fritters are best eaten the day they are made.

CHAPTER 4

Laminated Pastries

"and yet however
hard we try to

find the great nothingness
to escape the layers they

are always there unforget-
tably wrapped around us re-

calling what we were deter-
mining what we'll always be."

—J. Laughlin, "Layers"

If you have any of my other books, you know that I am a big fan of Danish pastries. In my previous cookbooks, I used a different recipe for Danish dough, but for this one I came up with a flakier version, which is now the recipe I use (see Note). For an extra flaky Danish, the Cheater Croissant Dough can be used. I love my Danish with cream cheese filling and jam or lemon curd, but fresh fruit, such as sliced strawberries, is incredible as well.

MAKES
8 DANISH

Cream-Filled Danish

CREAM CHEESE FILLING

4 oz [113 g] cream cheese, at room temperature

3 tablespoons granulated sugar

1 teaspoon lemon juice

ASSEMBLY

All-purpose flour, for dusting

½ recipe Danish Dough (page 276) or ½ recipe Cheater Croissant Dough (page 271)

Egg wash (see page 14)

1 lb [455 g] sliced strawberries or 1 cup [300 g] jam or Lemon Curd (page 288)

Granulated sugar, for sprinkling

1) FOR THE CREAM CHEESE FILL-ING In the bowl of a stand mixer fitted with a paddle, beat the cream cheese on medium speed until smooth. Add the granulated sugar, beating until the mixture is completely smooth. Scrape down the sides, lower the mixer speed to low, and add the lemon juice, beating until incorporated. Refrigerate the filling until ready to use. (The filling can be refrigerated in an airtight container for up to 2 days.) 2) TO ASSEMBLE AND BAKE Line two sheet pans with parchment paper. Generously flour your work surface, and divide the dough in half. Roll each half of the dough into a 10 in [25 cm] square. Cut each square into four 5 in [12 cm] squares. Fold each square in half to form a triangle.

Using a bench scraper (or a sharp knife), cut along the inside of each triangle ½ in [12 mm] from the edge, but don't cut all the way to the top of the point. Unfold of the triangle, then repeat with the remaining triangles, for a total of eight squares. 3) Take the cut strip of one side of the square and fold it over; you want the corner point to rest on the corner point of the smaller square. Repeat with the other side. Place the shaped Danish on the prepared sheet pan, then repeat with the other squares. You should have four shaped Danish on each prepared sheet pan. *See how-to photos, page 181.*

cont'd

4) Cover the sheets lightly with plastic wrap and let rise at room temperature until puffy (the dough should feel like a marshmallow when pressed), 1½ to 2 hours. (Danish can also do a slow rise in the refrigerator overnight. See "For overnight Danish.") 5) Position the oven racks to the upper-middle and lower-middle of the oven and preheat the oven to 400°F [200°C]. 6) Just before baking, gently press down the center of each Danish to make a place for the filling. Lightly brush the edges of the dough with egg wash and then place 1 heaping tablespoon of the cream cheese filling in the center of each piece. Use the back of a spoon to spread the cream cheese evenly in the center, then top with the fresh sliced strawberries or 2 tablespoons of jam. Sprinkle the exposed dough with a generous amount of granulated sugar. Bake for 10 minutes, then rotate the pans and bake until the pastries are golden brown, 8 to 10 minutes more. Transfer the sheet pans to wire racks and let the pastries cool to room temperature. Danish are best eaten the same day they are made.

FOR OVERNIGHT DANISH Shape the Danish, but do not let them rise at room temperature. Instead, cover them loosely with plastic wrap and refrigerate for at least 8 and up to 18 hours. When ready to bake, let the dough sit at room temperature (still covered in plastic wrap) until puffy, 1½ to 2 hours. Preheat the oven about 30 minutes before the dough is finished rising, and bake as directed.

NOTE Danish dough will make a softer pastry, and the croissant dough will make a flakier one. Both are delicious.

60

Raspberries, hazelnut cream, and a rich, flaky crust—this braid never fails to impress.

MAKES
2 BRAIDS

Raspberry Hazelnut Danish Braid

BRAID

All-purpose flour, for sprinkling

½ recipe Danish Dough (page 276)

½ cup [150 g] Hazelnut Cream (see variation, page 292)

¼ cup [75 g] Raspberry Jam (page 287)

Egg wash (see page 14)

ICING

1 to 2 tablespoons water

1 tablespoon Frangelico (optional)

1 tablespoon unsalted butter, melted

½ teaspoon pure vanilla extract

Pinch of salt

1 cup [120 g] confectioners' sugar

½ cup [50 g] hazelnuts, chopped

1) FOR THE BRAID Line two sheet pans with parchment paper. Generously flour your work surface. Cut the dough in half, then roll one piece of the dough into a 10 by 14 in [25 by 35.5 cm] rectangle, using enough flour so the dough doesn't stick to the surface or the rolling pin. Repeat with the remaining piece of dough. 2) Transfer each piece of dough to a prepared pan with a short side facing you and spread half of the hazelnut cream down the center of the dough, about 2 in [5 cm] wide. Spread half of the raspberry jam over the cream. Working from the filling out to the edge of the dough, carefully cut horizontal strips of dough ½ in [12 mm] wide (a pastry cutter works best here), doing your best to make the strips even and equal on both sides of the filling.

cont'd

3) Starting with the top two strips, gently cross them over the top of the filling, twisting them once. Continue crossing the strips all the way down the length of the braid. When you get to the end, tuck the loose ends underneath the braid (so they won't pop out during baking). *See how-to photos, page 185.* Repeat with the remaining piece of dough and filling. 4) Cover the braids loosely with plastic wrap and let rise until puffy (it should feel like a marshmallow when pressed), about 1½ hours. (The braids can also do a slow rise in the refrigerator overnight; see page 180.) 5) Position an oven rack in the middle of the oven and preheat the oven to 350°F [180°C]. 6) Lightly brush the braids with the egg wash and bake until golden brown, 25 to 30 minutes. Transfer the sheet pan to a wire rack and let cool until just warm to the touch. Meanwhile, make the icing.

7) FOR THE ICING In a medium bowl, whisk together 1 tablespoon of the water, the Frangelico (if using), butter, vanilla, and salt. Add the confectioners' sugar and mix together, then whisk until well combined and smooth. Add more water, 1 tablespoon at a time if needed, until the icing is thick but pourable. Pour the icing over the braid and scatter the chopped hazelnuts over the top.

These buns are (of course) inspired by the famous morning buns created at Tartine: orange and cinnamon and sugar and butter all wrapped up in a flaky dough. For the best flavor, let the buns rise overnight in the refrigerator.

Morning Buns

 MAKES 12 BUNS

3 tablespoons unsalted butter, melted and cooled, plus more, at room temperature, for greasing the muffin pan

1 cup [200 g] granulated sugar, plus more for coating the muffin pan and the baked buns

2 tablespoons grated orange zest

1 tablespoon ground cinnamon

Pinch of salt

All-purpose flour, for dusting

1 recipe Cheater Croissant Dough (page 271)

1) Generously butter the muffin wells and top of a standard twelve-cup muffin pan (see Muffin Tins and Greasing the Pans, page 24). Generously sprinkle each muffin well with sugar to coat, tapping out any excess. 2) In a small bowl, mix together the sugar, orange zest, cinnamon, and salt. 3) Generously flour your work surface. Roll out the croissant dough into a 10 by 24 in [25 by 60 cm] rectangle. Brush the dough with the melted butter, then sprinkle the sugar mixture evenly over the dough, gently pressing it into the butter to adhere. Starting at a long side, roll up the dough into a tight cylinder and position the dough seam-side down. Cut the dough crosswise into twelve equal pieces, about 2 in [5 cm] wide. Transfer the pieces to the prepared pan and place them with a cut side facing up. Cover the pan loosely with plastic wrap and let rise until doubled in size and the dough feels like a marshmallow when pressed, 2 to 2½ hours. (The buns can also do a slow rise in the refrigerator overnight. See "For overnight morning buns.") 4) Position an oven rack in the middle of the oven and preheat the oven to 400°F [200°C]. Place a sheet pan on a lower rack to catch any drips. Line another sheet pan with parchment paper. 5) Remove the plastic and gently press down on the top of each bun with a lightly greased spatula. Bake the buns for 15 minutes, then carefully press down on the tops of the buns again with a spatula. Rotate the pan and continue baking until the rolls are golden brown, 10 to 15 more minutes. Immediately flip the hot buns onto the prepared sheet pan. Using tongs, pick up one bun at a time and evenly coat them in the sugar mixture. Place the coated buns on a wire rack

and let cool. Morning buns are best eaten the day they are made.

FOR OVERNIGHT MORNING BUNS Put the twelve pieces of dough in the muffin pan, but do not let them rise at room temperature. Cover them loosely with plastic wrap and refrigerate for at least 8 and up to 18 hours. When ready to bake, preheat the oven and let the buns sit at room temperature (still covered in plastic) until puffy (the dough should feel like a marshmallow when pressed), 1½ to 2 hours. Bake as directed.

61

The humble raisin is elevated to new heights in this laminated pastry. First it takes a brief soak in rum, then it is rolled in brown sugar and baked inside pillows of flaky layers.

Rum Raisin Buns

MAKES
10 BUNS

BUNS

3 tablespoons unsalted butter, melted, plus more, at room temperature, for greasing the ramekins

½ cup [70 g] raisins

3 tablespoons dark rum

½ cup [100 g] brown sugar

¼ cup [50 g] granulated sugar

1 tablespoon grated orange zest

1 tablespoon grated lemon zest

½ teaspoon ground cinnamon

Pinch of salt

All-purpose flour, for dusting

1 recipe Cheater Croissant Dough (page 271)

GLAZE

1 to 2 tablespoons reserved dark rum

1 tablespoon unsalted butter, melted

⅛ teaspoon ground cinnamon (optional)

Pinch of salt

1½ cups [180 g] confectioners' sugar

1 to 2 tablespoons water (or more rum, if you like things boozy)

62

1) FOR THE BUNS Grease ten 3 by 2 in [7.5 by 5 cm] 6 oz [180 g] ramekins and line the bottoms with parchment paper (this makes for easier flipping). Place the ramekins on a sheet pan lined with parchment paper. 2) In a small bowl, combine the raisins and rum. Let the raisins soak for 20 minutes. Drain the raisins, reserving the rum. In another small bowl, mix together the brown and granulated sugars, the orange zest, lemon zest, cinnamon, and salt. 3) Generously flour your work surface. Roll out the croissant dough into a 10 by 24 in [25 by 60 cm] rectangle. Brush the dough with the melted butter, then sprinkle the sugar mixture evenly over the dough, gently pressing it into the butter to adhere. Scatter the raisins evenly over the top of the sugar. Starting at a long side, roll up the dough into a tight cylinder and position the dough seam-side down. Cut the dough into ten equal pieces. Transfer the pieces to the prepared ramekins and place them with a cut side facing side up. Cover the pan loosely with plastic wrap and let the dough rise until doubled in size and puffy (it should feel like a marshmallow when pressed),

2 to 2½ hours. (The buns can also do a slow rise in the refrigerator overnight; see page 187.) 4) Position an oven rack in the middle of the oven and preheat the oven to 400°F [200°C]. Line another sheet pan with parchment paper and place a wire rack on top. 5) Remove the plastic wrap and bake the buns until golden brown, 24 to 28 minutes. Flip each ramekin over onto the wire rack, and turn the buns right-side up. Let cool for 5 minutes. 6) FOR THE GLAZE While the buns are baking, in a medium bowl, whisk together the rum, butter, cinnamon, if using, and salt. Add the confectioners' sugar and mix together, then whisk until well combined and smooth. Add the water, 1 tablespoon at a time, until the glaze is thick but pourable. Pour the glaze over the warm buns. The buns are best eaten the day they are made.

Kouignettes are the mini version of kouign amann, a French pastry traditionally made in Brittany. They are sugar-coated pastries made from croissant dough that are rolled out in sugar, which creates deep caramelization as they bake. Some recipes often finish with a sprinkle of salt after baking; do as you see fit.

Kouignettes

MAKES 8
KOUIGNETTES

Butter, at room temperature, for greasing the baking rings

1¼ cups [250 g] granulated sugar, plus more for coating the baking rings

½ recipe Cheater Croissant Dough (page 271)

Finishing salt, such as fleur de sel, for sprinkling (optional)

1) Line a sheet pan with parchment paper. Butter eight 3½ in [9 cm] baking rings or English muffin rings and coat them generously with sugar (see Note). Place them on the prepared sheet pan. 2) On a clean work surface, sprinkle ½ cup [100 g] of the sugar and lay the dough on top. Sprinkle the surface of the dough evenly with another ¼ cup [50 g] of sugar. Using a rolling pin, roll out the dough into a 10 by 20 in [25 by 50 cm] rectangle, using more sugar as needed to keep the dough from sticking to the surface. With a pastry cutter, cut the rectangle in half lengthwise, then cut each half into four 5 in [12 cm] squares. 3) Fold the corners of the square so they meet in the center, and gently press them into the dough. Place the pastries in the rings, folded-side up, cover them loosely with plastic wrap, and let them rest for 1 hour. 4) Position an oven rack in the middle of the oven and preheat the oven to 400°F [200°C]. 5) Remove the plastic and bake the kouignettes until they are golden brown and the sugar has caramelized, 18 to 24 minutes. Transfer the sheet pan to a wire rack and remove the pastries from the baking rings as soon as the rings are cool enough to handle. Sprinkle with finishing salt, if desired. Let the pastries cool completely on a wire rack before eating. Kouignettes are best eaten the same day they are made.

NOTE If you don't have baking rings, you can bake the kouignettes in a buttered and sugared muffin tin.

63

64

This recipe came about because I wanted to mimic the streusel Danish I can always find in the grocery store; they are often rectangular in shape and left plain with just streusel, or filled with cream cheese and jam. I use a biscotti pan here because it is the perfect shape for this pastry, but disposable pans are also available in this size.

Streusel Danish

 MAKES ONE 12 IN [30.5 CM] DANISH

DANISH

All-purpose flour, for dusting

½ recipe Danish Dough (page 276) or ½ recipe Cheater Croissant Dough (page 271)

2 tablespoons granulated sugar

Egg wash (see page 14)

1 cup [140 g] Pecan Streusel (page 291)

GLAZE

1 to 2 tablespoons water

1 tablespoon unsalted butter, melted

Pinch of salt

1 cup [120 g] confectioners' sugar

1) FOR THE DANISH Line a 12 by 5½ in [30.5 by 14 cm] biscotti pan with parchment paper. Generously flour your work surface. Roll out the Danish dough to a 10 by 12 in [25 by 30.5 cm] rectangle. Sprinkle the surface with the granulated sugar and use the rolling pin to gently roll the sugar into the top of the dough. Fold the dough in half lengthwise, and place in the prepared pan. Let the dough rise until puffed, 1 to 1½ hours. 2) Position an oven rack in the middle of the oven and preheat the oven to 350°F [180°C]. 3) Brush the dough with egg wash. Sprinkle the top of the pastry with the streusel in two vertical strips, each about 1 in [2.5 cm] wide and leaving 2 in

[5 cm] between the strips. Bake the pastry until golden brown, rotating the pan halfway through baking, 22 to 28 minutes. Transfer the pan to a wire rack and let cool for a few minutes. 4) FOR THE GLAZE While the Danish is baking, in a medium bowl, whisk together 2 tablespoons of the water, the butter, and salt. Add the confectioners' sugar and mix together, then whisk until well combined and smooth. Add water, 1 tablespoon at a time, until the glaze is thick but pourable. Pour the glaze over the warm Danish. Let sit until warm to the touch, then serve. The Danish is best eaten the same day it is made.

This sheet pan Danish is inspired by the Good Morning Cheese Danish Slab Pie from Cathy Barrow's cookbook *Pie Squared*, made with a puff pastry crust, a cream cheese and jam filling, and a dusting of confectioners' sugar. My version is made with Danish dough, for a softer yet still flaky base and a cream cheese and lemon curd filling. It is delicious—a perfect way to start the day.

Sheet Pan Danish

 **MAKES 16 SERVINGS**

CREAM CHEESE FILLING

8 oz [227 g] cream cheese, at room temperature

¼ cup [50 g] granulated sugar

1 teaspoon lemon juice

Pinch of salt

ASSEMBLY

All-purpose flour, for dusting

½ recipe Danish Dough (page 276)

Egg wash (see page 14)

1 cup [320 g] Lemon Curd (page 288) or your favorite jam

ICING

1 to 3 tablespoons water

1 tablespoon unsalted butter, melted

½ teaspoon pure vanilla extract

Pinch of salt

1 cup [120 g] confectioners' sugar

1) **FOR THE CREAM CHEESE FILLING** In the bowl of a stand mixer fitted with a paddle, beat the cream cheese on medium speed until smooth. Scrape down the sides of the bowl and add the granulated sugar, lemon juice, and salt, mixing until completely combined. Transfer to a small bowl and refrigerate until ready to use. 2) **TO ASSEMBLE AND BAKE** Line a sheet pan with parchment paper. Generously flour your work surface. Roll out the Danish dough to an 11 by 15 in [28 by 38 cm] rectangle and transfer the dough to the prepared pan. With a pastry cutter or a sharp knife, score the surface of the dough, nearly all the way through, to create the outlines of sixteen equal portions, each approximately a 3¾ in [9.5 cm] by 2¾ in [7 cm] rectangle. Let the dough rise until puffed, 1 to 1½ hours.

3) Position an oven rack in the middle of the oven and preheat the oven to 350°F [180°C]. **4)** Brush the dough with egg wash. Use a small scoop or two spoons to dollop the cream cheese filling on top of each portion, about 1 tablespoon. Dollop 1 tablespoon of lemon curd right next to it. Bake the pastry until golden brown, rotating the pan halfway through baking, 18 to 24 minutes. Transfer the pan to a wire rack and let cool for a few minutes.

5) FOR THE ICING Meanwhile, make the icing. In a medium bowl, whisk together 1 tablespoon of the water, the butter, vanilla, and salt. Add the confectioners' sugar and mix together, then whisk until well combined and smooth. Add more water, 1 tablespoon at a time, until the desired consistency is reached; the glaze should be thick but pourable. **6)** Use a pastry wheel or pizza cutter to cut through the rectangles you scored, then drizzle with the icing; serve slightly warm. The Danish is best eaten the same day it's made.

66

This recipe evolved after my friend Scott took me out to breakfast; on our way out of the restaurant I glanced at the bakery case and saw pretty little cinnamon twists neatly stacked in a row. It was too late to grab one to go—we were in a hurry, and there was a line too long to wait in. So I went home and made my own. I use my Danish dough in this recipe, which makes them flaky and rich. This is also a great way to use up leftover Danish dough scraps.

Cinnamon Twists

 MAKES 10
TWISTS

TWISTS
¾ cup [150 g] granulated sugar

1 tablespoon ground cinnamon

Pinch of salt

All-purpose flour, for dusting

½ recipe Danish Dough (page 276)

Egg wash (see page 14)

ICING
2 oz [57 g] cream cheese, at room temperature

1 to 2 tablespoons water

1 tablespoon unsalted butter, melted

1 teaspoon pure vanilla extract

1¼ cups [150 g] confectioners' sugar

1) FOR THE TWISTS Line a sheet pan with parchment paper. In a small bowl, combine the granulated sugar, cinnamon, and salt. **2)** Generously flour your work surface. Roll out the Danish dough into a 15 in [38 cm] square. Brush the dough with the egg wash, then sprinkle the sugar mixture evenly over the dough, gently pressing it into the egg wash to adhere. **3)** Use a pastry cutter to cut the dough into ten pieces, each 1½ in [4 cm] wide. Twist each strip, then bend it into a horseshoe. Twist the two ends of the horseshoe around each other to form one long twist, then place it on the prepared sheet pan. Repeat with the remaining horseshoes. *See how-to photos, page 199.* Cover the twists loosely with plastic wrap and let rise for 45 minutes to 1 hour.

cont'd

4) Position an oven rack in the middle of the oven and preheat the oven to 350°F [180°C].

5) Bake the twists until golden and baked all the way through, 18 to 22 minutes. Transfer the pan to a wire rack with a piece of parchment paper underneath and let cool for 10 minutes. 6) FOR THE ICING While the twists are baking, make the icing. In a medium bowl, whisk together the cream cheese, 1 tablespoon of the water, the butter, and vanilla. Add the confectioners' sugar and mix together, then whisk until well combined and smooth. Add more water, 1 tablespoon at a time, until the desired consistency is reached; the glaze should be thick but pourable. Pour the icing over the warm twists and let cool until just warm to the touch; serve immediately. 7) Twists are best eaten the day they are made, but they can be stored in an airtight container at room temperature for up to 2 days.

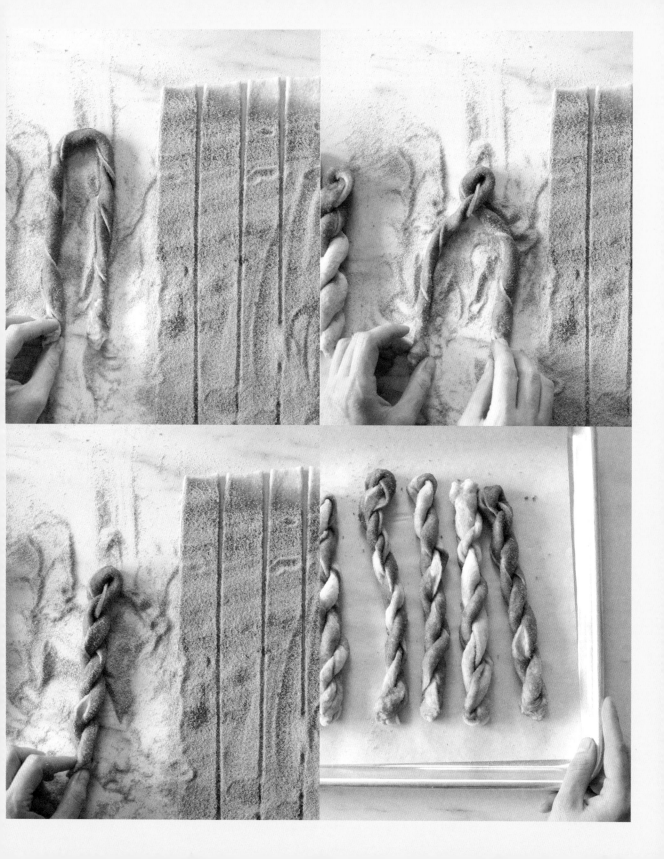

This recipe was named on a whim when one of my children asked me what I was making and I replied, "Some kind of apple flip thing?" The name stuck. It all started with a photograph of a flaky, moon-shaped apple pastry I came across while scrolling through social media one morning; I decided I had to make it. I later learned that an apple flip is actually a breakfast cookie, but I was so taken with the name that I kept it anyway. This flip is made with laminated Danish dough, filled with apples and brandy, and covered with an apple cider icing.

Apple Flips

MAKES 7
OR 8 FLIPS

FILLING

2 tablespoons unsalted butter

¼ cup [50 g] granulated sugar

¼ cup [50 g] brown sugar

¼ cup [60 g] apple cider

2 tablespoons cornstarch

1 teaspoon lemon juice

1 teaspoon ground cinnamon

¼ teaspoon salt

3 cups [426 g] peeled, cored, and chopped Gala apples

1 tablespoon applejack brandy (optional)

FLIPS

All-purpose flour, for dusting

½ recipe Danish Dough (page 276)

Egg wash (see page 14)

ICING

1 tablespoon unsalted butter, melted

1 to 3 tablespoons apple cider or water

½ teaspoon pure vanilla extract

Pinch of salt

¾ cup [90 g] confectioners' sugar

1) FOR THE FILLING Place the butter in a large saucepan and heat over medium heat until melted. Add the granulated and brown sugars, apple cider, cornstarch, lemon juice, cinnamon, and salt and heat until the sugar has dissolved, 2 to 3 minutes. Add the apples and cook until the apples are soft but still hold their shape, 20 to 25 minutes. Remove the pan from the heat and stir in the applejack, if using. 2) FOR THE FLIPS Line a sheet pan with parchment paper. Generously flour your work surface. Roll out the dough into a 15 in [38 cm] square. Cut out 5 in [12.5 cm] circles, using the rim of a glass or other circular object to measure. Reroll and cut any remaining dough scraps, for a total of seven or eight circles. Place 2 tablespoons of the apple filling on one half of each circle. Fold the empty half over the apple filling and gently press down. Place the apple flips on the prepared sheet pan. Cover gently with plastic wrap and

67

let rise until the dough is puffy, 1½ to 2 hours.
3) Position an oven rack in the middle of the
oven and preheat the oven to 375°F [190°C].
4) Brush the top of each flip with egg wash
and bake until golden brown, rotating the
pan halfway through baking, 18 to 22 minutes.
Transfer the sheet pan to a wire rack and let
cool. 5) FOR THE ICING While the flips are
cooling, in a medium bowl, whisk together
the butter, 1 tablespoon of the apple cider,
the vanilla, and salt. Add the confectioners'
sugar and mix together, then whisk until well

combined and smooth. Add more cider, 1 tablespoon at a time, until the desired consistency is
reached; the icing should be thick but pourable.
Pour the icing over the warm flips. Flips are
best eaten the day they are made.

NOTE If, while the filling is cooking, the apples
begin to stick at all to the bottom of the pan,
add a little more apple cider or water to the
pan, 1 tablespoon at a time.

I like to use pears in my turnovers rather than apples because they bake much faster, resulting in a tender fruit center that pairs beautifully with the golden brown flaky pastry. I prefer mine made with homemade puff pastry, but store-bought will work in a pinch.

Pear Turnovers

 MAKES 8 TURNOVERS

1½ cups [210 g] peeled and chopped Bartlett pears

2 tablespoons granulated sugar, plus more for sprinkling

⅛ teaspoon ground cinnamon

Pinch of salt

All-purpose flour, for dusting

1 recipe Rough Puff Pastry (page 278), cut into two pieces

Water, for brushing

Egg wash (see page 14)

1) Line a sheet pan with parchment paper. In a medium bowl, combine the pears, granulated sugar, cinnamon, and salt.

2) Generously flour a work surface. Roll one piece of the pastry dough into a 10 in [25 cm] square. Cut into four 5 in [12 cm] squares. Repeat with the second piece of dough, for a total of eight squares. Divide the pear mixture evenly among the squares of dough. Brush the edges of each square with water, fold the dough to make a triangle, and crimp the edges with a fork to seal. Transfer the triangles to the prepared sheet pan and place in the freezer while the oven preheats.

3) Position an oven rack in the middle of the oven and preheat the oven to 400°F [200°C].

4) Brush the tops of the turnovers lightly with egg wash and generously sprinkle with granulated sugar. Slide another sheet pan underneath so the pans are double stacked (this helps keep the bottoms from overbrowning). Bake the turnovers until golden brown, rotating the pan halfway through baking, 20 to 25 minutes. Remove from the oven and use a spatula to transfer the turnovers to a wire rack to cool slightly. Serve warm. Turnovers are best eaten the day they are made.

69

Cruffins are a tedious but fun project. My recipe uses a combination of my own croissant dough, a popover pan for height, and a mix of ingenious rolling methods from across the interweb. This combination of croissant and muffin makes for a tall, flaky, extravagant morning bun. For the best flavor, let the cruffins rise overnight in the refrigerator.

Cruffins

 MAKES 12
CRUFFINS

3 tablespoons unsalted butter, melted, plus more for greasing the pans

¾ cup [150 g] granulated sugar, plus more for sprinkling in the pans and coating the cruffins

All-purpose flour, for dusting

1 recipe Cheater Croissant Dough (page 271)

Pastry Cream (page 288, optional)

1) Line a sheet pan with parchment paper. Butter the wells of two large six-cup popover pans, then generously sprinkle each well with sugar. 2) Generously flour your work surface. Cut the croissant dough into six equal pieces. Leave one on your work surface and place the remaining five on the sheet pan. Cover loosely with plastic wrap and refrigerate until ready to use, one at a time. Roll out the first piece until it's as long, wide, and thin as possible, about 8 by 18 in [20 by 46 cm]. Brush with some of the melted butter and sprinkle with 1 heaping tablespoon of the granulated sugar, pressing it into the butter gently to adhere. Starting from a short edge, roll up the dough into a log, then cut the log in half lengthwise, so the layers of dough and filling are visible. One at a time, fold each half of the dough in half with the layers fanning out, so it's in a horseshoe shape. Twist one side of the horseshoe over the other, making a loop. Place the ends of the dough into one of the wells in the prepared popover pan so the ends are resting on the bottom and the top loop is sticking out slightly. Repeat with the other horseshoe. Repeat with the remaining five pieces of dough, for a total of twelve cruffins. *See how-to photos, page 206.*

cont'd

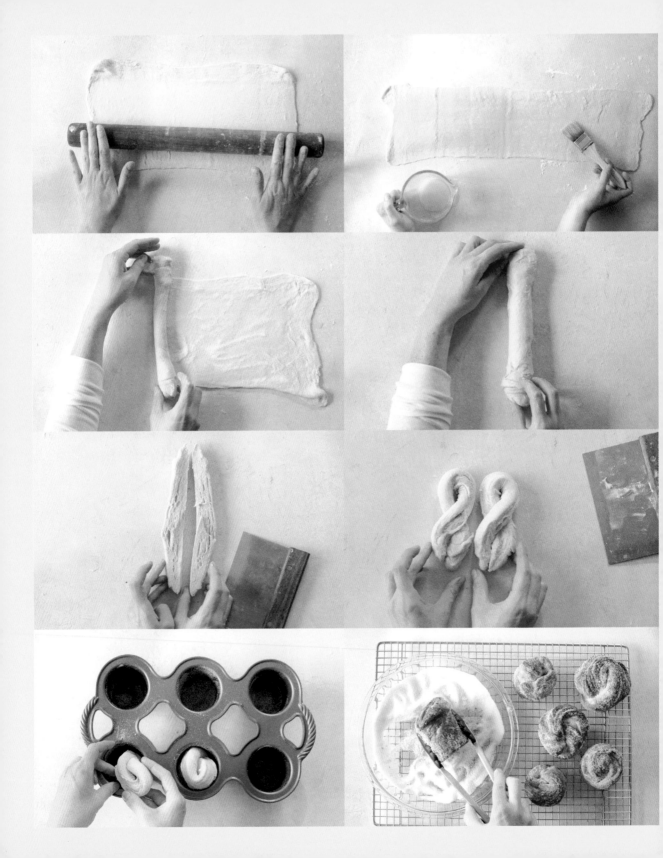

3) Cover the pans loosely with plastic wrap and let the dough rise at room temperature until doubled in size and it feels like a marshmallow when pressed, 2 to 3 hours. (Cruffins can also do a slow rise in the refrigerator overnight. See "For overnight cruffins.") 4) Position an oven rack in the middle of the oven and preheat the oven to 400°F [200°C]. Line a sheet pan with parchment paper. Put some sugar in a shallow dish. 5) Remove the plastic wrap from the pans and bake the cruffins until they are golden brown, 25 to 35 minutes. Let the cruffins sit in the pans for 1 to 2 minutes, then flip them out onto the prepared sheet pan. Roll each cruffin in the sugar, and transfer to a wire rack to finish cooling. 6) To fill the cruffins with pastry cream, if desired, fill a piping bag fitted with a plain tip with the pastry cream. Gently push the tip into the top of the cruffin (find a divot or space) and pipe in 1 to 2 tablespoons of pastry cream. Serve the cruffins the day they are made.

FOR OVERNIGHT CRUFFINS Prepare the cruffins, but do not let them rise at room temperature. Instead, cover the pans loosely with plastic wrap and refrigerate for at least 8 and up to 18 hours. When ready to bake, preheat the oven and let the buns sit at room temperature (still covered in plastic wrap) until puffy, 1½ to 2 hours. Bake as directed and fill with pastry cream, if desired.

VARIATION

• **Cruffins with Fruit Filling:** *Add ¼ cup [8 g] of freeze-dried berry powder (strawberry, raspberry, or blueberry; see page 14) to the sugar before sprinkling over the rolled-out dough.*

70

I fell in love with almond croissants before any other kind; chocolate was always too rich, and straight-up croissants were delicious but not as appealing to my sugar-loving self. I couldn't help but be drawn to that flaky treat studded with toasted almonds and a rich, creamy almond center.

Almond Croissants

MAKES 8 CROISSANTS

All-purpose flour, for dusting

½ recipe Cheater Croissant Dough (page 271)

½ cup [150 g] Almond Cream (page 292)

Egg wash (see page 14)

½ cup [50 g] sliced almonds

Confectioners' sugar, for dusting (optional)

1) Line a sheet pan with parchment paper. Generously flour your work surface and roll out the croissant dough into a rectangle measuring 10 by 15 in [25 by 38 cm]. With a long side facing you, trim the dough so the edges are straight and it measures 14 in [35.5 cm] in length. 2) Measure along the long side of the dough and cut long triangles measuring 10 in [25 cm] long and 3½ in [9 cm] wide at the base, for a total of eight croissants. 3) Hold the base of the triangle and gently stretch the triangle until it is 12 in [30.5 cm] long. Place the triangle on the work surface and evenly spread 1 tablespoon of almond cream on the wide end of the croissant, leaving a ½ in [12 mm] border. Roll up the dough from the wide end to the tip. Place the rolled croissant on the prepared pan and make sure the pointy end is tucked under (if it is on top, it can pop up during baking). Repeat with the remaining dough and space the croissants evenly out on the sheet pan (they will puff up quite a bit as they rise and bake). Cover the croissants loosely with plastic wrap, and let them rise until they are doubled in size and puffed, 2 to 2½ hours. 4) Position an oven rack in the middle of the oven and preheat the oven to 400°F [200°C]. 5) Remove the plastic and brush the croissants with egg wash. Sprinkle the tops with the sliced almonds. Bake until the croissants are deep golden brown and the layers do not look underbaked, 25 to 30 minutes. Move the sheet pan to a wire rack and let the croissants cool completely. Dust with confectioners' sugar, if desired. Croissants are best eaten the same day they are made.

71

These tarts are very easy to make and a great way to use up fresh fruit. I will advocate for making your own puff pastry, but store-bought also works well here. A streak of pastry cream in the center makes these extra fancy, but they also taste great without it.

Blackberry Puff Pastry Tartlets

 MAKES 8 TARTLETS

All-purpose flour, for dusting

1 recipe Rough Puff Pastry (page 278), cut into two pieces

1 lb [455 g] fresh blackberries

¼ to ½ cup [50 to 100 g] granulated sugar, plus more for sprinkling

Egg wash (see page 14)

1 cup [226 g] Pastry Cream (page 288, optional) or Lemon Curd (page 288, optional)

1) Line two sheet pans with parchment paper. Generously flour your work surface. Roll out one piece of the dough into a 10 in [25 cm] square. Cut into four 5 in [12 cm] squares. Repeat with the second piece of dough, for a total of eight squares. Using a sharp paring knife, score a ¾ in [2 cm] border around each square, making sure not to cut all the way through the dough. Use a fork to prick the center of each square (to prevent puffing while the pastry is baking). 2) Place four squares on each sheet pan and freeze the pastry while the oven is preheating. (If you don't have room in your freezer for two sheet pans, you can put them all on one to chill, then transfer half to a separate pan before baking.)

3) Position an oven rack in the middle of the oven and preheat the oven to 400°F [200°C]. 4) In a medium bowl, combine the blackberries and ¼ cup [50 g] of sugar. If the berries are especially tart, add more of the sugar as needed. Let the fruit sit in the sugar until ready to bake. 5) Brush each pastry square with the egg wash, being careful not to let any drip down the sides. Spread the pastry cream in the center of each tart, if using. Divide the fruit filling evenly among the pastries. Sprinkle a little more granulated sugar over the edges and the fruit. Bake one sheet at a time until the edges are golden brown and the fruit is bubbling, 20 to 24 minutes. Transfer the tarts to a wire rack to cool. Tarts are best eaten the same day they are made.

CHAPTER 5

The Weekend

"**Time for you** and
time for me, And time
yet for a **hundred
indecisions,** And for
a **hundred visions** and
revisions, Before the
taking of **a toast** and **tea.**
In the room the women
come and go,
Talking of Michelangelo."

—T. S. Eliot, "The Love Song of J. Alfred Prufrock"

This is the perfect way to use up any leftover or stale cinnamon swirl bread (my favorite version), brioche bread, or milk bread you may have lying around. Put the bread on a wire rack overnight so it's really stale; I find that dried-out bread makes the best French toast. I like to add a little cornstarch to the batter, which makes the toast nice and crisp on the outside.

Cinnamon Swirl French Toast

MAKES 4 SERVINGS

1 cup [240 g] half-and-half, at room temperature

1 large egg, at room temperature

2 tablespoons unsalted butter, melted and cooled, plus more for frying and serving

1 tablespoon granulated sugar

1 tablespoon pure vanilla extract

¼ teaspoon salt

2 tablespoons cornstarch

Eight ¾ in [2 cm] thick slices Cinnamon Swirl Bread (page 156), Milk Bread (page 262), or Brioche (page 259); or 8 thick slices store-bought challah or Texas toast bread

Maple syrup or jam, for serving

1) Line a sheet pan with parchment paper. In a large bowl or liquid measuring cup, whisk together the half-and-half, egg, melted butter, granulated sugar, vanilla, and salt. 2) Pour 3 tablespoons of the mixture into a small bowl and add the cornstarch, whisking until there are no lumps and the mixture is a smooth paste. Pour the cornstarch mixture into the liquid ingredients and whisk to fully combine. 3) Pour the mixture into a pie plate or shallow bowl. Dip the bread slices, one at a time, into the egg mixture, soaking the bread and making sure both sides are coated completely. Allow any excess egg mixture to drip back into the plate. Place the bread slices on the prepared pan and let the mixture soak into the bread while the skillet heats up.

4) Heat a 12 in [30.5 cm] skillet over medium heat until hot, 3 to 4 minutes. Swirl a scant tablespoon of butter in the skillet, then cook one or two slices of bread until golden brown, 2 to 3 minutes per side. Repeat until all the slices are cooked (see Note). The butter will brown and the mixture will melt, so use tongs to pick up a paper towel and wipe out the pan between batches. Serve immediately with butter and maple syrup and/or jam. French toast is best eaten the same day it's made.

NOTE French toast can be kept warm in a 175°F [80°C] oven on a wire rack placed over a sheet pan while the other slices are being cooked.

72

73

The most inspired overnight waffle recipe comes from Marion Cunningham, in her wonderful book *The Breakfast Book*. Her recipe in turn is from an early Fannie Farmer cookbook (an instance of Ecclesiastes ringing true: *The thing that hath been, it is that which shall be . . . there is no new thing under the sun*). I love this recipe because most of it is prepped the evening before. I use crème fraîche in my version here, and they cook into perfectly crisp but creamy waffles.

Overnight Crème Fraîche Waffles

 MAKES ABOUT 8 WAFFLES, DEPENDING ON THE SIZE OF YOUR WAFFLE IRON

½ cup water, warm (100 to 110°F [35 to 42°C])

1 tablespoon active dry yeast

1½ cups [360 g] milk, at room temperature

¾ cup [180 g] crème fraîche, homemade (page 290) or store-bought, at room temperature

8 tablespoons [1 stick or 113 g] unsalted butter, melted and cooled, plus more for serving

2 tablespoons cornstarch

1 tablespoon granulated sugar

1 teaspoon salt

2½ cups [355 g] all-purpose flour

2 large eggs

½ teaspoon baking soda

Maple syrup or jam, for serving

1) In a large mixing bowl, add the water and yeast, and let sit until the yeast is foamy, about 5 minutes. 2) Add the milk, crème fraîche, melted butter, cornstarch, granulated sugar, and salt and whisk until smooth and combined. Add the flour and whisk again until no lumps remain. Cover the bowl with plastic wrap and place in the refrigerator for 8 hours and up to overnight. 3) When ready to make the waffles, whisk in the eggs until completely combined, then add the baking soda and mix until combined. The batter will be thin. 4) Heat the waffle iron and cook the waffles according to the manufacturer's instructions. Serve the hot waffles immediately with plenty of butter and maple syrup or jam.

This is my favorite way to make pancakes; these cakes fall somewhere between a thin and a fluffy pancake and have good vanilla flavor. I love to add pear (see variation below), but a few blueberries or raspberries can also be added to each pancake—sprinkle them on the batter right after pouring it into the pan.

House Pancakes

 MAKES ABOUT 12 PANCAKES

2 cups [284 g] all-purpose flour

2 teaspoons baking powder

½ teaspoon baking soda

1 large egg, at room temperature

3 tablespoons unsalted butter, melted and cooled

2½ cups [600 g] buttermilk, at room temperature

3 tablespoons granulated sugar

2 teaspoons pure vanilla extract

½ teaspoon salt

Vegetable oil, for frying

1) In a large bowl, whisk together the flour, baking powder, and baking soda. In another large bowl or liquid measuring cup, whisk together the egg and melted butter, and then add the buttermilk, granulated sugar, vanilla, and salt, whisking until combined. Make a well in the center of the dry ingredients, pour the buttermilk mixture into the well, and stir very gently until the buttermilk mixture is just incorporated (a few lumps should remain in the batter). Be careful not to overmix the batter. Let the batter sit for 5 minutes while the skillet or griddle heats. 2) Heat a griddle or 12 in [30 cm] skillet over medium heat for 3 to 5 minutes. Brush the griddle with 2 teaspoons of vegetable oil. Using ¼ cup [60 g] of batter per pancake, add the batter to the hot griddle. Cook until large bubbles begin to appear on the surface of the pancake and the bottom of the pancake is golden brown, about 2 minutes. Flip the pancake and cook until golden brown on the other side, a minute or two longer. Repeat with the remaining batter, adding more oil as needed to the griddle. Serve immediately. 3) Leftover pancakes can be reheated; our family pops them in the toaster and heats until toasted. This also works with French Toast (page 216).

VARIATION
• **Pear Pancakes:** *Add 1 peeled, grated pear to the batter, stirring until just incorporated.*

My first encounter with a Dutch baby was at our local (now defunct) restaurant Pannen-koeken, which was a homey diner that offered breakfast and lunch, but most famously, of course, served Dutch-style pancakes. When I was in elementary school, my grandma often took me there for a late breakfast on the weekends, and I would stare in awe at the servers in their Dutch-inspired costumes, as each carried one giant plate containing a freshly baked puffed pancake above their heads, shouting "pannenkoeken!" as loud as they could while rushing to get that risen beauty to a table before it deflated.

MAKES 6
DUTCH BABIES

Mini Dutch Babies

1 cup [142 g] all-purpose flour

2 tablespoons cornstarch

1 cup [240 g] skim milk, at room temperature

4 large eggs, at room temperature

2 tablespoons granulated sugar

2 tablespoons unsalted butter, melted and cooled, plus 3 tablespoons

1 teaspoon pure vanilla extract

½ teaspoon salt

Confectioners' sugar, for sprinkling

Maple syrup, whipped cream, fresh fruit, or jam, for serving, in any combination

1) Position an oven rack in the lower third of the oven and preheat the oven to 450°F [230°C]. Line a sheet pan with parchment paper and place six crème brûlée ramekins on it. 2) In a large bowl, whisk together the flour and cornstarch. In another large bowl or liquid measuring cup, whisk together the milk, eggs, granulated sugar, melted butter, vanilla, and salt until completely combined. Add one-third of the wet ingredients to the flour mixture, whisking until no lumps remain, then slowly add the remaining wet ingredients, whisking until smooth. Let the batter rest for 5 minutes. 3) Cut the remaining 3 tablespoons of butter into six pieces and divide among the ramekins. Place the ramekins in the oven and heat

them for 2 to 3 minutes, until the butter melts completely. 4) Using an oven mitt, carefully remove the pan from the oven and divide the batter evenly among the ramekins. Immediately return the pan to the oven. Bake until the edges are golden brown and crisp and the pancakes have risen and puffed, 12 to 16 minutes. (If you like the edges extra crispy, you can bake the Dutch babies for a few minutes longer.) 5) Transfer the pan to a wire rack and sprinkle the pancakes with confectioners' sugar. Serve with maple syrup, whipped cream, fresh fruit, or jam.

75

Popovers are similar to Dutch babies; they have the same ability to "pop" out of the pan as they bake. I love them warm and slathered in butter; I have a recipe for Fig Butter here, but any flavored butter you may have on hand will work beautifully too.

Popovers
with Fig Butter

 MAKES 6 POPOVERS

FIG BUTTER

6 tablespoons [84 g] unsalted butter, at room temperature

3 tablespoons fig jam

1 teaspoon grated orange zest

POPOVERS

1¼ cups [178 g] all-purpose flour

4 large eggs, at room temperature

1½ cups [360 g] skim milk, at room temperature

2 oz [58 g] Parmesan, grated

2 tablespoons unsalted butter, melted, plus 2 tablespoons

1 teaspoon granulated sugar

½ teaspoon salt

1) FOR THE FIG BUTTER In a medium bowl, mix together the butter, jam, and orange zest until well combined and creamy. Cover and refrigerate until ready to use. 2) FOR THE POPOVERS Position an oven rack in the middle of the oven and preheat the oven to 400°F [200°C]. 3) Put the flour in a large bowl. In another large bowl or liquid measuring cup, whisk together the eggs, milk, Parmesan, melted butter, granulated sugar, and salt until completely combined. Add one-third of the wet ingredients to the flour, whisking until no lumps remain, then slowly add the remaining wet ingredients, whisking until smooth. 4) Cut the remaining 2 tablespoons of butter into six pieces and put one in each well of a large six-cup popover pan. Put the pan in the oven and heat for 2 to 3 minutes, until the butter melts completely. 5) Using an oven mitt, carefully remove the pan from the oven and divide the batter evenly among the wells of the popover pan. Immediately return the pan to the oven. Bake until the popovers have popped up nice and high and the edges are deep golden, 40 to 45 minutes. 6) Carefully remove the popovers from the pan. Serve immediately with the fig butter.

Because my Cheater Croissant Dough is used here, I can't claim these are genuine croissants. I will say, though, that they are flaky and delicious and bake up beautifully. A swirl of prosciutto and Gruyère makes these suitable for breakfast on their own, but you could also use them in Croissant Breakfast Sandwiches (page 229).

Prosciutto Gruyère Croissants

MAKES 8
CROISSANTS

All-purpose flour, for dusting

½ recipe Cheater Croissant Dough (page 271)

8 slices prosciutto

8 slices Gruyère

Egg wash (see page 14)

1) Line a sheet pan with parchment paper. Generously flour your work surface. Roll out the croissant dough into a rectangle measuring 10 by 15 in [25 by 38 cm]. With a long side facing you, trim the dough so the edges are straight and the long sides measure 14 in [35.5 cm]. 2) Using a ruler, mark along the bottom of the dough every 3½ in [9 cm]. Cut long triangles measuring 10 in [25 cm] long and 3½ in [9 cm] wide at the base. 3) Holding the base of a triangle, gently stretch the triangle until it is 12 in [30.5 cm] long. Place the triangle on the work surface. Lay one slice of prosciutto over the wider part of the triangle, and top with a slice of Gruyère. Roll up the dough from the wide end to the tip. Place the rolled croissant on the prepared pan, making sure

the pointy end is tucked under (if it is on top, it can pop up during baking). Repeat with the remaining triangles of dough, and space the croissants evenly on the sheet pan (they will puff up quite a bit as they rise and bake). See how-to photos, page 210. 4) Cover the croissants loosely with plastic wrap and let them rise for 2 to 2½ hours, until they are doubled in size and puffed. 5) Position an oven rack in the middle of the oven and preheat the oven to 400°F [200°C]. 6) Remove the plastic and brush the croissants with egg wash. Bake until the croissants are deep golden brown and the layers do not look underbaked, 25 to 30 minutes. Transfer the sheet pan to a wire rack and let the croissants cool completely. Croissants are best eaten the same day they are made.

About twenty (or so, ahem) years ago I was frequently working the early barista shift at the Blue Heron. On one particular morning, I was starving and wanted something more substantial than a scone or muffin. Erik, the owners' son (who was about twelve at the time), had popped in the back to make himself breakfast and offered to make me some too. (Erik and I were buddies; my own brother was the same age, and being away at school, I missed him something fierce.) I said yes to breakfast. He then proceeded to make me the BEST breakfast sandwich I had ever had in my life. It was just scrambled eggs and cheese on a croissant, but the eggs were cooked perfectly (see the variation below), the croissant was lightly toasted, and the cheese melted in my mouth. I was highly impressed by his culinary skills at such a young age (and can report they have only improved over the years). This recipe is slightly elevated, with bacon, cheese, and a fried egg, and can easily be doubled or tripled.

Croissant Breakfast Sandwiches

 MAKES 2 SANDWICHES

2 Croissant Sandwich Buns (page 275), baked and cooled, or store-bought

2 slices (2 oz [56 g]) Cheddar cheese, deli-thin

2 to 4 slices of your favorite bacon

2 tablespoons unsalted butter

1 tablespoon olive oil (optional)

2 large eggs

Salt and freshly ground pepper

Sriracha mayo, for serving (optional)

Salad greens, for serving (optional)

Sliced tomato, for serving (optional)

1) Position an oven rack in the middle of the oven and preheat the oven to 400°F [200°C]. Line a sheet pan with parchment paper. 2) Slice the croissants in half horizontally and place cut-side up on the sheet pan. Bake the croissants until light golden brown, 5 to 6 minutes.

cont'd

Add a slice of Cheddar to each croissant bottom and bake again until the cheese has melted, 1 to 2 minutes. Remove from the oven and set aside while assembling the rest of the sandwich. 3) Line a plate with paper towels. In a large pan over medium heat, cook the bacon until crisp and brown, about 10 minutes (I like my bacon VERY crispy, but you can cook yours however you like it). Transfer the bacon to the prepared plate to drain. 4) Pour off the bacon fat, setting aside 1 tablespoon for cooking the eggs, if desired. Wipe out the pan. Heat the pan over medium heat and add 1 tablespoon of the butter and either the reserved bacon fat or the olive oil. Crack the eggs into a small bowl, then pour the eggs into the hot pan. Season the eggs with salt and pepper. 5) Here is where you come in, as everyone likes their eggs cooked differently. If you prefer sunny-side up, cover the pan and cook the eggs until the whites are set, about 2 minutes. For eggs over easy or hard, cook the eggs until the whites are set and starting to turn golden, then carefully flip and cook until the yolks are the way you like them. (Or you may prefer your eggs cooked a completely different way, and that will work here too!) Remove from the heat. 6) Lay the bacon over the cheese on each croissant, then top with the eggs. Spread the top inside of the croissants with sriracha mayo, if desired, and add greens and tomato, if desired. Close the buns and eat immediately.

VARIATION

• **Souffléed Eggs:** My whole family loves soft eggs and yolks, but I am a firm well-cooked scrambled eggs person, because of one fateful sleepover at my grandma's house, where the most undercooked, runny scrambled eggs that ever landed on a plate were served to me at breakfast. My seven-year-old self was forever traumatized when my grandma insisted I take at least three bites before I could switch to Cinnamon Toast Crunch cereal. So here are "souffléed" eggs, similar to the ones Erik made me twenty years ago, and what I always make for myself.

In a medium bowl, whisk together 4 large eggs, a good pinch of salt, and 1 tablespoon half-and-half. In a medium pan over medium-high heat, melt 1 tablespoon of unsalted butter until sizzling. Add the eggs, sprinkle ⅓ cup [25 g] of grated sharp Cheddar cheese over the top, if you'd like, and cook, undisturbed, until the edges show signs of firming, about 1 minute. Lower the heat slightly, then use a rubber spatula to push the edges in toward the center about 1 in [2.5 cm], and gently tilt the pan so the uncooked liquid drains down to the now-clear spots in the pan, just as you would to make an omelet. Repeat pushing the eggs into the center and prodding the liquid down until the "omelet" is no longer runny and the bottom is golden in spots. Use a spatula to flip it over. Cook until the second side is starting to brown in spots and the eggs have puffed slightly. Split in half and divide between the two croissant buns.

This recipe was inspired by several people. First, by Polina Chesnakova, or really, by a photograph in her book *Hot Cheese* of the most incredible-looking croque monsieur sandwich I had ever seen, with melted, broiled cheese completely covering the top. (One glance at the photo led me down a rabbit hole of questions: Why hadn't I been broiling cheese? Why have I been putting it inside, always not melty enough? Why wasn't I toasting the bread first, so the bread was perfectly golden and buttery and crisp, and then adding the cheese? All my future grilled cheese sandwiches are ruined forever.)

Around the same time, I was visited by Larry and Colleen Wolner, my Blue Heron family. They surprised my son by bringing all the fixings for his favorite sandwich, the Southwest turkey, from their coffeehouse. There was a giant bag full of freshly baked bread, thinly sliced smoked turkey, lettuce, tomato, red onions, and a container of their Southwest mayo. Not long after their visit, I was brainstorming breakfast sandwiches early one morning, and I decided to put the two sandwiches together: grilled Southwest turkey on a single slice of homemade bread, covered with melty, bubbly cheese. It's technically a tartine, but filling enough to be considered a sandwich.

MAKES 2
SANDWICHES

Southwest Turkey Breakfast Sandwiches

SOUTHWEST MAYO

1 cup [240 g] mayonnaise

2 oz [57 g] chipotle peppers in adobo sauce, seeded if desired (see Notes)

2 garlic cloves

2 tablespoons chopped fresh parsley

1½ teaspoons red wine vinegar

1 teaspoon ground cumin

¼ teaspoon salt

ASSEMBLY

4 tablespoons [57 g] unsalted butter, at room temperature

Two 1 in [2.5 cm] thick slices Milk Bread (page 262) or Brioche Bread (page 259), or thick slices store-bought Texas toast bread

2 slices Cheddar cheese, deli-thin

4 slices smoked turkey, deli-thin

½ medium red onion, thinly sliced

2 slices provolone cheese, deli-thin

cont'd

1) FOR THE MAYO Add all the ingredients to the bowl of a food processor and blend until smooth. You should have about 1½ cups [360 g]. (Southwest mayo can be stored in an airtight container in the refrigerator for up to 1 week; you will have quite a lot left over.) 2) TO ASSEMBLE Position an oven rack in the upper third of the oven and preheat the broiler on high. 3) Butter the bread slices, making sure to cover the entire surface. Heat a large, ovenproof skillet (cast iron works nicely) over medium heat. Place the bread butter-side down and cook until the bottoms are golden and crispy, 2 to 3 minutes. Remove the bread, and move to a work surface. On the toasted side, spread a generous amount of Southwest mayo (depending on your preference). Add the Cheddar, smoked turkey, and onion, and cover each sandwich with a slice of provolone. Put the sandwiches back in the skillet butter-side down and cook until the untoasted side is light golden brown. Place the skillet under the broiler. Broil until the cheese on top is lightly browned and bubbling, 3 to 5 minutes. Serve immediately.

NOTES This recipe can easily be doubled or tripled; you will have enough Southwest mayo.

Chipotle peppers in adobo sauce can be spicy! I remove the seeds from the peppers to cut back on the heat, but if you like things spicy, you can keep them in.

I have made this with many different spreads, meats, and cheeses. Sriracha mayo also works well here, as does habanero Jack cheese or Muenster. I find that pre-sliced sandwich cheese works best; it is already in the perfect shape and thickness, and it melts well. It also ensures that you don't add too much or too little cheese—it is just the right amount.

There are many recipes for honey mustard, ham, and cheese sliders across the internet, but most are made with store-bought buns. The inspiration for this version was a recipe I came across in *Baking School: The Bread Ahead Cookbook* by Matthew Jones, Justin Gellatly, and Louise Gellatly, who make their "Baker's Sandwich" with homemade dough and let the sandwiches rise with their fillings inside. You can also set these up the night before and hold them in the fridge until the next morning. Let them come to room temperature while the oven preheats (about 45 minutes to an hour) and then bake as directed.

Ham and Cheese Breakfast Sliders

 MAKES 12 SLIDERS

SLIDERS

All-purpose flour, for dusting

1 recipe Pull-Apart Dough (page 269)

⅓ cup [80 g] plain or sriracha mayonnaise

12 slices sliced deli ham, halved

12 slices sliced provolone cheese, halved

3 tablespoons Dijon mustard

1 tablespoon honey

Egg wash (see page 14)

2 tablespoons poppy seeds

POURING SAUCE

4 tablespoons [57 g] unsalted butter, melted

1 tablespoon honey

1 teaspoon Dijon mustard

80

1) **FOR THE SLIDERS** Grease a 9 by 13 in [23 by 33 cm] pan. Line with a parchment sling (see page 14). Generously flour your work surface. Divide the dough in half, and roll each half into a 9 by 13 in [23 by 33 cm] rectangle. Cut each half into twelve squares. 2) Place half of the dough squares in the prepared pan; they should line the whole bottom. Use a spoon to spread a generous amount of mayo on each piece. Top the squares with the ham and provolone so they are all covered, folding the pieces in half to fit them on the bun. 3) In a small bowl, mix together the mustard and honey. Spread 1 teaspoon on each of the remaining twelve squares of dough, the tops of the sliders. Place the tops, mustard-side down, over the filled bottoms

in the pan, and press down gently. Loosely cover the sandwiches with plastic wrap and let them rise for about 45 minutes at room temperature. 4) Meanwhile, position an oven rack in the middle of the oven and preheat the oven to 350°F [180°C]. 5) Brush the tops of the sandwiches with egg wash and generously sprinkle with the poppyseeds. Bake the buns for 8 minutes. 6) FOR THE POURING SAUCE

While the buns are baking, in a small bowl or liquid measuring cup, whisk together the melted butter, honey, and mustard until well combined. Pour over the partially baked buns (remember, the pan is hot!). Continue baking until the buns are golden brown, 13 to 15 minutes. Move the pan to a wire rack and let cool for about 15 minutes, then serve. Sliders are best eaten the same day they are made.

This is a stellar way to start the day—a rich pastry crust filled with crème fraîche, Cheddar, sausage, spinach, and eggs. I like to use 6 eggs here; less is more for me. But my testers wanted more eggs, so you can use up to 8 if desired.

Sheet Pan Breakfast

MAKES 3 OR 4
SERVINGS

⅓ cup [80 g] crème fraîche, homemade (page 290) or store-bought

1 tablespoon heavy cream

1 garlic clove, minced

Salt

All-purpose flour, for dusting

½ recipe Danish Dough (page 276)

Egg wash (see page 14)

4 oz [113 g] breakfast sausage, cooked and crumbled into small pieces

⅓ cup [15 g] frozen spinach, thawed and drained

⅓ cup [25 g] grated sharp Cheddar cheese or Gruyère

6 or 8 large eggs

Freshly ground pepper (optional)

Grated Parmesan, for sprinkling, and olive oil, for drizzling (optional)

1) Line a sheet pan with parchment paper. 2) In a medium bowl, whisk together the crème fraîche, heavy cream, garlic, and a pinch of salt. Set aside. 3) Generously flour your work surface. Roll out the Danish dough to an 11 by 15 in [28 by 38 cm] rectangle, and transfer the dough to the prepared pan. Let the dough rise until puffed, 1 to 1½ hours. 4) Position an oven rack in the middle of the oven and preheat the oven to 350°F [180°C]. 5) Brush the dough with egg wash. Use an offset spatula to spread the crème fraîche filling on top of the risen dough. Scatter the sausage and spinach over the filling, then top with the Cheddar. 6) Bake the pastry until light golden brown, rotating the pan halfway through baking, 17 to 22 minutes. Leave the oven on. 7) Crack an egg into a small bowl, then slide it on top of the dough. Repeat with the remaining eggs, spacing them apart over the filling, trying to stay closer to the middle than the edges so they don't run off the sides as they bake. (Crack them one at a time into a bowl so that if a yolk isn't intact, you can easily discard it.) Season with salt and pepper, if desired. 8) Return the pan to the oven and bake until the egg whites are set but the yolks are still runny, 4 to 5 minutes more. Place the pan on a wire rack. Drizzle with olive oil and sprinkle on grated Parmesan, if desired. Let the pastry cool for a few minutes. Slice and serve immediately.

These are really mini crustless quiches—but that title didn't sound quite as exciting. However! These little egg bakes are really delicious, and so much easier to put together than a traditional quiche. Adding a little flour to the quiche before it bakes helps stabilize the custard. You can customize these to your taste (see Note).

MAKES FOUR 6 IN
[15 CM] QUICHES

Individual Quiche Bakes

1 cup [240 g] whole milk

½ cup [120 g] heavy cream

½ cup [120 g] crème fraîche, homemade (page 290) or store-bought

3 large eggs

2 large egg yolks

¾ teaspoon salt

¾ teaspoon Italian seasoning

Freshly ground pepper

2 tablespoons all-purpose flour

1 cup [80 g] grated Gruyère cheese

1) Position an oven rack in the middle of the oven and preheat the oven to 400°F [200°C]. Line a sheet pan with parchment paper. Grease four individual 6 in [15 cm] baking dishes or pie plates and place them on the sheet pan. 2) In a large bowl or liquid measuring cup, whisk together the milk, cream, crème fraîche, eggs, egg yolks, salt, and Italian seasoning. Season with pepper. Place 3 tablespoons of the mixture in a medium bowl, slowly whisk in the flour, and continue whisking until there are no flour lumps and the mixture is a smooth paste. Add to the liquid ingredients, whisking until fully incorporated. Stir in ½ cup [40 g] of the cheese.

3) Divide the filling among the prepared dishes and sprinkle the remaining ½ cup [40 g] of cheese over the top. Bake for 10 minutes, then turn down the heat to 325°F [165°C] and bake until the quiches are golden brown, puffed, and firm when shaken gently, 30 to 35 minutes more. Move the pan to a wire rack and let cool for 20 to 30 minutes, until the custard sets. Serve warm or at room temperature. The quiches can be stored, wrapped in plastic, in the refrigerator for up to 3 days.

NOTE You can add more ingredients to the quiche if desired. For example, ¾ cup [15 g] of chopped spinach stirred into the custard, or ¾ cup [110 g] of chopped ham (bite-size pieces) sprinkled over the tops is delicious.

82

"He that but looketh on a plate of ham and eggs to lust after it, hath already committed breakfast with it in his heart," wrote C. S. Lewis in a letter that always makes me laugh. Sin or no, this is a delicious way to start the day, and the croissants make the dish very indulgent.

 MAKES ONE 9 IN [23 CM] CASSEROLE

Cheesy Croissant Casserole

6 croissants, homemade (page 275) or store-bought, split in half lengthwise

2 tablespoons unsalted butter

¾ cup [105 g] minced onion

¾ teaspoon salt

1 teaspoon Italian seasoning

⅓ cup [80 g] dry white wine

5 large eggs, at room temperature

1½ cups [360 g] half-and-half, at room temperature

Freshly ground pepper

3 slices deli ham, cut into 12 pieces each

6 oz [170 g] Gruyère cheese, grated

⅓ cup [6 g] spinach leaves, torn in half

1) Position an oven rack in the middle of the oven and preheat the oven to 400°F [200°C]. Line a sheet pan with parchment paper. Generously butter a 10 by 7 in [25 by 17 cm] oval baking dish or other similar-size pan. 2) Place the croissants halves, cut-side up, in a single layer on the prepared sheet pan. Toast until golden, about 10 minutes. Transfer to a wire rack to cool. When the croissants have cooled, tear each half into smaller pieces, about 2 in [5 cm] each. 3) In a medium skillet over medium heat, melt the butter. Add the onion and ¼ teaspoon of the salt and sauté the onion until fragrant and translucent, 3 to 4 minutes. Add the Italian seasoning and sauté until fragrant, about 30 seconds. Add the wine and simmer until reduced slightly, 2 to 3 minutes. Remove from the heat.

4) In a large bowl or liquid measuring cup, whisk together the eggs, then slowly add the onion mixture, half-and-half, and remaining ½ teaspoon of salt. Season with pepper and continue whisking until completely combined. **5)** In the prepared baking dish, toss the croissant pieces, ham, 4 oz [113 g] of the cheese, and spinach leaves, making sure everything is evenly distributed. **6)** Pour the egg mixture evenly over the top of the casserole, cover the top with plastic wrap, and gently press down on the croissant layers to help them absorb the liquid. Refrigerate for at least 2 hours or overnight. **7)** When ready to bake, remove the casserole from the refrigerator and let sit at room temperature while the oven preheats. **8)** Position an oven rack in the middle of the oven and preheat the oven to 350°F [180°C]. **9)** Remove the plastic wrap from the casserole and top with the remaining 2 oz [55 g] of cheese. Bake until the center is puffed, firm to the touch, and golden brown, 45 to 50 minutes. Transfer to a wire rack and cool for 10 minutes. Serve warm.

83

This is a savory version of pull-apart bread; I use pesto and mozzarella here for a cheesy bread. It is a great addition to a brunch or breakfast table. Adding a little prosciutto along with the mozzarella is also delicious.

Pesto Pull-Apart Bread

 MAKES ONE 9 IN [23 CM] LOAF

All-purpose flour, for dusting

1 recipe Pull-Apart Bread Dough (page 269)

One 6.5 oz [184 g] jar pesto

10 slices (8 oz [226 g]) mozzarella cheese, deli-thin

1) Line a 9 by 4 by 4 in [23 by 10 by 10 cm] Pullman pan with a parchment sling (see page 14). 2) Generously flour your work surface. Roll out the dough into a 12 by 20 in [30.5 by 50 cm] rectangle with a short edge facing you. 3) Using a pastry wheel or pizza cutter, cut the dough crosswise into five strips, about 12 by 4 in [30.5 by 10 cm] each, then cut down the center of the rectangle to create a total of ten pieces. 4) Spread a generous 1 tablespoon of pesto over each piece, then top with a slice of cheese. 5) Fold each piece of dough in half, then fit the folded pieces into the prepared pan side by side, with the folds down in the pan and the cut edges facing up. (It will be a tight fit, but it is okay to press them close together.) Loosely cover the pan with plastic wrap and let the dough rise in a warm place until almost doubled in size, 45 minutes to 1 hour. (The bread can also do a slow rise in the refrigerator overnight. See "For overnight pesto pull-apart bread.") 6) Position an oven rack in the middle of the oven and pre-heat the oven to 350°F [180°C]. 7) Bake the bread until the top is golden brown and the bread registers 195°F [92°C] on an instant-read thermometer, 40 to 55 minutes. Check the bread half-way through baking—if the top is browning too quickly, put a piece of foil over the top. 8) Transfer the pan to a wire rack. Using the parchment sling, gently lift the loaf out of the pan, peel off the paper, and let the bread cool on the rack for 20 minutes. Pull apart the warm bread and enjoy. This bread is best the day it's made.

84

FOR OVERNIGHT PESTO PULL-APART BREAD
Put the filled pieces of dough in the pan, but do not let the bread rise at room temperature. Instead, cover the pan loosely with plastic wrap and refrigerate for at least 8 hours and up to overnight. When ready to bake, preheat the oven and let the bread sit at room temperature (still covered in plastic) for 45 minutes to 1 hour. Bake as directed.

This is an easy way to use up summertime fruit and leftover Bundt cake while creating a delicious breakfast. The roasted fruit is inspired by a recipe in *Everyday Food* magazine that I've been making for years. I like to keep the fruit pieces large when roasting them, then slice them into smaller pieces before serving. If you aren't crazy about rosemary, you can omit it. (You will have some roasted fruit and juice left over, but note: The fruit also tastes amazing over vanilla ice cream.)

 **MAKES 4 SERVINGS**

Roasted Fruit
with Toasted Pound Cake

3 apricots, halved and pitted

3 plums, halved and pitted

3 peaches, halved, pitted, and halved again

6 oz [170 g] fresh or frozen cherries, pitted

⅓ cup [65 g] granulated sugar

2 tablespoons olive oil

¼ teaspoon salt

1 vanilla bean, split, or 1 teaspoon pure vanilla extract

4 tablespoons [57 g] unsalted butter

2 or 3 sprigs rosemary (optional)

4 thick slices Everything Bundt Cake (page 96) or store-bought vanilla pound cake

Whipped cream, homemade (page 290) or store-bought, for serving (optional)

1) Position an oven rack in the middle of the oven and preheat the oven to 375°F [190°C]. 2) In a large baking dish, combine the apricots, plums, peaches, cherries, granulated sugar, olive oil, and salt and toss to combine. Nestle the vanilla bean, if using, into the fruit, or add the vanilla extract. Cut 2 tablespoons of the butter into eight pieces and scatter over the top. Scatter the rosemary sprigs, if using. Bake, uncovered, until the fruit is tender and juicy, 20 to 25 minutes. Let cool on a wire rack until slightly warm. 3) Meanwhile, in a large skillet over medium heat, melt the remaining 2 tablespoons of butter. Place the cake slices in the pan and toast until light golden brown on the bottom, about 3 minutes. Flip the slices and toast the other side until golden, about 2 minutes more. 4) If you like, slice the apricots, plums, and peaches into smaller pieces. Place the cake slices on individual plates and top with a good amount of the roasted fruit. Serve with whipped cream, if desired.

85

This amaretto cream filling has traveled with me many years, always finding its way into different flavored and shaped tarts. It is amazing paired with flaky puff pastry, and, topped with raspberries or strawberries, it can't be beat.

MAKES ONE 10 IN
[25 CM] TART

Amaretto Tart

86

PASTRY

All-purpose flour, for dusting

½ recipe Rough Puff Pastry (page 278), or 1 sheet store-bought

Egg wash (see page 14)

AMARETTO CREAM

8 oz [227 g] cream cheese, at room temperature

½ cup [100 g] granulated sugar

Pinch of salt

2 cups [480 g] heavy cream

2 to 3 tablespoons amaretto liqueur (see Note)

1 teaspoon pure vanilla extract

½ teaspoon almond extract

ASSEMBLY

10 oz [280 g] fresh berries (strawberries, raspberries, or blueberries work well)

1) FOR THE PASTRY Line a sheet pan with parchment paper. Generously flour your work surface. Roll out the dough into an 11 in [28 cm] square. Using a pastry cutter, cut off a 1 in [2.5 cm] strip from each side of the square, for a total of four, and set aside. Transfer the square of puff pastry to the prepared sheet pan. 2) Lightly brush the edges of the puff pastry square with egg wash. Lay the four reserved strips over the edges of the square so they line up exactly, overlapping at the corners, and trim them as necessary. Use a fork to prick the center of the square. Freeze the pastry while the oven is preheating. 3) Position an oven rack in the middle of the oven and preheat the oven to 400°F [200°C]. 4) When ready to bake, brush the tops of the four strips with egg wash, being careful not to let any drip down the sides. Bake the puff pastry until light brown and puffed, about 15 minutes. Using an offset spatula or the back of a spoon, press down on the center of the pastry, leaving the edges

puffed up. Return to the oven and bake until deep golden brown, 10 to 12 minutes more. Transfer the tart to a wire rack to cool and press down on the center again if needed. Let the tart cool completely before filling. 5) **FOR THE AMARETTO CREAM** In the bowl of a stand mixer fitted with a whisk, beat the cream cheese, granulated sugar, and salt on medium-high speed until light and fluffy, 1 to 2 minutes. 6) Lower the speed to low and add the heavy cream in a slow, steady stream. Scrape down the sides of the bowl, increase the speed to

medium, and beat until the mixture holds stiff peaks, 3 to 5 minutes. Lower the mixer speed to low and beat in the amaretto, vanilla, and almond extract. 7) **TO ASSEMBLE** Fill the center of the tart with the amaretto cream, then top with the fresh berries. This tart is best eaten the day it is made.

NOTE If you aren't a fan of amaretto, you can omit it, along with the almond extract, and just bump up the vanilla extract to 2 teaspoons.

I have always been a leftover-dessert-for-breakfast-the-next-day kind of person, but I decided to go all out here and straight-up serve fresh dessert. I've made this crisp slightly healthy with (of course) fruit, whole-wheat granola, and a yogurt whipped cream. This is perfect for a sleepyhead weekend breakfast or a gathering of friends.

Good Morning Berry Crisp

MAKES ONE 9 IN
[23 CM] CRISP

3 cups [420 g] Whole-Wheat Streusel (page 291)

1 cup [200 g] granulated sugar

¼ cup [25 g] cornstarch

½ teaspoon ground cinnamon

¼ teaspoon salt

16 oz [454 g] fresh or frozen blueberries

8 oz [227 g] fresh or frozen strawberries, quartered

8 oz [227 g] fresh or frozen raspberries

8 oz [227 g] fresh or frozen blackberries

2 tablespoons unsalted butter, melted

1 teaspoon pure vanilla extract

Yogurt Whipped Cream (page 290)

1) Position oven racks in the lower and middle of the oven and preheat the oven to 400°F [200°C]. Line a sheet pan with parchment paper and grease a 9 by 13 in [23 by 33 cm] baking pan. 2) Pour the streusel onto the sheet pan in an even layer. 3) In a medium bowl, whisk together the granulated sugar, cornstarch, cinnamon, and salt. 4) In a large bowl, combine all of the berries. Add the sugar mixture and stir until completely combined. Pour the butter and vanilla over the top and stir again until it is mixed in. Pour the fruit into the prepared baking dish and place in the oven on the middle rack. Place the streusel on the lower rack. Let the streusel bake for 8 to 12 minutes, until golden brown and crisp, stirring occasionally to make sure it doesn't burn. Remove the streusel from the oven and let cool. Let the fruit bake until it is soft and the liquid is thick and bubbling, 30 to 40 minutes (this may take longer if using frozen fruit). Make sure the liquid bubbles for at least 5 minutes. Carefully remove the pan from the oven and top the fruit evenly with the streusel. Transfer the baking dish to a wire rack and let cool slightly before serving. Serve topped with the yogurt whipped cream. 5) The crisp can be stored in an airtight container in the refrigerator for up to 2 days (without the yogurt whipped cream); reheat before serving.

87

I've been using this granola recipe for decades; it hasn't changed much, except for the addition of extra salt. I prefer my granola in small pieces, so I stir it often while it is baking to break up the oats. If you like your granola in larger clusters, stir most of the granola only once, when switching the pans between racks. But either way, stir the granola in the corners frequently to prevent burning.

At the bakeries where I have worked, we always toasted any add-ins on a separate sheet pan—nuts, dried fruit, unsweetened coconut—and then tossed them with the granola after cooling.

Granola

MAKES ABOUT
6 CUPS [840 G]

GRANOLA

½ cup [160 g] pure maple syrup

½ cup [112 g] vegetable or canola oil

¼ cup [50 g] brown sugar

2 tablespoons water

1 tablespoon pure vanilla extract

½ to ¾ teaspoon salt

5 cups [450 g] old-fashioned rolled oats

1 teaspoon ground cinnamon

OPTIONAL ADD-INS

1 cup [120 g] of your favorite nuts, toasted

1 cup [140 g] of your favorite dried fruit

1 cup [180 g] mini chocolate chips

½ cup [45 g] unsweetened coconut flakes

½ cup [60 g] pepitas

¼ cup [45 g] quinoa, toasted

3 tablespoons flaxseed

1) FOR THE GRANOLA Position the oven racks in the upper-middle and lower-middle of the oven and preheat the oven to 350°F [180°C]. Grease the edges of two sheet pans and line the bottoms with parchment paper. **2)** In a large bowl or liquid measuring cup, whisk together the maple syrup, oil, brown sugar, water, vanilla, and salt until combined. **3)** Put the oats in a large bowl and stir in the cinnamon. Add the wet ingredients and stir well, making sure the oats are completely coated. **4)** Spread out the oat mixture evenly between the prepared sheet pans and bake, stirring often, making sure to include the granola along the edges and in the corners of the pans, until the oats are golden brown and no longer wet, 24 to 30 minutes, rotating the pans halfway through baking. Transfer the sheet pans to a wire rack and let the granola cool, stirring once or twice. Transfer to a large bowl.

88

5) **FOR THE ADD-INS** While the oats are cooling, place whatever add-ins you are using (omitting chocolate chips) on a parchment-lined sheet pan and toss to combine. Bake until lightly toasted, 6 to 8 minutes. Let the pan cool on a wire rack, then mix into the cooled granola.

6) The granola can be stored in an airtight container at room temperature for up to 5 days.

VARIATION

• **Honey Granola:** *Substitute honey for the maple syrup. Honey heats a little differently than maple syrup, and I find I need to stir the granola more frequently when using it.*

I've seen granola bark everywhere from cookbooks to bakeries to the grocery store aisle and decided to take a stab at it myself. I used the peanut butter granola base from my first book, then added a layer of chocolate to the back to help keep it together (and also because chocolate is delicious). I like to add cacao nibs and roasted peanuts, but you could choose any of the add-ins from the granola recipe on page 250 as well.

Peanut Butter Granola Bark

MAKES ABOUT
48 PIECES

½ cup [100 g] brown sugar

½ cup [112 g] vegetable or canola oil

¼ cup [80 g] maple syrup

¼ cup [54 g] creamy peanut butter

2 tablespoons water

1 large egg white

1 teaspoon pure vanilla extract

½ teaspoon salt

5 cups [450 g] old-fashioned rolled oats

1 cup [140 g] chopped plain or honey-roasted peanuts

¼ cup [40 g] cacao nibs, chopped

1 lb [455 g] semisweet chocolate, melted

1) Position an oven rack in the middle of the oven and preheat the oven to 325°F [165°C]. Grease a sheet pan and line the bottom with parchment paper. 2) In a large bowl, combine the brown sugar, oil, maple syrup, peanut butter, water, egg white, vanilla, and salt. Add the oats and stir until completely coated. Add the peanuts and cacao nibs and stir again until evenly distributed. 3) Spread the mixture on the prepared pan and press into a nice, tight, even layer. Cover with a piece of parchment paper, and then place a second sheet pan on top. Bake for 25 minutes, then remove the top sheet pan. Continue to bake until the oats are golden brown and no longer wet, 10 to 15 minutes more.

4) Move the pan to a wire rack and run an offset spatula along the sides of the pan, just to make sure the granola is not stuck to the edges. Let cool to room temperature, running the offset spatula around the edges one more time. When the oats are completely cool, pour the melted chocolate over the top and use an offset spatula to spread it out in an even layer. Let cool until the chocolate is firmly set. 5) Cut the bark into pieces: you can either cut the bark into pieces in the pan, or place a spatula underneath the parchment paper and carefully loosen it, then pull it out of the pan and onto your work surface. Store the bark in an airtight container at room temperature for up to 1 week.

These cookies are inspired by the rye-cranberry chocolate chunk cookies in Dorie Greenspan's excellent book *Baking with Dorie*. Her cookie recipe is from Moko Hirayama, who serves them in her popular Paris restaurant, Mokonuts. I am obsessed with this cookie (it is perfect). It's known for its signature indentation on the top, which I've reproduced here, as well as its great flavor. But I couldn't resist putting my own spin on it in the form of a breakfast cookie. I use oats and whole-wheat flour, in addition to rye flour, cut out some of the butter, and use all my favorite add-ins: sesame seeds, pecans, orange pieces, poppy seeds, and, of course, chocolate. I would eat these every single morning if I could.

Sesame Chocolate Rye Breakfast Cookies

MAKES
16 COOKIES

1½ cups [213 g] all-purpose flour

1 cup [130 g] rye flour

¾ cup [68 g] old-fashioned rolled oats

¼ cup [36 g] whole-wheat flour

3 tablespoons white sesame seeds, plus more for sprinkling

2 tablespoons flaxseed

2 teaspoons baking powder

1 teaspoon baking soda

1 cup [2 sticks or 227 g] unsalted butter, at room temperature

1 cup [200 g] granulated sugar

1 cup [200 g] brown sugar

1 teaspoon salt

2 large eggs, at room temperature

1 tablespoon pure vanilla extract

4 oz [113 g] semisweet or bittersweet chocolate, coarsely chopped

½ cup [70 g] King Arthur Orange Jammy Bits or dried cranberries or cherries

½ cup [60 g] toasted pecans, chopped into bite-size pieces

⅓ cup [45 g] poppy seeds

Black sesame seeds, for sprinkling

Flaky sea salt, for sprinkling (optional)

1) Position an oven rack in the middle of the oven and preheat the oven to 425°F [220°C]. Line two sheet pans with parchment paper. Grease sixteen 3½ by 1 in [9 by 2.5 cm] English muffin rings (see Note) and place eight on each sheet pan. 2) In the bowl of a food processor, process the all-purpose flour, rye flour, rolled oats, whole-wheat flour, sesame seeds, flaxseed, baking powder, and baking soda until the rolled oats are broken down, about ten pulses. 3) In the bowl of a stand mixer fitted with a paddle, beat the butter on medium speed until creamy, about 1 minute. Add the granulated and brown sugars and the salt, and continue beating until light and fluffy, 3 to 5 minutes. Add the eggs and vanilla and beat until incorporated, scraping down the sides of the bowl as needed. Add the flour mixture on low speed, beating until incorporated. Add the chocolate, orange pieces, pecans, and poppy seeds

and mix until completely incorporated. 4) Form the dough into sixteen 3 oz [85 g] balls (about ¼ cup each), and place the balls in the center of the English muffin rings; there will be a little space between the dough and the rings. Sprinkle with the white and black sesame seeds and flaky sea salt, if using. Bake the cookies until the tops are golden brown and the dough has spread out into an even layer, 10 to 11 minutes. Transfer to a wire cooling rack. 5) Use an oven mitt or a pair of tongs to remove the English muffin rings from around the cookies. With the back of a spoon, tap the center of each cookie so it deflates and retains a slight indentation. It will look like the center isn't fully baked, but the centers will set as the cookies cool. Let the cookies cool on the sheet pans for 10 minutes, then transfer to a wire rack to finish cooling. 6) The cookies are best the day they are made, but they can be stored in an airtight container for up to 3 days. On the first day the cookies will have a crisp top and bottom shell, but they will soften with time. They are delicious both ways.

NOTE With the English muffin rings, the cookies bake up in perfect circles. If you don't have them, bake your cookies free-form instead. They will be ready 1 minute sooner, and will spread a little more.

CHAPTER 6

Base Doughs and Breads

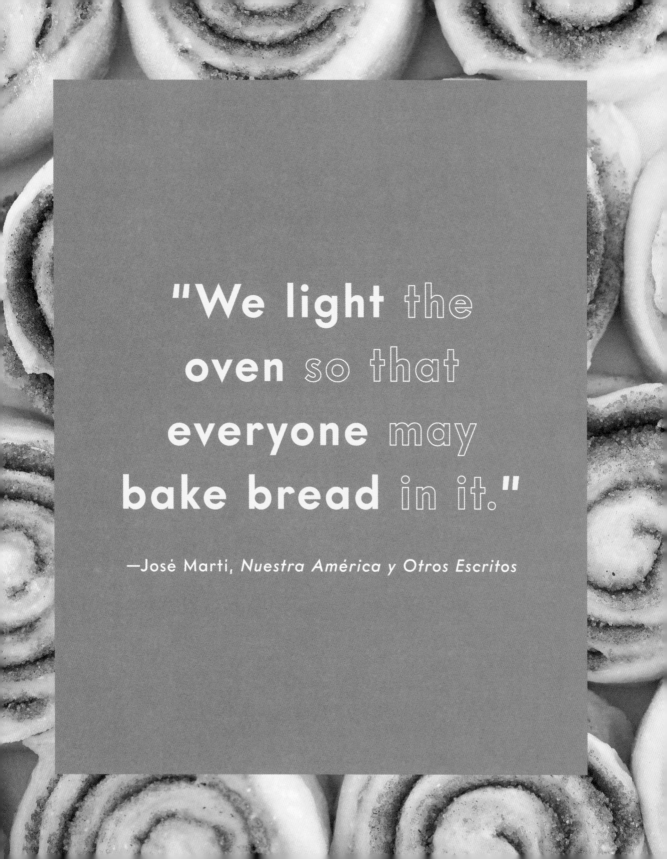

"We light the oven so that everyone may bake bread in it."

—José Marti, *Nuestra América y Otros Escritos*

I spent several months trying to get this recipe just right—as well as years of baking many, many different brioche recipes. This brioche has a fine texture and a tight crumb and is tender, rich, and dreamy to work with.

Brioche Dough

MAKES ABOUT 3 LBS [1.4 KG] OF DOUGH

½ cup [120 g] water, at room temperature

2 tablespoons granulated sugar

1 tablespoon active dry yeast

4 large eggs, at room temperature

3 large egg yolks, at room temperature

¼ cup [85 g] honey

2 teaspoons salt

1 teaspoon pure vanilla extract

4 cups [568 g] all-purpose flour

12 tablespoons [1½ sticks or 170 g] unsalted butter, cut into 12 pieces, at room temperature

1) In the bowl of a stand mixer fitted with a dough hook, stir together the water, granulated sugar, and yeast, and let sit until the mixture is foamy, about 5 minutes. Add the eggs, egg yolks, honey, salt, and vanilla and stir to combine. 2) Add the flour and mix on low speed until the ingredients come together and start to form a ball around the dough hook, 2 to 3 minutes; some of the dough will still be pooled at the bottom of the bowl. On low speed, add the butter, one piece at a time, until all the butter has been added and is fully incorporated into the dough. You will need to scrape down the sides of the bowl and the hook occasionally to get it all incorporated. Increase the speed to medium and beat until the dough is sticky but elastic, has formed a ball around the hook, and has mostly cleared from the sides and bottom of the bowl, 15 to 20 minutes. Resist the urge to add more flour to the dough to speed things along. Gently pull a small section of the dough; you should be able to count to 5 without it tearing apart. The dough will be elastic, satiny, and smooth and should not tear easily or be stiff and hard to stretch. Refrigerate the dough for at least 2 hours and up to 18 hours.

Brioche Loaves

1 recipe Brioche Dough (page 259)

All-purpose flour, for dusting

Egg wash (see page 14)

1) Grease two 8 by 4 in [20 by 10 cm] loaf pans or two 9 by 4 by 4 in [23 by 10 by 10 cm] Pullman pans. 2) After the dough has risen and chilled, transfer to a floured work surface and divide it into four pieces. Pat each piece into a disk 4 or 5 in [10 or 12 cm] in diameter. Fold the edges of the dough toward the center. Turn the dough over and use your hands to gently form the dough into a ball. Use your hands to move the ball around the work surface to form the dough into a smooth ball, using a little flour if necessary. Repeat with the three remaining pieces of dough.

3) Place two balls of dough, seam-side down, in each prepared pan. Cover the loaves loosely with plastic wrap and let rise at room temperature until almost doubled in size, 1½ to 2 hours. 4) Position an oven rack in the middle of the oven and preheat the oven to 350°F [180°C]. 5) Brush the tops of the loaves with egg wash. Bake until the loaves are golden brown and register 190°F [88°C] on an instant-read thermometer, 35 to 45 minutes. Transfer the pans to a wire rack and let the loaves cool in the pans for 5 minutes. Flip them out, turn them over, and let cool completely before slicing. 6) The loaves will keep, wrapped in plastic wrap, at room temperature for up to 4 days.

Milk bread dough has many names throughout Asia, but its defining characteristic is the inclusion of tangzhong, which is a roux made with either milk or water (or both) and flour. When baked, the dough is fluffy and soft, and it's often compared to cotton candy in texture. It can be used in many applications: swirled buns, savory twists, even pizza. I love it as a simple loaf baked tall, and then toasted and spread with a little butter for breakfast.

I have made many loaves of milk bread over the years and have found most recipes to be quite similar; after some tinkering (a little less sugar, a little more yeast), I've landed here. Kristina Cho's book *Mooncakes and Milk Bread* was a helpful guide for getting this dough and bread just right. The dough can be doubled.

Milk Bread Dough

MAKES 1½ LBS [685 G]
OF DOUGH

TANGZHONG
⅓ cup [80 g] water

2 tablespoons bread flour

DOUGH
½ cup [120 g] milk

3 tablespoons granulated sugar

1 teaspoon salt

1½ teaspoons active dry yeast

1 large egg, at room temperature

2½ cups [355 g] bread flour, plus more for dusting

4 tablespoons [57 g] unsalted butter, cut into 4 pieces, at room temperature

1) **FOR THE TANGZHONG** In a small saucepan, combine the water and flour. Heat over low heat, whisking constantly, until the mixture is shiny and thick, 2 to 3 minutes. Scrape into a small bowl and set aside to cool slightly. 2) **FOR THE DOUGH** In the same pan, combine the milk, granulated sugar, and salt. Heat, stirring constantly, until just simmering and the sugar and salt have dissolved, 2 to 3 minutes. Set aside to cool until the milk registers 100 to 110°F [35 to 42°C] on an instant-read thermometer.

92

3) Grease a large bowl and set aside. In the bowl of a stand mixer fitted with a dough hook, combine the warm milk and the yeast and let sit until foamy, 5 minutes. Add the slightly cooled tangzhong and egg and stir to combine. 4) With the mixer on low speed, add the flour and mix until incorporated and the dough is smooth and has formed into a cohesive ball, 2 to 3 minutes. Add the butter, one piece at a time, mixing until incorporated and scraping down the sides of the bowl and the hook as needed. Increase the speed to medium and knead the dough until it is sticky but elastic. It should be pulling away from the sides of the bowl and starting to gather around the hook while still pooling on the bottom of the bowl, 7 to 10 minutes. Gently pull a small section of the dough; you should be able to count to 5 without it tearing off. Lightly flour your hands and pull the ends of the dough to

form a smooth ball. Transfer the dough to the large greased bowl and let the dough rise until doubled in size, 1½ to 2 hours. The dough can be used immediately or refrigerated for up to 2 days.

Working with Yeast

Most people are nervous when they first start working with yeast. I was always a little afraid myself, until I realized that yeast wants to live, and will live through almost everything except hot water. Just make sure your water is around 110°F [42°C] and you will be fine (yeast begins to die at around 120°F [50°C]).

Milk bread loaves are usually made in three or four segments. You can also make this loaf in two segments; follow the directions on page 260 for Brioche Loaves.

Milk Bread Loaf

MAKES
1 LOAF

All-purpose flour, for dusting

1 recipe Milk Bread Dough (page 262)

Egg wash (see page 14)

1) Grease a 9 by 5 in [23 by 12 cm] loaf pan or 9 by 4 by 4 in [23 by 10 by 10 cm] Pullman pan. 2) Generously flour your work surface. Divide the dough into three equal pieces and pat each piece into a 4 in [10 cm] long oval. Use a rolling pin to roll out the oval into a long rectangle, about 8 in [20 cm] long. Fold in any protruding edges from the long sides of the rectangle. Starting at a short end, roll up the rectangle into a log. Repeat with the remaining pieces of dough. 3) Place the logs side by side in the prepared pan, seam-side down. Cover the pan loosely with plastic wrap and let the dough rise until it almost reaches the top of the pan, 1½ to 2 hours (if using a Pullman pan, the dough will be just below the rim).

4) Position an oven rack in the middle of the oven and preheat the oven to 350°F [180°C]. 5) Brush the top of the loaf with egg wash and bake until golden brown and an instant-read thermometer registers 190°F [88°C], 28 to 35 minutes. Transfer the pan to a wire rack and let cool for 5 minutes, then flip the loaf onto the wire rack, turn right-side up, and cool completely. 6) The loaf will keep, wrapped in plastic wrap, at room temperature for up to 4 days.

This dough makes an amazing dinner roll type of bun. I like to cut the dough into ten pieces and make the buns in a 12 by 5½ in [30.5 by 14 cm] biscotti pan, but you can also cut it into nine pieces and bake in a 9 by 9 in [23 by 23 cm] square pan.

Milk Bread Buns

MAKES 9
OR 10 BUNS

All-purpose flour, for dusting

1 recipe Milk Bread Dough (page 262)

Egg wash (see page 14)

1) Butter a 12 by 5½ in [30.5 by 14 cm] biscotti pan or a 9 in [23 cm] square pan. Generously flour your work surface, then use a bench scraper or scissors to divide the dough into nine or ten pieces, depending on your pan size. Roll each piece into a ball, then place the balls in a single layer in the pan. Cover the pan loosely with plastic wrap and let rise until doubled in size, 1 to 1½ hours. 2) Position an oven rack in the middle of the oven and preheat the oven to 350°F [180°C]. 3) Brush the tops of the buns with egg wash. Bake until the buns are golden brown, 18 to 24 minutes. Place the pan on a wire rack. Let the buns cool completely in the pan before serving. 4) The buns will keep, wrapped in plastic wrap, at room temperature for up to 2 days.

This dough is almost no-knead; it is gently folded over itself a few times during the rise time (this helps improve the dough's structure, ensures gluten will form, and makes it easier to handle). It is enriched with butter and milk and bakes up fluffy and delicious.

Sweet Dough

MAKES ABOUT 2½ LBS
[1.1 KG] OF DOUGH

¾ cup [180 g] warm whole milk (100 to 110°F [35 to 42°C])

2¼ teaspoons active dry yeast

4 large eggs, at room temperature

¼ cup [85 g] honey

2 teaspoons salt

4 cups [568 g] all-purpose flour

10 tablespoons [142 g] unsalted butter, cut into 1 in [2.5 cm] pieces, at room temperature

1) Grease a large bowl. In the bowl of a stand mixer fitted with a paddle, combine the milk and yeast on low speed, then let sit until the yeast has dissolved, about 5 minutes. Add the eggs, honey, and salt and mix until well combined. Add the flour, mixing on low speed until incorporated, 1 to 2 minutes. Add the butter, one piece at a time. When all the butter has been added, increase the speed to medium and beat the butter into the dough until all the little butter pieces are incorporated, 1 minute. Transfer the dough to the prepared bowl. The dough will be very sticky and you will need a spatula to scrape the dough into the bowl. 2) Cover the bowl with plastic wrap and let the dough rise for 30 minutes. Place

your fingers or a spatula underneath the dough and gently pull the dough up and fold it back over itself. Give the bowl a quarter turn and fold the dough over again. Repeat six to eight more times, until all the dough has been folded over on itself. *See how-to photos, page 267.* Re-cover the bowl with plastic and let the dough rise for 30 minutes. Repeat this series of folding the dough three more times, every 30 minutes, for a rise time of 2 hours. 3) Tightly cover the bowl with plastic wrap and refrigerate for at least 2 hours and up to 2 days. (The dough needs to be chilled after folding it, which will help with the rolling-out process. If you don't chill the dough, it will be hard to roll out because it will be sticky.)

This is a buttermilk version of my Sweet Dough,
and it bakes up light and fluffy, with a hint of tang.

MAKES ABOUT 2 LBS
[910 KG] OF DOUGH

Buttermilk Dough

½ cup [120 g] buttermilk (100 to 110°F [35 to 42°C])

2 teaspoons active dry yeast

3 large eggs, at room temperature

3 tablespoons granulated sugar

1½ teaspoons salt

1 teaspoon pure vanilla extract

3 cups plus 2 tablespoons [444 g] all-purpose flour, plus more for dusting

8 tablespoons [1 stick or 113 g] unsalted butter, cut into 8 pieces, at room temperature

1) Grease a large bowl. In the bowl of a stand mixer fitted with a paddle, combine the buttermilk and yeast on low speed, and let sit until the yeast has dissolved, about 5 minutes. Add the eggs, granulated sugar, salt, and vanilla and mix until well combined. 2) Add the flour, mixing on low speed until incorporated, 1 to 2 minutes Add the butter, one piece at a time. When all the butter has been added, increase the speed to medium and beat the butter into the dough, until all the little butter pieces are incorporated, 1 minute. Transfer the dough to the prepared bowl. The dough will be very sticky and you will need a spatula to scrape the dough into the bowl. 3) Cover the bowl with plastic wrap and let the dough rise for 30 minutes. Remove the plastic wrap and place your fingers or

a spatula underneath the dough to gently pull the dough up and fold it over itself. Give the bowl a quarter turn and fold the dough over again. Repeat six to eight more times, until all the dough has been folded over on itself. *See how-to photos, page 267.* Cover the bowl with plastic wrap and let the dough rise for 30 minutes. Repeat this series of folding the dough three more times, every 30 minutes, for a rise time of 2 hours. 4) Tightly cover the bowl with plastic wrap and refrigerate overnight or up to 3 days.

This dough is a slightly scaled-down version of my Sweet Dough (page 266). As the name suggests, I use it for pull-apart bread, such as the Cinnamon Roll Pull-Apart Bread (page 135), but also in a few other applications, like the Giant Carrot Cake Cinnamon Roll (page 125).

Pull-Apart Bread Dough

 MAKES ABOUT 2 LBS [910 KG] OF DOUGH

½ cup [120 g] warm milk (100 to 110°F [35 to 42°C])

2 teaspoons active dry yeast

3 large eggs, at room temperature

2 tablespoons honey

1 tablespoon granulated sugar

1½ teaspoons salt

3 cups plus 2 tablespoons [444 g] all-purpose flour, plus more for dusting

8 tablespoons [1 stick or 113 g] unsalted butter, cut into 8 pieces, at room temperature

1) Grease a large bowl. In the bowl of a stand mixer fitted with a paddle, combine the milk and yeast on low speed. Let sit until the yeast has dissolved, about 5 minutes, then add the eggs, honey, granulated sugar, and salt and mix until well combined. 2) Add the flour, mixing on low speed until incorporated, 1 to 2 minutes Add the butter, one piece at a time. When all the butter has been added, increase the speed to medium and beat the butter into the dough until all the little butter pieces are incorporated, 1 minute. Transfer the dough to the prepared bowl. The dough will be very sticky and you will need a spatula to scrape the dough into the bowl. 3) Cover the bowl with plastic wrap and let the dough rise for 30 minutes. Remove the plastic wrap and place your fingers or

a spatula underneath the dough to gently pull the dough up and fold it over itself. Give the bowl a quarter turn and fold the dough over again. Repeat six to eight more times, until all the dough has been folded over on itself. *See how-to photos, page 267.* Cover the bowl with plastic wrap and let the dough rise for 30 minutes. Repeat this series of folding the dough three more times, every 30 minutes, for a rise time of 2 hours. 4) Tightly cover the bowl with plastic wrap and refrigerate overnight or up to 3 days.

VARIATION
• **Carrot Sweet Dough:** *After the butter is incorporated into the dough, add 1½ cups [150 g] finely grated carrots and mix until well distributed. Proceed with the recipe as written.*

I developed this recipe while trying to find the perfect base for Kolaches (page 133). It is a dreamy dough to work with—soft and elastic, and it rolls out so smooth.

Sour Cream Dough

MAKES 2.5 LBS
[1.1 KG] OF DOUGH

½ cup [120 g] water, at room temperature

1 tablespoon active dry yeast

¾ cup [180 g] sour cream, at room temperature

1 large egg, at room temperature

4 large egg yolks, at room temperature

½ cup [100 g] granulated sugar

1½ teaspoons salt

4 cups plus 2 tablespoons [577 g] all-purpose flour

8 tablespoons [1 stick or 113 g] unsalted butter, cut into 8 pieces, at room temperature

1) Grease a large bowl. In the bowl of a stand mixer fitted with a dough hook, combine the water and yeast on low speed. Let sit until the yeast has dissolved, about 5 minutes, then add the sour cream, egg, egg yolks, granulated sugar, and salt and mix until well combined. Add the flour, mixing on low speed until incorporated, 1 to 2 minutes (the dough will be very sticky and will be in a puddle at the bottom of the bowl). Add the butter, one piece at a time, mixing until completely incorporated after each addition. Scrape down the sides of the bowl and the hook. Increase the speed to medium and mix until the dough is sticky but elastic, is starting to gather around the hook, and has mostly pulled away from the sides but is still sticking to the bottom, 8 to 10 minutes. 2) Gently pull on a small piece of the dough; you should be able to count to 5 without it tearing off. Transfer the dough to the greased bowl, cover with plastic, and let it rise for about 2 hours. The dough will have risen slowly during this time, increasing its volume by about half. Refrigerate the dough for at least 2 hours or overnight before using.

96

This dough is inspired by many different recipes, but specifically Dominique Ansel's croissant MasterClass and Mandy Lee's laminated dough in her book *The Art of Escapism Cooking*. Mandy skips using the butter in a block, instead spreading room-temperature butter over the surface of the dough, and then proceeds with the folding. The results are still amazingly flaky, and it works great in applications such as Morning Buns (page 186), Prosciutto Gruyère Croissants (page 227), and Cruffins (page 205).

Cheater Croissant Dough

 MAKES ABOUT 2½ LBS [1.1 KG] OF DOUGH

1½ cups [360 g] warm water (100 to 110°F [35 to 42°C])

1 tablespoon plus 1 teaspoon active dry yeast

4 cups plus 1 tablespoon [577 g] all-purpose flour, plus more for dusting

¼ cup plus 1 tablespoon [65 g] granulated sugar

2 teaspoons salt

2 tablespoons unsalted butter, melted

1½ cups [3 sticks or 339 g] European butter (preferably 83 to 84 percent butterfat), at room temperature (68°F [20°C]) and pliable

1) Grease a large bowl and set aside. In a small bowl or liquid measuring cup, stir together the water and yeast and let sit until the yeast has dissolved, about 5 minutes. 2) In the bowl of a stand mixer fitted with a dough hook, whisk together 4 cups [568 g] of the flour, the granulated sugar, and salt. Start the mixer on low speed and add the water-yeast mixture, followed by the melted butter. Continue to mix until all the ingredients are combined, 3 or 4 minutes (see Notes). The dough will be rough and bumpy, but it should be in one piece. Transfer the dough to the greased bowl and cover with plastic wrap. Let rise at room temperature until doubled in size, 1½ to 2 hours. 3) With your fist, gently press down on the dough, releasing as much gas as possible. Place the dough on a large piece of plastic wrap and shape into a 10 by 12 in [25 by 30.5 cm] rectangle. Cover the dough with more plastic wrap, place it on a sheet pan, and refrigerate for at least 2 hours or overnight.

cont'd

97

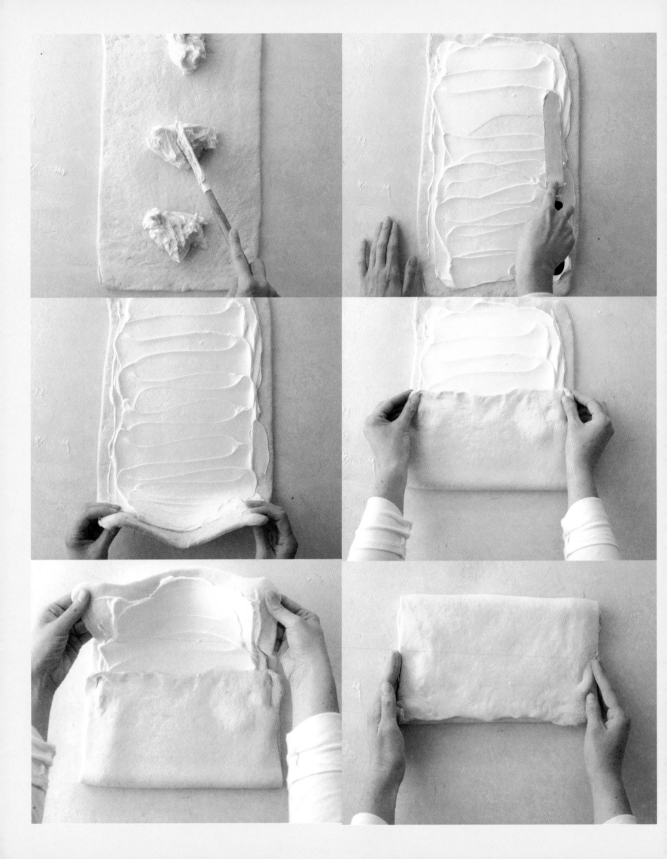

4) In the bowl of the stand mixer now fitted with a paddle, beat together the European butter and the remaining 1 tablespoon of flour until combined and creamy, 2 to 3 minutes. The mixture should be pliable, but not melting; it should have the texture of cream cheese and should spread easily. 5) Remove the dough from the refrigerator, unwrap it, and place it on a lightly floured work surface. Roll out the dough into a 12 by 20 in [30.5 by 50 cm] rectangle. Spread the entire rectangle evenly with the butter, leaving a ½ in [12 mm] border around the rectangle. Make the first turn, or letter fold: Starting with a short side facing you, fold one-third of the dough onto itself, making sure the edges are lined up with each other. Then fold the remaining one-third of the dough on top of the side that has already been folded. Rotate the dough so the seam is facing to the right and one open end is facing you. Gently roll out the dough into a 10 by 18 in [25 by 46 cm] rectangle. (Each time you roll, the rectangle will get a bit smaller; *see how-to photos, page 272*.) Repeat the letter fold. Sprinkle flour on a sheet pan or plate, place the dough on it, and freeze the dough for 6 minutes—set a timer so you don't forget (see Notes)! (The freezer helps cool the dough slightly and makes the last turn less messy.) 6) Remove the dough from the freezer and repeat the letter fold again, making sure the seam is facing to the right. Roll out the dough again into a rectangle, this time about 8 by 16 in [20 by 40.5 cm]. Repeat the steps for one letter fold. Gently compress the dough with the rolling pin, and, depending on the recipe you are using it in, keep the dough in one piece or cut it into two equal portions. 7) If using the

dough immediately, place the piece being used in the freezer for 6 minutes to chill, and then proceed with the recipe. Otherwise, wrap the dough in plastic, place it in a freezer-safe bag, and freeze for up to 2 weeks. The dough can be removed from the freezer the night before using and placed in the refrigerator to thaw.

NOTES Don't overmix the dough when combining the ingredients; this can result in a tough, chewy texture.

If the butter is left in the freezer for more than 6 minutes, it will start to freeze, and then break apart as you roll it out. If you didn't remove the dough on time, let it sit at room temperature for a while until it rolls out easily.

The laminating process will help strengthen the dough.

These sandwich buns are folded up into a square, instead of the classic triangle, which makes them perfect vessels for Croissant Breakfast Sandwiches (page 229).

Croissant Sandwich Buns

MAKES 8
SANDWICH BUNS

All-purpose flour, for dusting

½ **recipe Cheater Croissant Dough (page 271)**

Egg wash (see page 14)

1) Line a sheet pan with parchment paper. 2) Generously flour your work surface and roll out the croissant dough into a 10 by 20 in [25 by 50 cm] rectangle. Measure along the long side of the dough and cut eight long rectangles measuring 10 in [25 cm] long and 2½ in [6 cm] wide at the base. 3) Holding the base of a rectangle, gently stretch until it is 15 in [38 cm] long. Place on the work surface and fold the dough over itself every 2 in [5 cm] for a total of four folds. Flip the pastry so the free end is on the bottom. Repeat with the remaining rectangles and space them out evenly on the prepared sheet pan (they will puff up quite a bit as they rise and bake). Cover the croissants loosely with plastic wrap and let them rise until they are doubled in size and puffed, 2 to 2½ hours. 4) Position an oven rack in the middle of the oven and preheat the oven to 400°F [200°C]. 5) Brush the croissants with egg wash. Bake until the croissants are deep golden brown and the layers look completely baked, 25 to 30 minutes. Transfer the croissants to a wire rack and let them cool completely. Croissants are best eaten the day they are made.

This dough is similar in technique to my Cheater Croissant Dough (page 271), but the added egg and extra sugar make it a more tender affair.

Danish Dough

MAKES ABOUT 3 LBS
[1.4 KG] OF DOUGH

1½ cups [360 g] warm water (100 to 110°F [35 to 42°C])

4 teaspoons active dry yeast

½ cup [100 g] granulated sugar

4 tablespoons [57 g] unsalted butter, melted

1 large egg, at room temperature

2 large egg yolks, at room temperature

2 teaspoons salt

5 cups plus 1 to 2 tablespoons [710 g] all-purpose flour, plus more for dusting

1½ cups [3 sticks or 339 g] unsalted European butter (preferably 83 to 84 percent butterfat), at room temperature (68°F [20°C]) and pliable

1) Grease a large bowl and set aside. In the bowl of a stand mixer fitted with a dough hook, stir together the water and yeast on low speed and let sit until the yeast has dissolved, about 5 minutes. Add the granulated sugar, melted butter, egg, egg yolks, and salt and mix to combine. 2) Add 5 cups [710 g] of the flour and mix on low speed until incorporated, 3 to 4 minutes. If the dough is really sticking to the sides of the bowl after 2 minutes of mixing, add 1 tablespoon more of flour. The dough will start to gather around the hook but will still be sticking to the bottom of the bowl. Transfer the dough to the greased bowl and cover loosely with plastic wrap. Let the dough rise at room temperature until doubled in size, 1½ to 2 hours.

3) With your fist, gently press down on the dough, releasing as much gas as possible. Place the dough on a large piece of plastic wrap and shape it into a 10 by 12 in [25 by 30.5 cm] rectangle. Cover the dough with more plastic wrap, place it on a sheet pan, and refrigerate for at least 2 hours or overnight. 4) In the bowl of a stand mixer now fitted with a paddle, beat together the European butter and the remaining 1 tablespoon of flour until combined and creamy, 2 to 3 minutes. The mixture should be pliable but not melting; it should have the texture of cream cheese and should spread easily.

98

5) Remove the dough from the refrigerator, unwrap it, and place it on a lightly floured work surface. Roll out the dough into a 12 by 20 in [30.5 by 50 cm] rectangle. Spread the entire rectangle evenly with the butter, leaving a ½ in [12 mm] border around the rectangle. Make the first turn, or letter fold: Starting with a short side facing you, fold one-third of the dough onto itself, making sure the edges are lined up with each other. Then fold the remaining one-third of the dough on top of the side that has already been folded. Rotate the dough so the seam is facing to the right and one open end is facing you. Gently roll out the dough into a 10 by 18 in [25 by 46 cm] rectangle. (Each time you roll, the rectangle will get a bit smaller; see how-to photos, page 272.) Repeat the letter fold. Sprinkle flour on a sheet pan or plate, place the dough on it, and freeze the dough for 6 minutes—set a timer so you don't forget! (The freezer helps cool the dough slightly and make the last turn less messy.)

6) Remove the dough from the freezer and repeat the letter fold again, making sure the seam is facing to the right. Roll out the dough again into a rectangle, this time 8 by 16 in [20 by 40.5 cm]. Repeat the steps for one letter fold. Gently compress the dough with the rolling pin and, depending on the recipe you are using it in, keep the dough in one piece or cut it into two equal portions. 7) If using the dough immediately, place the piece being used in the freezer for 6 minutes to chill, and then proceed with the recipe. Otherwise, wrap the dough in plastic wrap, place it in a freezer-safe bag, and freeze for up to 2 weeks. The dough can be removed from the freezer the night before using and placed in the refrigerator to thaw.

This is my shortcut to puff pastry; it's not as exacting as the real thing but still results in rich, flaky layers, just like the more labor-intensive version.

MAKES ABOUT 2 LBS
[910 G] OF PUFF PASTRY

Rough Puff Pastry

2 cups [284 g] all-purpose flour, plus more for dusting

1½ cups [3 sticks or 339 g] unsalted butter, cut into 20 pieces

¼ cup [60 g] ice water, plus 1 to 2 tablespoons, as needed

½ teaspoon lemon juice

1 tablespoon granulated sugar

½ teaspoon salt

1) Dust a sheet pan or plate with flour and set aside. Put the butter pieces in a small bowl and place in the freezer for 5 to 10 minutes. 2) In a liquid measuring cup, combine the ¼ cup [60 g] ice water and lemon juice. 3) In the bowl of a stand mixer fitted with a paddle, mix together the flour, granulated sugar, and salt on low speed. Add the chilled butter and mix until only slightly incorporated. The pieces of butter will be smashed and in all different sizes, most about half their original size. Add the lemon juice and water mixture and mix until the dough just holds together and looks shaggy. If the dough is still really dry and not coming together, add more ice water, 1 tablespoon at a time, until the dough just starts to hold. 4) Transfer the dough to a lightly floured work surface and flatten it slightly into a square. Gather any dry loose pieces and place them on top of the square. Gently fold the dough over on itself and then flatten into a square again. Repeat this process five or six times, until all the loose pieces are worked into the dough. Flatten the dough one last time and form it into a 6 in [15 cm] square. Transfer the dough to the prepared sheet pan and sprinkle the top of the

dough with flour. Refrigerate until firm, 20 minutes. 5) Return the dough to the lightly floured work surface and roll it into an 8 by 16 in [20 by 40.5 cm] rectangle. If the dough sticks at all, sprinkle more flour underneath it. Brush any excess flour off the dough, and, using a bench scraper, fold the short ends of the dough over the middle, like a business letter, making three layers. This is the first turn. (If the dough still looks shaggy, don't worry; it will become smooth and will even out as you keep rolling.) 6) Flip the dough over, seam-side down, give the dough a quarter turn, and roll away from you, this time into a 6 by 16 in [15 by 40.5 cm] rectangle. Fold the short ends over the middle. This is the second turn. Sprinkle the top of the dough with flour, return it to the sheet pan, and refrigerate for 20 minutes.

7) Return the dough to the work surface and repeat the process of folding the dough for the third and fourth turns. On the fourth turn, use a rolling pin to gently compress the layers together slightly. Depending on the recipe you are using it in, keep the dough in one piece or cut the dough into two equal portions. Wrap tightly in plastic wrap. Refrigerate for at least 1 hour before using. Otherwise, wrap the dough in plastic wrap, place it in a freezer-safe bag, and freeze for up to 2 weeks. The dough can be removed from the freezer the night before using and placed in the refrigerator to thaw.

This bread is based on the classic anadama bread, but instead of cornmeal I've used oats, and I've swapped the molasses for granulated sugar. It is delicious toasted or for making sandwiches.

Toasting Bread

100

MAKES ONE 9 IN
[23 CM] LOAF

½ cup [45 g] old-fashioned rolled oats

¼ cup [50 g] granulated sugar

1 teaspoon salt

1 cup [240 g] boiling water

2 tablespoons sour cream

¼ cup [60 g] warm water (100 to 110°F [35 to 42°C])

2 teaspoons active dry yeast

2¼ cups [320 g] all-purpose flour, plus more as needed and for dusting

1 tablespoon unsalted butter, melted, plus more for greasing the bowl and pan

1) Grease a large bowl. In a food processor, process the oats, granulated sugar, and salt until the oats are broken down and finely ground. Transfer to a medium heatproof bowl. Pour the boiling water over the oats and whisk together until smooth. Add the sour cream and whisk again to combine. Let the mixture cool to room temperature. 2) In the bowl of a stand mixer fitted with a dough hook, whisk together the warm water and yeast. Let the mixture stand until the yeast has dissolved, about 5 minutes. Add the cooled oat mixture to the yeast and stir by hand to combine. With the mixer on low speed, add the flour, mixing until incorporated. Increase the speed to

medium and knead until the dough is smooth and elastic and starting to gather around the dough hook but still slightly sticky, 8 to 10 minutes. Add more flour, 1 tablespoon at a time, if needed. 3) Transfer the dough to a lightly floured work surface and shape into a ball. Add the butter to the greased bowl, add the dough, and then turn it seam-side down. Cover with plastic wrap and let rise until doubled, 1 to 1½ hours. 4) Position an oven rack in the middle of the oven and preheat the oven to 350°F [180°C]. Grease a 9 by 4 by 4 in [23 by 10 by 10 cm] Pullman pan or an 8 by 4 in [20 by 10 cm] loaf pan and line it with a parchment sling (see page 14).

5) Move the risen dough to a lightly floured surface, then flatten the dough with your hands. Use a rolling pin to roll out the dough into a rectangle about 8 in [20 cm] long and ½ in [12 mm] thick. Starting with the long side facing you, roll the dough into a tight cylinder, then pinch the seam closed. Place the dough in the prepared pan and cover lightly with plastic wrap. Let the dough rise again until the loaf is about 1 in [2.5 cm] from the top of the pan if using a Pullman pan, or 1 in [2.5 cm] above the pan if using a regular loaf pan, about 1 hour.

6) When ready to bake, use a pastry brush to brush the melted butter over the top of the bread. Bake until the loaf is golden brown and registers 200°F [400°C] on an instant-read thermometer, 30 to 40 minutes. Remove the bread from the pan using the parchment sling, peel off the paper, and transfer the bread to a wire rack. Immediately brush the loaf with more melted butter. Cool completely before slicing.

7) The bread can be stored in an airtight container for up to 3 days; it's best toasted on following days.

CHAPTER 7

Extras

"Mr. Darcy said very little, and Mr. Hurst nothing at all. . . . The latter was thinking only of his breakfast."

—Jane Austen, *Pride and Prejudice*

Pomegranate Sparkler

I'm not much of a mixed drink kind of person—more of a beer with dinner on the weekend type. Although I do have a cabinet stuffed full of liqueur bottles, they are all for baking. But! Sometimes the weekend calls for a little extra, and this is a simple, delicious way to trade the beer in for something more sassy.

MAKES 4 DRINKS

One 12 oz [340 g] can frozen pomegranate juice concentrate, slightly thawed and scoopable (see Note)

4 oz [113 g] vodka, or more or less to taste

2 cups [480 g] ginger ale

Place 3 tablespoons of the pomegranate concentrate in each glass. Add 2 tablespoons of vodka (or more or less if desired) and stir to combine. Pour in the ginger ale until each glass is three-quarters full. Top with ice, then stir again, and serve.

NOTE This can easily be made with other flavors—use any frozen juice concentrate you prefer.

Rhubarb Lemonade

A most refreshing drink, courtesy of the Blue Heron Coffeehouse. Colleen notes that if you'd like your lemonade to be a deeper shade of pink, add a slice of beet to the rhubarb and sugar mix while it simmers.

MAKES ABOUT 4 CUPS [960 G]

RHUBARB SYRUP

3 cups [375 g] diced rhubarb, 1 in [2.5 cm] pieces

2 cups [480 g] water

1½ cups [300 g] granulated sugar

1 vanilla bean, split (optional)

Pinch of salt

ASSEMBLY

One 12 oz [340 g] can of your favorite frozen lemonade concentrate

Water as suggested on package directions

1) FOR THE SYRUP In a medium saucepan, combine the rhubarb, water, granulated sugar, vanilla bean, if using, and salt. Bring to a simmer over medium heat, and continue simmering until the rhubarb is very tender, about 15 minutes. 2) Strain the syrup through a sieve into a heatproof bowl, discarding the rhubarb, and let cool to room temperature before using. (The syrup will keep, in an airtight container in the refrigerator, for up to 2 weeks.) 3) TO ASSEMBLE In a large pitcher, mix together the lemonade concentrate and water. Stir in ¾ cup [175 g] of the rhubarb syrup. Refrigerate until cold. Fill glasses with ice and pour the lemonade over before serving.

Easy Strawberry Smoothie

This has become a favorite family breakfast staple. I use frozen strawberries, so the smoothie is wonderfully cold and there is no need to use ice.

MAKES 3 OR 4 SMOOTHIES

One 24 oz [680 g] container plain or vanilla Greek yogurt

2 to 4 tablespoons honey (see Note)

1 teaspoon pure vanilla extract

Pinch of salt

12 oz [340 g] frozen strawberries

In a blender, combine the yogurt, honey, vanilla, and salt. Blend until smooth and the honey is completely incorporated. Add the strawberries and blend again until the strawberries are completely broken down. Divide among glasses and serve. This smoothie is best drunk immediately but can be covered and refrigerated overnight. Stir before drinking.

NOTE If using plain, unsweetened yogurt, you may want to add more honey. You may also want to add more honey if your strawberries are on the tart side (sometimes frozen strawberries are). You can start with 2 tablespoons, blend, taste, and always add more if needed.

VARIATION

• **Strawberry Basil Smoothie:** *Add 2 to 4 tablespoons fresh basil leaves to the blender along with the yogurt.*

Fruit-Flavored Syrup

When I was growing up, going out to dinner at a sit-down restaurant was a rare occasion. Occasionally, however, we would venture out to the Cottage, a breakfast-all-day restaurant. It seemed so fancy to my young eyes: The lights were always slightly dimmed and in the center of the restaurant was a gazebo-like platform. Each time we went, I crossed my fingers, hoping to sit in that special section, but we were always brought to a booth. One evening, however, I got the most incredible two-for-one special: We were seated in the center, and my parents let me order the adult-size pancakes, complete with blueberry syrup. I can still see the plate of pancakes disappearing before me as I poured more syrup over the top. I only made it about halfway through my plate, but it was a dreamy evening nonetheless.

MAKES ABOUT 2 CUPS [480 G]

6 oz [170 g] fresh or frozen raspberries, blueberries, or blackberries

1 teaspoon water

Pinch of salt

1½ cups [510 g] maple syrup

In a medium saucepan, combine the berries, water, and salt and heat over medium-low heat until the berries are broken down, 4 to 5 minutes. Remove from the heat, pour in the maple syrup, and stir to combine. Let cool to room temperature, then transfer to a container and refrigerate for at least 8 hours before using. The syrup will keep, in an airtight container in the refrigerator, for up to 1 week.

Coffee Syrup

This recipe is also in my first book. I'm including it here because it is still a favorite for slathering on waffles and pancakes. It is a little buttery and full of coffee flavor.

MAKES ABOUT 1½ CUPS [360 G]

2 cups [480 g] strong coffee, at room temperature

2 cups [400 g] granulated sugar

¾ teaspoon salt

2 tablespoons unsalted butter

1 teaspoon pure vanilla extract

2 tablespoons Frangelico (optional)

1) In a medium saucepan over medium-high heat, bring the coffee, granulated sugar, and salt to a boil. Continue boiling until reduced to 1½ cups [360 g], 10 to 12 minutes. 2) Remove the pan from the heat and add the butter, vanilla, and Frangelico, if using, and stir to combine. Let the mixture cool for 10 minutes before serving. The syrup will keep, in an airtight container in the refrigerator, for up to 1 week.

Quick Berry Jam

I tried canning jam a few times over the years, and then I discovered quick jam and never looked back. It is a great way to use up ripe fruit or frozen fruit that is buried in the back of your freezer.

MAKES ABOUT 1 CUP [300 G]

4 cups [450 g] fresh or frozen blueberries, strawberries, or raspberries (see Note)

½ to ¾ cup [100 to 150 g] sugar

¼ cup [8 g] freeze-dried berry powder (see page 14, optional)

2 teaspoons lemon juice, plus another squeeze or two if needed

1 vanilla bean, split, or 1 teaspoon pure vanilla extract (optional)

Pinch of salt

1) Combine the berries, granulated sugar, freeze-dried berry powder, lemon juice, vanilla bean pod (but not the vanilla extract), and salt in a large saucepan. Bring to a simmer over medium-low heat and continue simmering for 30 to 40 minutes, stirring often, until the berries have broken down and the jam is thick enough to cling to a wooden spoon Remove from the heat and remove the vanilla bean pod, or stir in the vanilla extract. Taste your jam—if it is a little flat, stir in another squeeze or two of lemon juice to brighten the flavor. 2) Let the jam cool to room temperature before using. The jam will keep, in an airtight container in the refrigerator, for up to 2 weeks.

NOTE If using frozen berries, they will take a little longer to break down. You may need to add 1 or 2 tablespoons of water to the pot while waiting for the frozen fruit to release their juice.

VARIATION
• **Rhubarb Berry Jam:** *Use 2 cups [250 g] of chopped rhubarb and 6 oz [170 g] of berries.*

Lemon Curd

I've never been crazy about store-bought lemon curd and find that making it at home is worth the effort involved. I leave out the zest for a smooth, not-too-tart curd, but you can add some to ramp up the lemon flavor, if you like (see Note).

MAKES ABOUT 2 CUPS [640 G]

8 tablespoons [1 stick or 113 g] unsalted butter, at room temperature

1½ cups [300 g] granulated sugar

¼ teaspoon salt

5 large egg yolks, at room temperature

1 large egg, at room temperature

⅓ cup [80 g] fresh lemon juice

1) In the bowl of a stand mixer fitted with a paddle, beat the butter on medium speed until creamy, about 1 minute. Add the granulated sugar and salt and mix until incorporated, 1 minute more. Scrape down the sides of the bowl, lower the mixer speed to low, and add the egg yolks (but not the egg). Increase the speed to medium and beat until smooth and light, 3 to 4 minutes. Lower the speed to low, add the whole egg, and mix until incorporated. Add the lemon juice and mix, scraping down the sides as needed. 2) Transfer the mixture to a medium, heavy-bottom saucepan. Cook over medium heat, stirring constantly with a heat-proof spatula, until the curd is thick enough to coat the spatula and registers 170°F [75°C] on an instant-read thermometer, about 10 minutes. Strain the mixture through a fine-mesh sieve into a medium bowl, then lay a sheet of plastic wrap directly on the surface of the curd to keep it from forming a skin. Refrigerate until well chilled. 3) The curd can be stored in the refrigerator in an airtight container for up to 5 days.

NOTE Add 2 tablespoons of lemon zest to the mixing bowl with the granulated sugar for a more tart and acidic flavor.

VARIATIONS

• **Blood Orange Curd:** *Replace the lemon juice with an equal amount of blood orange juice.*

• **Passion Fruit Curd:** *Replace the lemon juice with ½ cup [120 g] of passion fruit purée.*

Pastry Cream

Pastry cream is the filling that enriches my Blackberry Puff Pastry Tartlets (page 213) and Cruffins (page 205), but it has many other applications. And, if you have any leftover pastry cream, you can turn it into buttercream (see Variation).

MAKES ABOUT 2 CUPS [450 G]

1 vanilla bean

1 cup [240 g] whole milk

1 cup [240 g] heavy cream

5 egg yolks, at room temperature

1¼ cups [250 g] granulated sugar

¼ teaspoon salt

¼ cup [35 g] cornstarch

1 tablespoon unsalted butter

2 teaspoons pure vanilla extract

1) Split the vanilla bean in half, scrape the seeds out into a small dish, and put the pod in a medium, heavy-bottom saucepan. Add the milk

and heavy cream and heat over medium-low heat until just about to simmer. Remove from the heat, cover the pan, and set aside. 2) In the bowl of a stand mixer fitted with a paddle, beat the egg yolks on low speed until combined. Slowly add the granulated sugar, followed by the salt and vanilla bean seeds (see Note). Increase the mixer speed to medium-high and beat the egg-sugar mixture until very thick and pale yellow, about 5 minutes. Scrape down the sides of the bowl, lower the mixer speed to low, and beat in the cornstarch. 3) Pour the hot milk and cream into a medium liquid measuring cup, leaving the vanilla bean pod behind in the pan. With the mixer still on low speed, very slowly add the hot mixture, beating until completely incorporated. Transfer the mixture to the saucepan and cook over medium-low heat, stirring constantly with a wooden spoon, until the pastry cream becomes very thick and begins to boil, 5 to 7 minutes. Switch to a whisk and whisk the pastry cream until glossy and smooth, 3 to 4 minutes. Remove from the heat and strain the pastry cream through a fine-mesh sieve into a medium heatproof bowl. Stir in the butter and vanilla. 4) Lay a sheet of plastic wrap directly on the surface of the pastry cream to keep it from forming a skin and refrigerate until well chilled. Use right away or transfer to an airtight container. The pastry cream will keep, covered in the refrigerator, for up to 5 days.

NOTE The reason it's important to continuously beat egg yolks while adding sugar is to prevent the sugar from burning the yolks, causing them to harden and form little egg bits in whatever you are making.

VARIATION

• **German Buttercream (also known as crème mousseline):** *Put the entire recipe of pastry cream in the bowl of a stand mixer and add 1 cup [2 sticks or 227 g] of room-temperature butter. Beat until incorporated.*

Caramel

This is another staple that is fine store-bought but so much better homemade.

MAKES 1½ CUPS [270 G]

1¼ cups [250 g] granulated sugar

⅓ cup [80 g] water

2 tablespoons corn syrup

½ teaspoon salt

½ cup [120 g] heavy cream

5 tablespoons [70 g] unsalted butter, cut into 5 pieces

1 tablespoon pure vanilla extract

1) In a large, heavy-bottom saucepan, combine the granulated sugar, water, corn syrup, and salt, stirring very gently to combine while trying to avoid getting any sugar crystals on the sides of the pan. Cover the pan, bring to a boil over medium-high heat, and boil until the sugar has dissolved and the mixture is clear, 3 to 5 minutes. Uncover and cook until the sugar has turned light golden. Turn the heat down and cook until the mixture is deep golden and registers 340°F [170°C] on an instant-read thermometer. Remove immediately from the heat and add the heavy cream. The cream will foam a lot, so be careful pouring it in. Add the butter next, followed by the vanilla, and stir to combine. Set aside to cool. 2) Transfer the caramel to an airtight container. It will keep in the refrigerator for up to 2 weeks.

Crème Fraîche

Crème fraîche is similar to sour cream but is less sour and often has a higher percentage of butterfat. It also withstands heat much better and doesn't break when introduced to high temperatures.

MAKES ABOUT 4 CUPS [960 G]

3 cups [720 g] heavy cream

¾ cup [180 g] buttermilk

In a large bowl, whisk together the cream and buttermilk. Cover the top of the bowl with several layers of cheesecloth and secure with a rubber band or tie a string around the bowl to keep the cheesecloth in place. Let the bowl sit out at room temperature until it has thickened considerably, at least 24 hours and up to 3 days (see Note). When it is thick and ready to use, gently stir the crème fraîche and transfer it to an airtight container. It will keep in the refrigerator for up to 1 week.

NOTE Buttermilk contains active cultures ("good" bacteria), which prevent the cream from spoiling. And it's acidic enough to deter "bad" bacteria from growing.

The time required for the mixture to thicken will depend on the temperature inside your home. On cold winter days, it will take much longer than on hot summer ones.

Whipped Cream

Recently, Zoë François schooled me on my "whipped-creaming" technique. She insisted that low and slow whipping is the way to go. Of course, she was right.

MAKES ABOUT 3 CUPS [720 G]

1½ cups [360 g] heavy cream

2 tablespoons granulated or confectioners' sugar

2 teaspoons pure vanilla extract

Pinch of salt (optional)

1) Place a bowl and whisk attachment from a stand mixer in the freezer for 10 minutes or in the fridge for 20 minutes. Whisk together the heavy cream, sugar, vanilla, and salt, if using, on low speed for 30 to 45 seconds. Increase the speed to medium and beat until the cream has thickened and nearly doubled in volume, 2 to 3 minutes. 2) Remove the bowl from the mixer and continue whisking by hand with the whisk attachment or a handheld whisk for a few more seconds, until the whipped cream is the desired consistency. Whipping by hand gives you more control and makes it more difficult for you to whip the cream too much. Whipped cream is best used right away, but it can be made up to 2 hours ahead of time and stored in an airtight container in the refrigerator.

VARIATION

• **Yogurt Whipped Cream:** *In the bowl of a stand mixer fitted with a whisk, whisk together ½ cup [120 g] of vanilla Greek yogurt and 2 tablespoons of honey on low speed until combined. With the mixer still running, add 1 cup [240 g] of heavy cream in a slow, steady stream, then add 1 teaspoon of pure vanilla extract. Follow the directions above for whipping the whipped cream.*

Streusel

I often keep a bag of streusel in my freezer and find it comes in quite handy. I use it on top of the Streusel Coffee Cake (page 83), but I also sometimes throw it on top of banana bread, muffins, Bundt cakes, and the like.

MAKES 4 CUPS [500 G]

1⅓ cups [189 g] all-purpose flour

1 cup [100 g] almond flour

⅔ cup [135 g] granulated sugar

⅔ cup [135 g] light brown sugar

1 tablespoon ground cinnamon

¼ teaspoon salt

12 tablespoons [1½ sticks or 170 g] unsalted butter, cut into 12 pieces, at room temperature

In the bowl of a stand mixer fitted with a paddle, combine both flours, both sugars, the cinnamon, and salt on low speed. Add the butter, one piece at a time, beating just until the mixture comes together but is still quite crumbly. Store the streusel in an airtight container in the refrigerator for up to 1 week or in a freezer-safe bag in the freezer for up to 1 month.

Pecan Streusel

MAKES 5 CUPS [740 G]

1½ cups [180 g] toasted pecans, finely chopped

1⅓ cups [189 g] all-purpose flour

⅔ cup [130 g] granulated sugar

⅔ cup [130 g] brown sugar

2 teaspoons ground cinnamon

½ teaspoon salt

10 tablespoons [140 g] unsalted butter, melted

In a large bowl, mix together the pecans, flour, both sugars, cinnamon, and salt. Pour the melted butter over the top and use a spatula to stir everything together until well combined. Store the streusel in an airtight container in the refrigerator for up to 1 week or in a freezer-safe bag in the freezer for up to 1 month.

Whole-Wheat Streusel

MAKES ABOUT 3 CUPS [400 G]

½ cup [78 g] whole-wheat flour

½ cup [71 g] all-purpose flour

½ cup [45 g] rolled oats

¼ cup [50 g] granulated sugar

¼ cup [50 g] brown sugar

¼ teaspoon salt

7 tablespoons [100 g] unsalted butter, cut into 7 pieces, at room temperature

In the bowl of a stand mixer fitted with a paddle, combine both flours, the oats, both sugars, and the salt on low speed. Add the butter, 1 tablespoon at a time, until the mixture comes together but is still quite crumbly. Store the streusel in an airtight container in the refrigerator for up to 1 week or in a freezer-safe bag in the freezer for up to 1 month.

Candied Nuts

Nuts are perfect by their lonesome, but adding some caramelized sugar and salt makes them extraordinary.

MAKES ABOUT 3 CUPS [420 G]

2 cups [280 g] walnuts, peanuts, hazelnuts, cashews, almonds, or pepitas

½ cup [100 g] granulated sugar

¼ teaspoon salt

Line a sheet pan with parchment paper. In a large skillet over medium heat, stir together the nuts, granulated sugar, and salt. Cook until the sugar begins to melt and the nuts begin to toast, stirring almost constantly. Turn the heat down to low and cook until the nuts are lightly caramelized. Pour the nuts onto the prepared sheet pan. Cool completely before chopping them. The nuts will keep, in an airtight container at room temperature, for up to 1 week.

Almond Cream

Almond cream is also known as frangipane cream and is often used in traditional French baking. Most recipes contain quite a bit of sugar, but because I usually use the cream in a rich pastry that has plenty of sugar already, I can get away with less.

MAKES 1 CUP [300 G]

4 tablespoons [57 g] unsalted butter, at room temperature

¼ cup [50 g] granulated sugar

Pinch of salt

½ cup [50 g] almond meal

3 tablespoon all-purpose flour

1 large egg, at room temperature

⅛ teaspoon almond extract

1 tablespoon brandy (optional, see Note)

In the bowl of a stand mixer fitted with a paddle, beat the butter on medium speed until creamy, about 1 minute. Add the granulated sugar and salt and mix until well incorporated and creamy, 1 to 2 minutes. Add the almond meal and flour and mix until incorporated. Add the egg and mix again until incorporated, scraping down the sides of the bowl if needed. The mixture may look broken at this point, but that is normal. Add the almond extract and brandy, if using, and stir to combine. The cream will keep, in an airtight container in the refrigerator, for up to 1 week.

NOTE Stir in ⅓ cup [75 g] of Pastry Cream (page 288) at the end for a richer version, or replace the brandy with ¼ teaspoon of orange essence.

VARIATION

• **Hazelnut Cream:** *Replace the almond meal with an equal amount of hazelnut flour, and replace the brandy with Frangelico.*

Caramelized Onion Jam

I'm a big fan of caramelized onions and like to sneak them into anything savory I'm making. This jam can be doubled or tripled, and it freezes well.

MAKES 1 CUP [300 G]

1 lb [455 g] yellow onions

2 tablespoons unsalted butter

½ teaspoon salt

Pinch of cayenne, or more to taste

1 teaspoon balsamic vinegar

Halve the onions around the equator and slice the halves into ¼ in [6 mm] thick half rounds. Melt the butter in a large, heavy-bottom pot over medium-high heat. Add the sliced onions, salt, and cayenne and cook until the onions begin to brown, 10 to 12 minutes. Turn the heat down to medium-low and cover the pan. Cook, stirring occasionally, for 20 to 30 minutes. Uncover the pot and continue cooking over medium-low heat until the onions are dark and jammy, about 30 more minutes. Remove from the heat and stir in the vinegar. Let cool to room temperature, then transfer the jam to a jar and store, tightly sealed, in the refrigerator for up to 1 week.

Brown Butter

Brown butter adds a nice, nutty flavor to many dishes, but please note: It's not a perfect swap for regular butter in most recipes, because some of the liquid evaporates from the butter as it cooks. You can use any amount of butter for this; the process will be the same.

YIELD VARIES

Unsalted butter

In a light-colored, heavy-bottom skillet, such as stainless steel, melt the butter over medium-low heat, swirling it with a heatproof rubber spatula. When it starts to bubble, turn up the heat to medium and keep stirring until it begins to foam, 3 to 5 minutes. You will start to see brown bits at the bottom of the skillet and the butter will smell nutty. Keep stirring as the butter browns, making sure to gently scrape the bottom of the pan. The butter will quickly change from light brown to golden brown. Immediately remove it from the heat and pour the butter and any flecks on the bottom of the pan into a heatproof bowl. The brown butter can be used immediately or cooled to room temperature and stored in a tightly sealed jar in the refrigerator for up to 5 days.

Maple Mustard Dressing

This dressing is inspired by the maple mustard vinaigrette in *Savoring the Seasons of the Northern Heartland*, by Beth Dooley and Lucia Watson. I always use it on my salads, but it is also great on so many other things, like chicken, quinoa, and couscous. If you are serving a salad at brunch, this is a great addition.

MAKES ABOUT 2 CUPS [480 G]

⅔ cup [230 g] maple syrup

⅓ cup [80 g] cider vinegar

2 tablespoons store-bought garlic paste, or 3 garlic cloves, minced

2 tablespoons Dijon mustard

Freshly ground pepper

1 cup [224 g] vegetable or canola oil

In a blender, combine the maple syrup, cider vinegar, garlic, mustard, and pepper. Blend on high speed until smooth, then lower the speed to low and pour in the oil in a slow, steady stream. Increase the speed to high and blend until the dressing is emulsified. The dressing will keep, in an airtight container in the refrigerator, for up to 2 weeks.

MORNING TUNES TO BAKE TO

BEBEL GILBERTO
Tanto Tempo

BILLIE MARTEN
Writing of Blues and Yellows

BOB DYLAN
The Freewheelin' Bob Dylan

THE CACTUS BLOSSOMS
One Day

CLEO SOL
Mother

ELLA FITZGERALD AND LOUIS ARMSTRONG
Ella and Louis

JONI MITCHELL
Ladies of the Canyon

THE LEGENDARY JIM RUIZ GROUP
Sniff

MILES DAVIS
Bye Bye Blackbird

NAT KING COLE TRIO
The Complete Capitol Recordings

OVER THE RHINE
Good Dog, Bad Dog

ST GERMAIN
Tourist

Conversions

Commonly Used Ingredients

1 cup flour = 142 g

1 cup granulated sugar = 200 g

1 cup brown sugar = 200 g

1 cup confectioners' sugar = 120 g

1 cup cocoa powder = 100 g

1 cup butter [2 sticks] = 227 g

1 egg white = 35 g

1 cup whole milk = 240 g

1 cup heavy cream = 240 g

1 cup sour cream = 240 g

1 cup cream cheese = 226 g

Oven Temperatures

300°F = 150°C

350°F = 180°C

375°F = 190°C

400°F = 200°C

425°F = 220°C

450°F = 230°C

Weights

½ oz = 14 g

1 oz = 30 g

1½ oz = 45 g

2 oz = 57 g

2½ oz = 71 g

3 oz = 85 g

3½ oz = 99 g

4 oz = 113 g

4½ oz = 128 g

5 oz = 142 g

8 oz = 227 g

10 oz = 280 g

12 oz = 340 g

16 oz (1 lb) = 454 g

Bibliography

Much of my baking training was hands-on experience that took place in the workplace, and many ideas, techniques, and recipe evolutions were picked up here and there over the years. It would be impossible to cite everything and everyone, but I must acknowledge (with so much gratitude) Larry and Colleen Wolner and Zoë François for their mentorship, guidance, and encouragement (you can sample the Wolners' amazing baked goods at the Blue Heron Coffeehouse in Winona, Minnesota. And Zoë offers help to all on her beautiful website, zoebakes.com, and her Instagram, @zoebakes).

Over the years, many books have both taught me new techniques and guided my baking knowledge. As Lindsey Remolif Shere wrote in her book *Chez Panisse Desserts*, "No cook starts absolutely fresh: there are thousands of contributors to the continuously evolving art of cookery." Here are some that have inspired a starting point or answered a baking question for this book.

Ansel, Dominique. *The Secret Recipes*. New York: Simon & Schuster, 2014.

Arefi, Yossy. *Sweeter Off the Vine*. Berkeley: Ten Speed Press, 2016.

Barrow, Cathy. *Pie Squared*. New York: Hachette Book Group, 2018.

Beranbaum, Rose Levy. *The Cake Bible*. New York: William Morrow, 1988.

Boyce, Kim. *Good to the Grain*. New York: Abrams, 2010.

Braker, Flo. *The Simple Art of Perfect Baking*. San Francisco: Chronicle Books, 1985.

Chang, Joanne. *Pastry Love*. Boston: Houghton Mifflin Harcourt, 2019.

Chesnakova, Polina. *Hot Cheese*. San Francisco: Chronicle Books, 2020.

Cho, Kristina. *Mooncakes and Milk Bread*. New York: HarperCollins, 2021.

Collucci, Stephen. *Glazed, Filled, Sugared, and Dipped*. New York: Clarkson Potter, 2013.

Cunningham, Marion. *The Breakfast Book*. New York: Knopf, 1987.

Dooley, Beth, and Lucia Watson. *Savoring the Seasons of the Northern Heartland*. New York: Alfred. A. Knopf, 1994.

Editors at America's Test Kitchen. *Bread Illustrated*. Brookline, MA: America's Test Kitchen, 2016.

François, Zoë. *Zoë Bakes Cakes*. Berkeley: Ten Speed Press, 2021.

François, Zoë, and Jeff Hertzberg. *Holiday and Celebration Bread in Five Minutes a Day*. New York: St. Martin's Press, 2018.

Gand, Gale. *Gale Gand's Brunch!* New York: Clarkson Potter, 2009.

Garten, Ina. *The Barefoot Contessa*. New York: Clarkson Potter, 1990.

Greenspan, Dorie. *Baking with Dorie*. Boston: Houghton Mifflin Harcourt, 2021.

Greenstein, George. *A Jewish Baker's Pastry Secrets*. Berkley: Ten Speed Press, 2015.

Heatter, Maida. *Maida Heatter's Book of Great Desserts*. New York: Alfred A. Knopf, 1965.

Keller, Thomas. *Bouchon Bakery*. New York: Artisan, 2012.

Kimber, Edd. *Patisserie Made Simple*. London: Kyle Books, 2014.

Lee, Mandy. *The Art of Escapism Cooking*. New York: HarperCollins, 2019.

Levine, Sarabeth. *Sarabeth's Bakery: From My Hands to Yours*. New York: Rizzoli, 2010.

Lomas, Vallery. *Life Is What You Bake It*. New York: Clarkson Potter, 2021.

Ortiz, Gayle, and Joe Ortiz. *The Village Baker's Wife*. Berkeley: Ten Speed Press, 1997.

Ottolenghi, Yotam, and Helen Goh. *Sweet*. Berkeley: Ten Speed Press, 2017.

Page, Karen, and Andrew Dorenburg. *The Flavor Bible*. New York: Little, Brown and Company, 2008.

Prueitt, Elisabeth, and Chad Robertson. *Tartine: A Classic Revisited*. San Francisco: Chronicle Books, 2019.

Seneviratne, Samantha. *The Joys of Baking*. New York: Running Press, 2019.

Sever, Shauna. *Midwest Made*. New York: Running Press, 2019.

Shere, Lindsey Remolif. *Chez Panisse Desserts*. New York: Random House, 1985.

Weller, Melissa. *A Good Bake*. New York: Alfred A. Knopf, 2020.

Williams, Odette. *Simple Cake*. Berkley: Ten Speed Press, 2019.

Resources

BREVILLE

www.breville.com

Kitchen equipment and essentials

EMILE HENRY

www.emilehenry.com

Ceramic cookware

KERRYGOLD

www.kerrygoldusa.com

European butter

KING ARTHUR FLOUR

www.kingarthurflour.com

Specialty flours and baking items

MATERIAL

www.materialkitchen.com

Beautiful and functional kitchen knives and cookware

MAUVIEL

www.mauviel-usa.com

Copper cookware

NORDIC WARE

www.nordicware.com

Baking pans and kitchen necessities

PENZEYS SPICES

www.penzeys.com

Spices

VALRHONA

www.valrhona-chocolate.com

Chocolates and cocoa powder

VERMONT CREAMERY

www.vermontcreamery.com

Butter and other fine dairy products

VOLLRATH

www.vollrath.com

Disher scoops that don't break

WILLIAMS SONOMA

www.williams-sonoma.com

Bakeware, baking utensils, and decorating tools

You can also find my favorite kitchen items at my Amazon storefront: amazon.com/shop/sarah_kieffer

Acknowledgments

First, thank you to my family, Adam, Winter, and River, for your support and encouragement. This book was hard for all of us, what with a pandemic, school constantly changing, friends and family sick, teacher strikes, that one month of May that nearly destroyed us, and the world burning, burning, burning in the background. But your constant love and laughter are truly the rock that this book was built on. Thank you for your kind words, silly songs, dad jokes, dinner making, dish washing, tap and snaps, hugs, and reminders to rest. There is still a whisper of hope that love and goodness will find us all the days of our lives. I love you all more than these words could ever convey.

Thank you, Jane Dystel, for *always* having my back, and for being a helpful guide these last eight years of our working together. Your steady guidance has shaped all my books, and I look forward to writing more with you. Thank you, also, to Miriam Goderich for all your help and hard work.

Thank you, Chronicle Books, and of course Sarah Billingsley and Jessica Ling. I pinch myself every time I realize I get to write books for my job, and I feel so lucky and grateful every single day when I head to my kitchen counter to test recipes. Thank you for caring so much about books, and for caring to make a book *together*. To Lizzie Vaughan, I am so glad to be designing another book with you; you have made all these books so beautiful. Thank you to all the copy editors that helped shape this book: Deborah Kops, Karen Levy, and Margo Winton Parodi, who has worked on all three books with me.

To Amanda Paa: Your organization and care over the last few years have helped me move forward and stay sane. I am so grateful for your friendship (and that you convinced us we needed kitties in our home).

To Sara Bartus, I'm so glad Zoë decided to share you! I appreciate all the hard work you have done for this book; all these recipes tested to perfection. Thank you for your honesty and attention to detail (and for your grace with all my typing errors).

A gigantic thank you to the Blue Heron bakers for baking through many of these recipes. And to Kelsey Tenney, Heidi Smith, and Linda Mueller, thank you again for your valuable help and testing expertise.

To Zoë François, always, always thank you. You are always a text away, and your words of encouragement, help, and humor have kept me sane all these years. Everybody loves you.

To Larry and Colleen, I am so grateful for all that you have taught me about baking and cooking and running a business, but your friendship over the years has been the most important. I love you both so much.

To Katie Peck and Melody Heide, thank you for the encouragement, laughter, and last-minute intro editing (every single time, every single book). I love you both.

To all the grandmas and grandpas and aunties and uncles and cousins and dear friends who have stopped by to pick up treats, sent kind words, babysat children, tested recipes, and offered to wash dishes—thank you. I love you all so much. And to Dad—I don't know how many copies of my books you have bought and given away; it's too many to count. Your support has meant so much.

And of course, thank you to all the lovely *Vanilla Bean Blog* readers. This book wouldn't be here without your support, and I am truly grateful each and every day. Thank you for making my recipes, pan-banging, sending kind notes, buying books, and being so wonderful. Much love.

Index

100 Morning Treats

SEE ALSO

100 COOKIES
BAKING FOR THE HOLIDAYS